D1520649

# Globalization, Social Movements, and Peacebuilding

*Syracuse Studies on Peace and Conflict Resolution*
Robert A. Rubinstein, *Series Editor*

**Other titles from Syracuse Studies on Peace and Conflict Resolution**

# Globalization, Social Movements, and Peacebuilding

Edited by

Jackie Smith and Ernesto Verdeja

Syracuse University Press

For a listing of books published and distributed by Syracuse University Press,
visit our website at SyracuseUniversityPress.syr.edu.

ISBN: 978-0-8156-3321-1

**Library of Congress Cataloging-in-Publication Data**

Globalization, social movements, and peacebuilding / edited by
Jackie Smith and Ernesto Verdeja. — First edition.
pages cm. — (Syracuse studies on peace and conflict resolution)
Includes bibliographical references and index.
ISBN 978-0-8156-3321-1 (cloth : alk. paper) 1. Peace-building.  2. Social movements.
I. Smith, Jackie, 1968–  II. Verdeja, Ernesto.
JZ5538.G586 2013
327.1'72—dc23      2013009976

*Manufactured in the United States of America*

*Dedicated to those struggling for justice*
*so that we may find peace*

# Contents

## Part One: Discourses of Conflict and Movement

# Part Two: Global Models and Local Conflicts

# Part Three: Peacebuilding from Below

*Opportunities and Challenges*

# Tables and Figure

# Acknowledgments

This project began as part of a conversation about the current state of peace research and its ability to help us account for and address the problem of violence and war in the contemporary world. Despite a proliferation of journals and the rise in prestige of the field of peace research over recent decades, we didn't see much movement toward developing real solutions to the problems that were fueling contemporary conflicts. At the same time, multidisciplinary scholarship framed as "global studies," "development studies," "women's studies," and "third world studies" was bringing new critical perspectives to discussions about interstate relations and the structures that govern the world political and economic system.

Contributors to this book met at the University of Notre Dame to consider questions about why violence and wars have persisted despite the massive expenditures on international peacekeeping and peacebuilding efforts. They brought a diverse array of expertise and perspectives to the conversations, which were lively and charged with energy and creativity. The workshop reflected the advantages of bringing scholars out of their disciplinary silos to engage in discussions about how to solve the real problems the world is facing. In this sense it reflects what the field of peace research has sought to do as a problem-focused arena of scholarship.

This book draws from this wealth of research that eludes classification within a single discipline or even multidisciplinary field. We sought contributors from distinct disciplines whose work reflected the best efforts to address the problems of persistent violence by looking to multiple disciplines and perspectives. Contributors here also bring a "sociological imagination" to this effort to understand the underlying causes of violent conflict, identifying the historical structures and systems of relations that allow injustice and violence to fester. In seeking solutions to the problem of violence, we have challenged our authors to look beyond what seems feasible in the existing interstate context, urging them to consider what sort of systemic changes might be more effective at ending violence. If, as one of our workshop participants insisted, wars can only be ended through a *radical redistribution of resources at the global level,* then what sorts of changes are needed to the larger organization of modern society? As readers will see, analyses in this volume link persistent wars and violence not only to the institutions that govern the world political and economic orders, but also to the predominant modes of thought and discourse.

As editors, we wish to extend our gratitude to our contributors, who persevered through several drafts as we worked to extend our thinking beyond disciplines and to forge new ground in the study of violence, conflict, and peacebuilding. We are grateful for the opportunity to think together with such a smart, critical, and creative group of people, and we hope that this project has been as positive an influence for all participants as it has been for us. Our thinking about the causes of violence and the paths to peace has been sharpened and advanced in new ways because of this opportunity to engage with such a diverse group of scholars. In addition to those contributing to this book, we also wish to thank the following workshop participants for their critical insights and reflections on the themes of globalization, social movements, and peacebuilding: Scott Appleby, Pascha Bueno Hansen, Topher McDougal, Katherine Marshall, Atalia Omer, and Balakrishnan Rajagopal.

Finally, we are grateful to the following entities and offices at the University of Notre Dame for providing the resources that allowed us to host the initial workshop and to bring these papers together into an edited collection: Kroc Institute for International Peace Studies, Center for the Study of Social Movements, Institute for Scholarship in the Liberal Arts, Office of Research, Nanovic Institute for European Studies, the Graduate School, the Department of Political Science, and the Department of

Sociology. Thanks to Kathy Smarrella, Cathy Laake, and other Kroc Institute staff who helped make the workshop productive and rewarding, and to Nhu Phan, who provided editorial assistance with the manuscript.

Jackie Smith and Ernesto Verdeja, Editors

Globalization, Social Movements, and Peacebuilding

# Introduction

## Jackie Smith and Ernesto Verdeja

In the wake of the Cold War, the attention of much work in peace research shifted to the problem of postwar peacebuilding. This was largely in response to the efforts of United Nations Secretary General Boutros Boutros-Ghali to expand the work of the United Nations beyond its traditional peacekeeping functions. It also was a response to the proliferation of new democracies during this time. International intervention was seen as an important tool for helping establish durable democratic institutions in states affected by the Cold War thaw. The effect of this has been a tendency in the field to focus on violent conflicts and postwar settings, with less research on other phases of conflict (including social movements), a neglect of the problem of structural violence, and an uncritical acceptance of the notion that neoliberal models of economic development are best suited to advancing development and peace.

This pattern parallels the tendency of researchers, in the words of Rivage-Seul, to "[accept] the politicians' vision of the best possible world," rather than to articulate alternatives that confront unequal power relations and focus attention on basic human needs. Quoting Jonathan Schell, Rivage-Seul argues that the logic of deterrence "deter[red] debate about itself," placing "sharp limits . . . on the definition of 'respectable' [and] so-called 'realistic' thinking about nuclear strategy" (1987, 153). In a similar way, the market ideology of neoliberal globalization has served to deter debate about itself throughout most of the 1980s and 1990s.[1] Critics of global markets were marginalized from major policy debates as the global financial institutions took on more influential roles in national and global economic policy during the 1980s and 1990s. A "market epistemology" has "infected" disciplines such as development studies and international relations (Da Costa and McMichael 2007, 588). Indeed, a key element of the neoliberal globalization project was the depoliticization of core questions about economic and social policy (Brunelle 2007). This was accomplished largely through the establishment of an "apparent homogeneity of discourse" about global economic policies (Dagnino 2008, 69), leading to the "discursive demobilization" of a wide range of social movements (see Lynch 1998). Following Fetherston (2000), we argue that effective peacebuilding needs to transform discourses and modes of thinking, and it must begin with a rigorous critique of the dominant social and political order.

In the academy, neoliberal approaches in economics displaced other theoretical tendencies, thereby silencing alternatives to global markets by channeling resources toward growing and legitimating business schools and by purging economics departments of scholars who ventured outside neoliberal orthodoxy (Sklair 1997; Hayes 2007). Within national and international institutions, neoliberal-friendly economists found more employment prospects over this time period (Markoff and Montecinos 1993; Montecinos 2001; Babb 2001). Even within the United Nations, attempts to address persistent poverty and rising inequality through redistributive and nonmarket measures were marginalized from the key policy arenas—including peacebuilding—as the UN sought to cultivate more cooperative ties with corporations (Smith 2008; Knight and Smith 2007).

The influence of market ideologies on both theory and practice is also evident in the field of peace research. While recent work in the field identifies some of the ways neoliberal reforms can exacerbate conflict,

---

1. This has been changing since the late 1990s as popular resistance to economic globalization has expanded in intensity and geographic scope and as the world witnesses multiple and successive crises caused by financial globalization and excessive reliance on international trade and finance as a means to development. The global economic crisis beginning in late 2007 has contributed further to the delegitimation of neoliberal ideology.

the recommendations emerging from this work are to merely reduce the speed at which such policies are introduced in postwar settings, rather than to allow space for alternative paths to economic development (e.g., Collier et al. 2003; Paris 2004). More structural critiques of the interstate system and its orientation toward markets are largely absent from this work. This may be due in part to the fact that a good deal of this research is funded by governments or intergovernmental agencies (notably including the World Bank) and therefore is largely articulated within existing policy discourses and frameworks. This book challenges dominant assumptions in much of the literature on peacebuilding, arguing that economic globalization is a major source of the structural violence[2] underlying most contemporary violent conflicts. While much of the literature in the field of peace research focuses on violent interstate and intrastate conflict, it is becoming increasingly difficult to address the transnational dimensions of conflict that are often working to affect localized conflict dynamics. As economic globalization shifts economic and other important policy decisions to supranational institutions, the ability of local actors to affect conflict and peacebuilding processes within their borders is diminished. Moreover, as resources such as energy, land, and water become increasingly scarce, decisions about these resources are increasingly shifted away from local policy arenas. Thus, it is vital that scholars, analysts, and practitioners engage in more critical reflection on *global* structures of power to improve our understandings of how these structures affect both inter- and intrastate conflict.

We also contend that studies of peacebuilding and violent conflict can benefit from greater dialogue with the extensive literature on social movements. This literature has focused largely on civil society and its relationship to the state and, increasingly, the interstate system (for reviews, see,

---

2. According to Webster and Perkins (2001, 330), "structural violence occurs when political and economic systems are organized in ways that oppress, exploit, and dominate certain segments of a population while privileging others who hold power and wealth." For Uvin, structural violence is the "denial, through the distribution of resources and opportunity, of people's means of realizing basic needs and potential" (2003, 148). Scholars of economic globalization use the term "social exclusion" to refer to similar phenomena (see Munck 2002).

e.g., Snow, Soule, and Kriesi 2004; Tarrow 2011; McCarthy 1997; Smith and Kutz-Flamenbaum 2010; Smith and Wiest 2012). While virtually all analyses of peacebuilding processes stress the important roles civil society plays in building peace, much of the work fails to adequately problematize the relationships between states and civil society or the operation of power within civil society. Social movement theory addresses how state power and practices affect both the character of civil society associations and the opportunities diverse actors have to affect social change. It also is concerned with dynamics of conflict and cooperation *within* civil society itself, including the conditions (both national and transnational) that contribute to or obstruct effective alliance building and coordination among civil society groups. Both of these dimensions are essential to understanding what makes postwar peace processes durable and what sort of structures and policies can help prevent the outbreak of violent conflict in the first place. Thus, a key aim of our project is to expand attention to social movement theory in the field of peace research.

Authors in this volume draw from work in multiple disciplines to uncover how the predominant, global neoliberal models of economic development affect the dynamics of conflict and peace in a variety of local settings. While there may indeed be relationships between economic liberalization and the conditions that foster peace, and while open markets might be associated with more open political systems, there is considerable debate among social scientists about the nature of these relationships. Market liberalization can proceed in highly authoritarian contexts, and highly democratic countries may in fact limit their participation in global markets in response to democratic pressures. Moreover, some analyses show that economic liberalization can seriously undermine efforts to rebuild social institutions and foster political liberalization in war-torn societies (Uvin 1998; McGinty 2006; Paris 2004).

In addition to questioning some basic assumptions in much of the mainstream peace research literature, we also want to shift attention away from the political projects and discourses of elites and toward the efforts of popular groups to respond to and redress problems in specific contexts. Our bottom-up approach seeks to uncover the visions, demands, and political projects being advanced in local settings in response to—and often despite—the constraints imposed by more powerful groups (Kaldor 2003). The case studies in this volume demonstrate how globalized models and norms can channel and constrain popular movements in ways that undermine emancipatory projects. Although global norms such as human rights and disarmament can legitimize challengers and provide opportunities for movements to mobilize transnationally, they can be a double-edged sword, for they can lead movements to engage with institutional processes that replicate power asymmetries and ultimately reinforce the interests of dominant powers (see Fetherston 2000).

Our perspective calls into question many assumptions about the nature of modern states. Peacebuilding missions have been described as "transmission mechanisms" of neoliberal models of the state, assisting the process of transforming national states into entities that facilitate the trade liberalization agenda of globalized capital (Paris 2002). In this sense, peacekeeping operations are a part of the "revolution from above," that helped expand the global economy in recent decades (Robinson 2004). Under neoliberalism, states around the world have been restructured to deemphasize their welfare-providing and regulatory functions while simultaneously strengthening their coercive capacity, particularly in regard to the protection of private property and the disciplining of labor (O'Brien 2004).

The neoliberal state is thus "lean and mean" (Evans 1997, 85–86), trimmed of its social welfare components but with strengthened military, policing, and prison capacities (see also Harvey 2005). This revolution from above has been even more brutal for people in the global South, where states were hollowed out before they had developed effective systems of representation and distribution (Ferguson 2006; see also Tilly 1990). And its effects have been especially harsh for society's most vulnerable groups, including women (Moghadam 2005; 2012). In more recent years, the "war on terror" has introduced new repressive tendencies in Western states, and traditional rights to political participation and assembly have been eroded there as well (della Porta et al. 2007). This has implications for future trajectories of violent conflict and therefore deserves more attention by peace researchers.

Clearly, countries experience different forms of violence, and this requires attention to their particular needs. Some nations are left with little infrastructure following civil war or genocide (such as Rwanda, the Democratic Republic of the Congo, and Sierra Leone) and must commit significant resources to rebuild their economies and societies. Elsewhere, pervasive structural violence is a consequence of uneven international development and social and cultural practices of discrimination over generations, even under conditions of formal democracy (for example, India and Brazil). The specific needs of countries are a consequence of their particular histories and contemporary challenges, and certainly there is no universal model of reform. Nevertheless, neoliberal prescriptions call for a reduction of state capacity, services, and public welfare protections and for the opening of national economies to generate economic growth.

For countries with a long history of international exploitation and other forms of structural violence, such policies may only exacerbate social exclusion, making a return to violent struggle more likely (Silver 2003). Neoliberal reforms tend to strengthen the power of well-positioned domestic and international economic elites while providing only tangential if any benefits to the poor. At the same time, these reforms tend to subject historically disadvantaged groups to even greater economic vulnerability (Jaggar 2001; Rajagopal 2003; Rudra 2002; Kingfisher 2003). Measuring progress only by looking at gross economic indicators, common to many neoliberal economic development strategies, neglects the complex and reinforcing patterns of marginalization that often accompany the rapid scaling back of state services (Bergman 2009; Babb 2005).

Neoliberal policies may also destabilize fragile postwar societies. By requiring state restructuring along neoliberal lines, contemporary frameworks for peace agreements constrain the policy space available to states recovering from wars. Take two common requirements for external aid, privatization and liberalization. In theory, privatization increases the efficiency of corrupt, unproductive state enterprises by subjecting them to new incentives of profitability (which presumably reflects their accountability and responsiveness to consumer demands). In transitional settings, however, privatization may only widen economic disparities, for often the only domestic actors capable of purchasing newly privatized businesses are those who already enjoy significant economic and political power, and frequently they contributed to the violence in the first place (Mani 2002,

138–41; Boyce 2002). Under these conditions, privatization may "be impossible or merely involve the enrichment of senior government officials" (Fitzgerald 2000, 58). In Sierra Leone, for example, privatization resulted in placing many profitable enterprises "in a few oligopolistic hands and deepening a popular sense of grievance" (Keen 2000, 40), rather than expanding wealth to broader sectors of the population.

Liberalization focuses on reducing restrictions to foreign investment and minimizing barriers to foreign trade. The goal is to stimulate the domestic economy by permitting the introduction of needed capital and generating employment. In postwar countries with fragile economies, however, liberalization can be destabilizing. Liberalization combined with a weakened state can depress wages and promote export-led "growth" that leaves societies vulnerable to fluctuations in world prices of their primary exports (Carbonnier 2002; Uvin 1998). Most postwar settings require extensive state intervention to provide for social welfare and redistribution of land and other sources of wealth, often an original source of the conflict. Greater state protection from international market competition is also vital to rebuilding local and national economies. Local workers must have a stake in national economic recovery. Yet, policies designed to attract international investment do not necessarily help—and may even hinder—efforts to expand local economic opportunities and thereby build loyalty and commitment to peacebuilding processes (see, e.g., Pugh and Cooper 2004). Also, an active and participatory state is often necessary to protect minorities and women and ensure the rule of law (Dagnino 2008). Neoliberal states cannot effectively achieve these aims, and therefore undermine peacebuilding processes. In the aftermath of civil war, where political and ethnic divisions may run deep and populations enjoy little economic or material security, policies that limit social protections diminish the public's stake in peace agreements and can further exacerbate tensions and conflict.

Of course, civil wars have many causes, such as elite radicalization, ethnic factionalization, and pervasive poverty in the face of growing inequality and politicization. We do not deny that there are numerous sources of civil wars, and that some of these are national or local (Fearon and Laitan 2003; Wood 2004; Collier and Sambanis 2005). What is remarkable, however, is the extent to which the peacebuilding literature focuses on short-term and national-level causes and ignores broader global factors contributing to instability and violence.

A critical review of the peacebuilding literature suggests that much more attention must be paid to questions of how the inequities of the global economic and political order affect the prospects for peace and peace processes at national and local levels. The dominant "liberal peace" framework, with its emphasis on conflict termination and the promotion of individual human rights, formal democracy, and a market economy, fails to address the deeper global economic and material causes of violence (Paris and Sisk 2009). Global institutions and processes have privileged rich, Western countries, leaving many without much stake in the existing global order. As Peter Uvin observes, "current modes of globalisation provoke structural violence, and, as a result, acute violence. At this level, structural reform of the world economy is advocated—including the establishment of major redistributive mechanisms" (Uvin 2002, 19–20). Recent years have also drawn heightened attention to how environmental devastation caused largely by the development policies pursued under neoliberal globalization can cause or exacerbate violent conflict. In short, the legitimacy and stability of global agreements and institutions depends upon work to integrate more equitably actors on the periphery—that is, non-Western states as well as civil society—into policy agendas and decision-making processes.

Some contemporary social movements have mobilized explicitly in response to the conflicts generated by this larger world economy and interstate system (e.g., Macdonald 1997; Paffenholz and Spurk 2006). Many have been working at local, national, and transnational levels to resist the neoliberal state and to promote redistributive and welfare policies. Movements in Latin America in particular have been successful in this regard, and have as a result begun to challenge global power relations. Movement actors have also developed transnational networks and organizations capable of fostering communication and dialogue that can contribute to peacebuilding (Kaldor 2003). The World Social Forum (WSF) process, for instance, is a deliberate attempt to bring together multiple and diverse movements to develop alternative visions aimed at addressing the most challenging conflicts of our day. The WSF process consists of a linked series of encounters organized across space (from local to global) and time. It aims to foster new forms of association and engagement that nurture mutual understandings, solidarity, and collective identities based on notions of equity and shared goals of a more just and ecologically sustainable global order. Such efforts help anticipate and give voice to conflicts over scarce resources *before* they escalate into organized violence. At the same time, they build support for nonviolent alternatives. More important for our purposes, the WSF process represents one of the largest and most sustained movements for the sort of large-scale systemic change that would address the structural violence fueling most major wars. As such, it deserves consideration as an essential part of the work of contemporary peacebuilding.

As noted above, most scholars of peacebuilding stress the crucial role that civil society actors play in postwar peacebuilding processes (Darby 2006; Mason and Meernik 2006). But few seriously consider questions about how to create the long-term structural conditions that can nurture strong and democratic (that is, tolerant and nonviolent) civil societies both in postwar settings as well as in contexts where conflict has not escalated into violence (but see Paffenholz 2010a). Indeed, part of the difficulty stems from the emphasis on what Michel Foucault (1991) referred to as "governmentality," or the process by which the state and elites employ a host of strategies and techniques to make a society "governable." Such a process often requires depoliticizing civil society, or at the very least reinscribing the domain of politics to draw a sharp distinction between legitimate and illegitimate policies and political ends.

In these contexts, critical civil society groups are redefined as spoilers, without careful distinctions between movements calling for greater democratic input and reactionary movements. This can exacerbate the discursive demobilization (Lynch 1998) of groups making legitimate claims and/or wielding significant, though nonmilitarized, influence in local settings. By delegitimizing critical local actors, conventional peacebuilding approaches undermine critical analysis and normalize state and elite interests (Fetherston 2000). As Neil Cooper has argued, "both the problematisation of war economies and the emphasis on the imperative of transformation can be understood as speech acts that securitise and pathologise the local in order to legitimise the extraordinary measures deemed necessary to bring about liberal governance" (Cooper 2006a, 87).

We examine in this volume the ways global institutions and practices affect the contexts in which contemporary peacebuilding efforts take place. In particular, we consider how global economic and structural forces serve to facilitate or constrain civil society actors, including humanitarian nongovernmental organizations (NGOs) and other social movements (see Paffenholz and Spurk 2010). We also explore the relevance of a major global mobilization of civil society actors, the WSF process, as a possible source of ideas about alternative models of social organization and as a space for experimenting with and developing practices that support peace and justice. What is required, therefore, is an alternative to the dominant "liberal peace" framework, one that deepens its commitment to human rights and democracy while eschewing damaging demands for privatization, liberalization, and weakened welfare states.

A more critical perspective on peacebuilding must be *systemic:* it must identify the underlying structural causes of violence, including their local, national, regional, and global sources, while also formulating a broader conception of peace that incorporates a wider set of actors. In this way, our conceptualization of peacebuilding returns us to Johan Galtung's original articulation of this idea in 1975, which focused on cultivating what he called "positive peace" rather than simply on ending violence, or "negative peace" (see Paffenholz 2010b, 43). Specifically, peace scholarship and practice should move beyond its focus on elite, transnational expertise and knowledge and resituate social movements and civil society at the center of debates about durable and just peace. It is this juncture— between peace studies, social movement theory, and globalization—that this volume explores.

**Core Propositions**

Based on the above analysis, we arrive at a set of core propositions that will guide the analyses that follow. Here, we briefly sketch these.

(1) The structural conditions that shape processes leading to violence or peace can be linked to the world capitalist economic system, and therefore attempts to prevent the outbreak of violence and to promote sustainable peace in postwar settings require attention to historic

and world-systemic factors (see Smith 2010; Silver 2003; Pugh et al. 2008a). Approaches to peacebuilding that focus strictly on the national level—such as those addressing problems of failed states, elite corruption, economic policies, and arms regulation—do not adequately address how those states' relations to the larger world economy and their historic relations with other states are shaping these dynamics (see, e.g., Farmer 2004; Burawoy 1998; McMichael 1990). If peace research is to offer solutions for long-term peace, it must examine more critically the global and systemic constraints that fragile, postwar societies face. This requires a close look at how these states are embedded within the world economy.

Indeed, scholars such as David Harvey (2006) have argued that the global capitalist economy is itself based on a political economy of violence, or "accumulation by dispossession" (see also Escobar 2004). It follows that local and national struggles must be understood within a larger network of local, national, and global relations that are oriented around this global capitalist logic. Effective peace processes thus require a reversal of the processes of dispossession that are inherent in neoliberal policies and practices.

(2) The contemporary context is one in which the dominant model for organizing the world-system is in crisis and is being challenged by various contenders. Glasius and Kaldor (2002) have usefully, if rather schematically, categorized these various actors as (a) neoliberals, who wish to accelerate the processes of trade deregulation, dismantlement of state capacity, and insertion of "peripheral" countries into the world economy; (b) regressive antiglobalizers, who resist the pressures of economic and societal transformation by reverting to "traditional" cultural practices that may be explicitly hostile to human rights and democracy; and (c) democratic progressives, who seek to expand popular participation and deliberation about the fundamental ends of society (see also Barber 1995). The first two are often coercive and pursue top-down policies on the population. The latter cosmopolitan and democratic approach is largely a bottom-up approach to global integration. Our project privileges this bottom-up vision of global integration, without presuming any single outcome or model. The goal is to identify paths toward political and social emancipation while taking seriously the heterogeneity of needs and context-appropriate strategies.

(3) Institutional and structural factors privilege powerful actors—including states, hegemons, capitalists, etc. This affects how alternatives are articulated and advanced. If they are to succeed at transforming social conflict, peacebuilding processes must disrupt the means through which powerful actors can reproduce their interests despite challenges. In other words, we must better understand processes such as "discursive demobilization" or the entrenchment of power in the "deep structures" (Rajagopal 2006) of the economy and political institutions. Pugh, Cooper, and Turner (2008b) call for a "politics of emancipation" that can yield new, ecologically informed thinking about societal organizing logics and goals. Concepts such as "social emancipation," "life welfare," and "gender justice" seek to sensitize analysts to the operation of power and to orient our thinking toward alternative structures that are more likely to generate the sustained peacebuilding outcomes we seek. Because it lacks a vested interest in the dominant institutional order, civil society is a primary locus for thematizing, securing, and sustaining these various forms of emancipation from a world economic system based in inequality and violence (Alexander 2006; Bohman 2007; Habermas 1996).

## Concepts

The book is oriented around the exploration of a set of core concepts, discussed below. The authors' contributions engage explicitly with these concepts, helping provide greater coherence to the project and uniting the various chapters in an ongoing and multiperspectival analysis. The concepts were originally chosen by the editors, but were refined through conversations and exchanges at an authors' workshop at the University of Notre Dame.

### Neoliberalism

We understand the term "neoliberalism" as a set of economic policies advanced by leading world economies and global financial institutions such as the World Bank, the International Monetary Fund, and the World Trade Organization beginning in the 1970s and continuing through the

1990s and beyond. The primary goal is to reduce constraints on international trade and expand opportunities for foreign investment, thereby integrating national economies into the global capitalist economy. Key policies include trade and financial liberalization, privatization, deregulation, and reductions of public sector employment and expenditures. An important effect of neoliberal policies has been the redistribution of wealth and political influence from lower income to higher-income groups within and across societies (Babb 2005; Harvey 2006).

*Social Movements*

We understand the term "social movements" as *collections* of organizational and individual actors who "who engage in *sustained* political or cultural *contestation* through recourse to institutional and extrainstitutional forms of action" (Escobar and Alvarez 1992, 321, emphasis added). We stress that for most analysts and for our purposes here, social movements are collective, sustained, popularly based engagements with authorities. They also may engage with formal political procedures where these are available, but typically combine formal political actions with extrainstitutional actions, including crime. While many movements cultivate explicit collective identities among participants, some movements are unified and defined more in terms of their shared social change goals. As will become clear in the following pages, not all movements are progressive or democratic. Furthermore, some of the "movements" we will explore in this book are somewhat nascent and less self-consciously organized. Examples of this sort of movement include the youth engaging in social leveling in Sierra Leone and the pirates off Somalia's coast.

*Gender Justice*

Most analyses of postwar peacebuilding processes identify the vital importance of attention to gender inequities in sustainable peace processes. The term "gender justice" indicates efforts to reform legal institutions and practices to remedy gender inequalities and address gender-based violence and war crimes. It also includes structural reforms aimed at improving women's access to resources and economic opportunities. The process of securing gender justice is a complex one that places a priority on the renegotiation of gender relations to prevent backlash against women in the aftermath of armed conflict (see Pugh, Cooper, Turner 2008). Given the significant redistributions of power required, explicit attention must be paid to the question of how gender justice might be achieved in particular contexts (both peaceful and postwar).

### Globalizing Projects

We might view our project as an exploration of contestation over different visions of how the world should be organized. Phil McMichael (2006) argues that neoliberal globalization reflects a particular "globalization project" that favors wealthy countries, corporations, and individuals at the expense of poorer countries, workers, and other people. Pugh and his colleagues refer to neoliberal peacebuilding as a "normative project," which imposes neoliberal policies on states attempting to rebuild after armed conflicts.

More recently, various actors have been articulating alternative globalization projects aimed at remedying the problems linked to neoliberal economic globalization. Many social movement activists represented in the WSF, for instance, stress the need to reorganize fundamentally global relations around the aims of inclusion, diversity, and participation.

Elite globalization projects are reflected in UN-led initiatives such as "Human Security." Pugh and his colleagues distinguish between "problem solving"[3] and "paradigm shifting" approaches, noting that the human security approach has been co-opted to justify military intervention and to help re-legitimize neoliberal agendas in the wake of failed structural adjustment programs (Pugh, Cooper, and Turner 2008, 393). They show

---

3. A problem solving approach is likened to what Paul Rogers (2010) refers to as "liddism"—i.e., keeping a lid on, or containing the problems emerging through the implementation of neoliberal reforms, without attention to the underlying causes of the problems. Pugh and his colleagues see analysts such as Joseph Stiglitz, Jeffrey Sachs, George Soros, and Amy Chua as offering such problem-solving approaches.

how the language of human security has failed to address the complexities of local geographies of power while privileging the atomized individual as the target of policy. Instead of "human security" they call for a "politics of emancipation" that helps create space for a "life welfare" approach that appreciates the importance of social relations and the ecology. For them, peacebuilding efforts must be "unsecuritized" and more attentive to local voices and power relations. In addition, they call for a shift in paradigms of peacebuilding that "rejects universalism in favour of heterodoxy, reconceptualises the abstract individual as a social being and limits damage to planetary life—in short, a 'life welfare' perspective" (393).

## From "Empowerment" to Social Emancipation?

Empowerment is the process whereby groups and individuals in a society gain greater control over their lives and destinies. Empowerment is seen as a key to peacebuilding, since it helps expand popular commitment to the peace process while also addressing some of the inequities that contribute to conflict escalation. Much of the research on peacebuilding suggests that this is one of the more neglected features of postwar peace operations (Paffenholz 2010a). Effective redistribution of the means of production and political influence rarely occurs, and this is clearly a part of the explanation for why so many peace agreements break down.

By understanding peacebuilding within the larger global political and economic context, we have given attention to the role that culture, ideas, and institutions play in reinforcing dominant power relations, even where actors aim to transform inequalities and related conflicts. Thus, we draw from the work of Boaventura de Sousa Santos (2007a) to argue for an approach to conflict transformation and peacebuilding that emphasizes *social emancipation* rather than empowerment. The latter term suggests that marginalized groups are essentially the addressees, or recipients, of reformist policies, and in many instances the term has been co-opted by external elites and institutions promoting neoliberal transformations (see Eliasoph 2011). We therefore use the term "social emancipation," which attributes more agency and control to those who are excluded from equitable participation in the economy, society, and polity. This emphasis on the agency of the marginalized also elicits different strategies for peace-building than does the term "empowerment." As Pugh, Cooper, and Turner have noted, "the political economy of post-conflict peace and state-building in a liberal peace framework has involved a simulacra of empowerment where peacebuilders transfer responsibilities to society without transferring power" (2008, 391). Thus, the social emancipation framework emphasizes the structural analysis of power relations and examines the possibilities for excluded groups to exercise agency, in contrast to less politicized forms of peacebuilding empowerment that focus more on charity toward the dispossessed.

## Chapter Summary

Part one of the book develops analyses of how discourses are used to reinforce dominant social relations, and how discourses are mobilized by social movements as they work to transform unequal social relations. Neil Cooper's chapter leads off this discussion with a consideration of how the discourses surrounding arms regulation, including those of "human security," have focused attention on the regulation of weapons systems and have not significantly impacted conventional arms trade or broader human security. He argues that peace movements and their supporters must look critically at the history of arms control campaigns in order to devise strategies that can reorient multilateral peace agendas and generate agreements that go beyond the token efforts to regulate international flows of weapons and move us more clearly in the direction of greater human well-being.

Cecelia Lynch explores the specialized and globalized discourses characterizing the world of humanitarian NGOs. Organizations working with grants or contracts from governments and intergovernmental agencies are increasingly required to document and demonstrate the effectiveness of their operations in postwar contexts. This results orientation, Lynch argues, has generated a set of benchmarks and criteria that are more linked with expanding a neoliberal economic agenda than with advancing peacebuilding.

Dia Da Costa's chapter demonstrates how *Janam*, an organization of the cultural and political left in India, has used street theater to challenge dominant neoliberal discourses. She critiques the ways the group has articulated class within its satirical plays, uncovering the challenges to movements that aim both to contest the larger debates over neoliberal globalization and build unity among a diverse array of social and class actors. Her analysis offers insights into the particular strategies and tactics movements use as they seek to transform relations based in large-scale structural violence.

Part two of the book examines how globalized models and concepts are applied in local contexts, and considers their implications for the transformation of violent conflicts. Valentine Moghadam begins the section by identifying linkages between the world economy and the structural violence that underlies violent conflicts. She argues that war and militarism are both fueled by and reproduce gendered identities that help perpetuate violence. She illustrates this through an examination of the gendered consequences of the wars in Iraq and Afghanistan, developing an argument for a more explicitly *gendered* approach to the global "human security" and peacebuilding agenda that privileges the goal of *gender justice*. She explores the roles that transnational feminist networks have played in fostering peace and gender justice, offering insights into strategies for improving peacebuilding as well as preventing the escalation of conflicts into violence.

Isaac Kamola uses the case of the Somali pirates to uncover how the concept of "failed states" has been used to justify selective international interventions that reinforce the interests of Western powers in controlling access to natural resources. According to Kamola, the concept obfuscates the nature of conflicts, thereby inhibiting effective efforts to address underlying causes. He argues that piracy is not simply reducible to localized greed or state failure, but is also part of a larger struggle over the governance and policing of international commodity flows.

Catherine Bolten then offers insights into how humanitarian aid gets translated into historically structured social networks in Sierra Leone. She examines the "Pull-You-Down Syndrome" of social leveling employed by local "big men" to shape the social distribution of resources. Large pools of undereducated and unemployed men are readily mobilized by would-be big men in the latter's efforts to mobilize foreign aid resources in ways that enhance their power. If aid is to contribute to peacebuilding, efforts to understand the local social context and counter these sorts of internally competitive dynamics are necessary.

Finally, in part three of the volume we consider the possibilities for building peace from below by cultivating movements and practices conducive to nonviolent conflict resolution. James Bohman explores how processes of democratic deliberation enacted within social movements can promote the aims of peacebuilding by enhancing trust among participants and strengthening the legitimacy of decisions. He explores the possibilities for constructing and sustaining public spheres that can promote effective deliberation at a scale appropriate to the contemporary globalized context.

Jackie Smith, Rebecca Burns, and Rachel Miller then provide an in-depth look at the activities of activists working within the WSF process, demonstrating how the work in that arena reflects the practices and aims of peacebuilding, particularly those identified in Bohman's chapter. They consider the lessons the WSF process provides for work in a variety of contexts to transform conflict and reduce violence.

We offer this volume as a contribution to important debates on how we might reimagine the possibilities for both preventing wars and violence and for securing and sustaining a just peace for fragile societies. We have endeavored to bring together certain scholarly literatures that have remained largely separated from one another—the social movements, peacebuilding, and globalization literatures—and thus generate a provocative conversation that can reframe the ways in which scholars and practitioners understand the work of peacebuilding.

Part One

# Discourses of Conflict and Movement

# I

# The Post–Cold War Arms Trade Paradox

*Humanitarian Arms Control, NGOs,*
*and the Strategic Complexes of the Liberal Peace*[1]

## Neil Cooper

A notable aspect of the post–Cold War arms control agenda has been the appearance, and in many respects the relative success, of what has been labeled as a humanitarian arms control (HAC) (Greene 2010; Hynek 2007) or humanitarian disarmament (Borrie 2009, 312; Borrie and Randin 2006) agenda. This has included, in particular, the campaign on landmines that led to the 1997 Ottawa Convention, the campaign to ban cluster munitions that resulted in the 2008 Convention on Cluster Munitions, and a range of initiatives designed to control the trade in small arms and light weapons, most notably, the 2001 UN Program of Action on Small Arms. To the extent that current efforts to negotiate an Arms Trade Treaty (ATT) are animated by humanitarian concerns, this initiative might also be classified as a further example of HAC in action. What all these cases of conventional arms regulation also have in common is that they have generally been discussed by commentators as examples of a control agenda that

1. Research for this article was conducted with the aid of grants from the British Academy (Ref: SG101199) and the Trust for Research and Education on the Arms Trade. Archival material from the National Archives of the UK is quoted with permission.

marks a striking departure from the traditional practices and foci of arms control and as instances of the transformative power of global civil society campaigners working to operationalize a benevolent human security agenda. This chapter aims to challenge these assumptions. Instead, it will argue that such initiatives are far more ambiguous in both their roots and their consequences than mainstream accounts might suggest.

Initiatives such as those on landmines and cluster munitions are actually part of a much longer history of regulation and taboos constructed around "pariah weapons." Following on from this, I will argue that the social construction of certain weapons as particularly odious has more to do with the interests of powerful actors and the relationship of such weapons to legitimized military technologies than any inherently inhumane characteristics claimed for them. These points will be illustrated by way of brief discussions on the way the meanings attached to both cluster munitions and small arms have altered over time. The chapter will then discuss the ways in which dominant models of economy and geographies of threat construction have worked to produce particular approaches to arms trade regulation in different eras. A key contention with regard to the post–Cold War era will be that it has been characterized by an (apparent) arms trade paradox, whereby the proliferation of formal instruments of international regulation, ostensibly designed to constrain the conventional arms trade, has also coincided with a shift to a more permissive approach to arms sales in general. Viewed at the system level however, the specific combination of permission and proscription characteristic of the post–Cold War era makes sense as a morphology of regulation that, in broad terms, aims to triangulate between efforts to discriminate against pariah actors, to support the bio-political goals of intrastate pacification in the global South, and to maintain military hierarchy. Understood from this perspective, the humanitarian arms control agenda has had far more ambiguous effects than its supporters allow. While it has certainly produced some notable arms control achievements, it has also served to reflect and reaffirm a new "new standard of civilization" centered around the distinction between discriminate and indiscriminate weapons and modes of warfare that are key elements in the legitimizing discourse of both contemporary militarism and liberal peace intervention.

This chapter then, represents an attempt to respond to the call from our editors, Jackie Smith and Ernesto Verdeja, for thinking about peacebuilding that is *systemic*. That is, scholarship that does not simply focus on the inside of the postconflict state but that, rather, considers how broader historic and world-system factors shape the global architecture of peace and violence that specific instances of liberal peacebuilding are both located in and conditioned by. Accordingly, the chapter will conclude by briefly considering the implications of this analysis for our understanding of the role played by arms trade NGOs as actors in the strategic complexes of the liberal peace and by briefly outlining the elements of a more emancipatory agenda for arms trade regulation.

## Humanitarian Arms Control

There are a number of common claims that are made about the various initiatives labeled under the rubric of humanitarian arms control. First, supporters claim that the bans on cluster munitions and landmines in particular represent novel moments in the history of arms control, a novelty that stems partly from the fact that commitments to ban specific categories of conventional weapons are considered to be unprecedented. As Thakur and Maley have suggested, for example, the Mine Ban Treaty was "historically significant for being the first to impose a ban on an entire class of weapons already in widespread use" (Thakur and Maley 1999; also see Williams 2008, 282).

Second, it is claimed that the bans on antipersonnel mines (APMs) and cluster munitions as well as international action to address small arms proliferation represent signal successes of a new post–Cold War human security agenda (Axworthy 1998, 451; Francheschet 2006, 33–34; Owen 2008). Third, advocates argue that a key element in the success of the campaigns on APMs and cluster munitions in particular has been a reframing of them as presenting specifically humanitarian problems. It is this discursive move on the part of campaigners that is deemed to have enabled them to promote HAC initiatives as issues necessitating action within the parameters of human security, rather than an arms control issue subject to the realpolitik logics of national security (Williams, Goose, Wareham

2008, 2; Cottrell 2009). In particular, the campaigns on landmines, cluster munitions, and small arms have all been grounded in a discourse that emphasizes the threat posed to innocent civilians—which, in the case of the first two in particular, is deemed a function of the "inherently inhumane" (Thakur and Maley 1999, 296) nature of the technology.

A final theme in the narratives on humanitarian arms control is the emphasis given to the transformative potential of global civil society (albeit in alliance with key like-minded states) acting as an expression of bottom-up power, to persuade the majority of foot-dragging states of the necessity to take action (Mathew and Rutherford 2003, 29–30; Roberts 2008, 183). In summary, this is a narrative of the post–Cold War humanitarian arms control agenda as a novel, radical, entirely benign, bottom-up endeavor that places the security of the human at the very heart of practice. The contribution of HAC initiatives to pre-conflict, in-conflict, and post-conflict peacebuilding would therefore appear to be both self-evident and indisputable, not least by reducing the frequency with which problem weapons are utilized in war and by limiting their deadly legacy after conflict.

There has, of course, been some dispute over the extent to which HAC initiatives have really produced changes in practice. For example, the failure of key producer or user states (e.g., the United States, China, India, Pakistan, Russia) to sign up to the bans on landmines and cluster munitions is widely acknowledged as a weakness. Similarly, detractors have criticized the tendency in initiatives on small arms to focus on illicit rather than legal supplies (Mutimer 2006) and have tended to be less positive about the effect of such initiatives in actually curbing the small arms trade (Karp 2006). These are certainly weaknesses that undermine the claims of HAC advocates. However, in the case of landmines at least, the attempt to construct a weapons taboo that influences the behavior of actors irrespective of their formal adherence to the Ottawa Treaty would appear to have been relatively successful (see table below).

Such debates on the scope of agreements and their implementation as well as studies of the modes of negotiation and campaigning are certainly important, but they also reflect a level of analysis problem inherent in much of the literature on humanitarian arms control; a literature that

Table 1.1

Use of Antipersonnel Mines (APMs) in Major Armed Conflicts

|  | 1999 | 2000 | 2001 | 2002 | 2003 | 2004 | 2005 | 2006 | 2007 | 2008 |
|---|---|---|---|---|---|---|---|---|---|---|
| No. of major armed conflicts | 21 | 19 | 20 | 17 | 17 | 13 | 16 | 15 | 14 | 16 |
| Use of APMs by governments | 12 | 13 | 14 | 9 | 4 | 4 | 3 | 2 | 2 | 2 |
| % of conflicts | 57% | 68% | 70% | 53% | 24% | 31% | 19% | 13% | 14% | 13% |
| Use of APMs by nonstate armed groups | 18 | 19 | 14 | 11 | 16 | 13 | 10 | 8 | 9 | 7 |
| % of conflicts | 85% | 100% | 70% | 65% | 94% | 100% | 63% | 53% | 64% | 44% |

Sources: Landmines Monitor Report 2009: Toward a Mine-Free World, p. 9 (see http://www.icbl.org/); Stockholm International Peace Research Institute, *SIPRI Yearbook 2009: Armaments, Disarmament, and International Security,* Oxford: Oxford University Press, Table 2A.2, p. 70.

NB: Landmines Monitor data cross over two calendar years (e.g., the 2009 Landmines Monitor provides data on landmines use for 2008 and key developments up to May 2009). In contrast, SIPRI data on the number of major armed conflicts are listed by calendar year. The data may not therefore be directly comparable but nevertheless provide a rough measure of the relative (as opposed to absolute) fall in the use of APMs in conflicts.

rarely goes beyond a narrow, time-bound and policy-orientated discussion of campaigning strategies, policy arguments, and implementation issues. There is, admittedly, a smaller literature that steps back from this kind of discussion and undertakes a second level of analysis focused on the politics of HAC agenda setting, explaining the adoption of particular initiatives as a function, for example, of the relative abilities of key NGOs to prescribe or proscribe particular campaigning agendas (Carpenter 2011, 69–102). This kind of approach certainly offers greater explanatory power compared to the first level of analysis, but it tends to be both ahistorical and grounded in an anemic conception of power. Consequently, it offers only a partial explanation of how specific control agendas come to be adopted instead of others. My concern, then, in the remainder of this chapter, is not so much to consider the success or failure of particular initiatives as understood in the first level of analysis nor to ponder the relative influence of narrowly defined sets of norm entrepreneurs. Instead, it is to undertake both a more historically informed examination of conventional arms trade regulation and one that seeks to explain the relative capacity of particular actors to set HAC agendas not only in terms of their own qualities but also as a function of much larger paradigm shifts in, for example, dominant approaches to economy, security, and war. In order to do this, however, it is first necessary to illustrate the ahistoricism at the heart of the literature on HAC by examining the longer history of both pariah weapons regulation and the way this reflects particular relationships between power, arms ethics, and legitimized weaponry.

This ahistoricism is perhaps most obviously highlighted by the fact that there is a long record of initiatives aimed at eliminating certain pariah weapons or restricting their use in particular contexts. Examples include the attempts to impose bans or limits on the use of poison, "Greek fire," the crossbow, the gun in seventeenth- and eighteenth-century Japan, dum dum bullets, and the submarine (Burns 2009). The specific mix of motivations underpinning these attempts has varied according to each particular case, with some, such as the attempt to restrict the operation of submarines, arguably more clearly rooted in state calculations of realpolitik (Manson 1992). The success of such initiatives has varied from case to case. For example, restrictions on the submarine failed to survive the exigencies of total war in World War II, while restrictions on the gun in seventeenth- and eighteenth-century Japan resulted in its almost total disappearance from society, despite the fact that it had originally been quite widespread (Perrin 1979). However, notwithstanding their different levels of success, such restrictions do illustrate that there is nothing particularly novel or unique to the post–Cold War era attempt to ban specific weapons technologies.

Moreover, the justification of such measures by appeals to some kind of principled discourse is not unusual. For example, the prohibition on the use of crossbows issued by the Second Lateran Council of 1139 (and reissued at the Fourth Lateran Council in 1215) was not only underpinned by the Church and reinforced by religious sanction (the penalty of anathema), but was also represented as a restriction imposed on "that deadly and God-detested art of slingers and archers" (Croft 1996, 24). Such views were also reflected in late eleventh- and early twelfth-century carvings on the pilgrimage churches on the way to Compostela depicting demons with crossbows (Strickland and Hardy 2011, 61–3). Similarly, prohibitions on the use of poison that appear as far back as the Hindu Laws of Manu (ca. 2000BC–200AD), have often been accompanied by some appeal to higher moral standards—whether grounded in religious ethics or notions of military honor. In particular—like many pariah weapons—discussions of both proscription and legitimacy have often evolved around rather fluid concepts of "the standard of civilization." This was particularly the case in Europe from the eighteenth century onward when the prohibition against poison became an accepted part of the laws of war, in part at least because it was subject to a dual and self-reinforcing construction as a weapon that was both typical of savages and one that had no place in war between civilized nations (Price 1997, 26).

Not that the standard of civilization always pointed in the direction of restraint with regard to pariah weapons. For instance, just as prohibitions on the use of the crossbow were not extended to their use against barbarians, so the British argued against the ban on dum dum bullets imposed at the 1899 Hague conference on the grounds that the greater destructive potential of expanding bullets was necessary for use in colonial wars because "the savage, like the tiger . . . will go on fighting even when desperately wounded" (Spiers 1975, 7). Indeed, the British even considered adopting a double stock of ammunition—one, consisting of expanding bullets, for use in colonial wars and another set for use against a European enemy (ibid.). As Price has noted, then, the categorization of weapons as humane or inhumane, civilized or uncivilized, not only naturalizes or delegitimizes particular practices of international violence but also serves to secure (and indeed construct) the identities of actors in the process (Price 1997, 9).

Both moral sentiment and concerns about the standard of civilization were also reflected in the arms trade provisions of the 1890 Brussels Act. Although principally an antislavery initiative, the agreement not only included restrictions on firearms aimed at preventing the slave trade and limiting their "pernicious and preponderating part" in "internal wars between the native tribes" (Burns 1993, 1329), but was also agreed against the backdrop of a pan-European civil society campaign rooted in ethical concerns for the colonized. Thus, the British government was bombarded by letters of support for the act from campaigners concerned at the way " . . . the indiscriminate trade in firearms and ammunition has been, and is, a great curse and injury to the native races of Africa" (Letter from Mr. F. W. Fox to Lord Salisbury, October 17, 1889, Fox 1889). The participants at the Brussels Conference, where the agreement was negotiated, also received numerous communications from groups supporting the restrictions on the slave, arms, and liquor trades under discussion. For example, the Aborigines Protection Society sent a memorial declaring its long-standing commitment to upholding "the right of uncivilized races to humane and equitable treatment" and arguing that the supply of firearms and other munitions of war

> should, as far as possible, be absolutely forbidden, and that their importation from the coast to the interior should be strictly limited to the purposes helpful to civilization [while the relevant local authorities should be] rigidly held responsible for any breach of duty in contributing to internecine war among native tribes (Aborigines Protection Society to the President of the International Conference in Brussels, December 16, 1889).

The eventual outcome was an agreement to restrict the importation of firearms (particularly sophisticated weapons) as well as powder and ammunition into an area extending from the middle of the Sahara to present-day Namibia and Zimbabwe.

However, while particular instances of arms regulation might be actively supported by campaigners concerned to promote human welfare, and be framed in the most principled language (of its era), this tells us little about the broader system of arms trade regulation in which they are embedded. For example, the passage of the Brussels Act occurred in a period that "saw the fewest restraints and regulations on the arms trade in modern history" (Krause and MacDonald 1992, 712), thus illustrating the way in which instances of apparently ethical restraint can exist within a highly permissive architecture of regulation. This raises two questions: what creates the facilitating conditions for ethical appeals for arms restraint to gain traction even in such circumstances, and how can we understand their relationship to the global system of arms regulation? Four factors are crucial: the relationship between arms regulation and the narrow political and material interests of powerful actors; the relationship between pariah weapons and legitimized military technology; the relationship between economic philosophy and the approach to arms regulation; and the relationship between the global system of arms trade regulation and the dominant framing of threats in particular eras. Only by examining the interplay of these factors can we properly reflect on the role played by global civil society campaigns on the arms trade and consider their effects on broader efforts to promote peace—both globally and in the aftermath of local conflicts.

### Power and Interest

Discussions of humanitarian arms control tend to represent campaigning NGOs as agents of the powerless acting (albeit in alliance with some like-minded states) to mobilize global public opinion and pressure the larger body of reluctant states to adopt principled measures designed to further human welfare. Alternatively, some analysts have also highlighted the way middle-ranking states such as Canada have used campaigns on landmines or small arms as vehicles to enhance their diplomatic status in international forums such as the UN (Cottrell 2009). Both of these frameworks certainly capture important ways in which power and interest have interacted in the HAC agenda. However, even a brief analysis of the longer history of pariah weapons restrictions illustrates the need for more consideration of the way current initiatives might mirror older initiatives in reinforcing the interests of powerful actors.

For example, one factor in the virtual eradication of the gun in seventeenth- and eighteenth-century Japan was that it represented a threat to the warrior class when in the hands of the lower classes (Perrin 1979, 25–33). Similarly, although the weapons restrictions in the 1890 Brussels Act were certainly grounded in an ethical discourse, they were primarily rooted in concerns about the impact of the arms trade on colonial order. For instance, one British official calculated at the time that eighty thousand to one hundred thousand firearms annually were entering Africa via East African ports (Beachey 1962, 453), while immediately before the Brussels Conference convened, six hundred thousand rifles destined for Africa were sold in Antwerp (Krause and MacDonald 1992). Consequently, as one British official observed:

> The chief value of the work of the Brussels conference lies . . . in the uniform rules to be applied to the introduction of arms and spirits. . . . Without such rules and provisions I regard the government of Africa by Europeans [as] impossible. The African Continent . . . is far from rich, it is tropical and feverish, and will prove not worth holding in the face of a population of savages supplied with firearms and degraded with trade spirits (Memorandum by Sir John Kirk, August 15, 1891).

Thus, as Engelbrecht and Hanighen would later observe, the arms elements of the Brussels Act were "a selfish measure of the great imperialist powers to keep modern weapons out of their colonies and to hold them in submission" (Engelbrecht and Hanighen 1934, 267). This same concern also prompted various efforts to ensure guns were stamped, registered, and licensed, as well as to restrict gun ownership to officials or "reliable persons." The signatory powers also agreed to exchange information with each other (Beachey 1962, 457). Other initiatives stemming from the same urge to control the proliferation of firearms included the imposition of a gun tax under the Uganda Agreement of 1900, resulting in the surrender of many obsolete weapons not considered worthy of such a tax (ibid., 461).

The history of pariah weapons regulation would therefore appear to demonstrate a persistent link between the material and political interests of states and/or powerful elites and the emergence of pariah weapons regulation. Of course, the material and political interests of the same, or other, powerful actors also provide countervailing pressures. For example, the immediate interests of nobles in winning wars with crossbows mostly won out over their broader class interests (McNeill 1982, 67–80). But the point is that attempts at pariah regulation cannot be explained purely by reference to popular pressure or humanitarian concerns. Yet despite this there has been little reflection on the part of commentators regarding the ways in which contemporary restrictions might reflect the interests of powerful states and other actors, albeit in ways that are subject to similar countervailing pressures—an issue that will be explored in more detail below.

### Constructing the "Other" of the Legitimized and Heroic Weapon

The relationship between power, interest, and regulation can sometimes be direct, as in the case of bans on swords or crossbows that pose a threat to elites. This relationship can also manifest itself in both more indirect and complex ways—one example being the manner in which the narratives deployed by hegemonic actors to legitimize dominant weapons and ways of war can have the effect of delegitimizing particular categories of weapons that fail to accord with such narratives. In some cases this may occur as an unintended consequence of the dominant framing. In other cases the process of delegitimization may be actively promoted, for example as part of a process by which other weapons are constructed as "heroic"—weapons deemed to embody positive values such as honor and/or values that are deemed central to national defense.

For example, the series of relatively successful acts implemented in England between 1508 and 1542 banning crossbows and handguns (albeit initially with an exemption for men worth more than £100 per annum) were largely rooted in a concern to preserve the use of the heroic longbow, deemed central to a long line of English military successes (Payne-Gallwey 2007, 34). The Japanese ban on the gun was similarly connected to the romanticization of the heroic samurai sword as the visible form of one's honor and as associated with grace of movement in battle (Perrin 1979). In effect both weapons became the "other" that defined legitimized military technologies and militarism. Similar themes also help explain the contemporary taboos constructed around particular sets of military technology such as cluster munitions.

### Cluster Munitions

What is notable about the campaign against cluster munitions is not that it succeeded in banning an inhumane weapon but that this success occurred when cluster munitions use was actually in decline compared to the peak years of the Vietnam era (Borrie 2009, 433–36). The latter was a period when some 790,000 cluster bombs containing 383 million submunitions were dropped on Vietnam, Cambodia, and Laos, a total greater than their combined populations (Prokosch 1995, 97). The United States also contemplated using them even more extensively. For example, the August 1966 JASON Report proposed an antipersonnel and antivehicle barrier along the demilitarized zone, which required the monthly use of approximately 20,000 CBU-24 cluster bombs. Given that each CBU-24 included between 640 and 670 submunitions (Borrie 2009, 11), this implied the distribution of at least 12.8 million submunitions *per month*. Although this proposal was never implemented, it reflected the fact that, in the opinion of the US military, "CBUs were categorized as a standard weapon, to be taken off the shelf—'conventional ironmongery'" (Krepon 1974, 600).

This is not to suggest that the United States use of cluster munitions in this period went unremarked. For example, there were efforts in the 1970s by the International Committee of the Red Cross (ICRC) to promote restrictions on their use (Borrie 2009, 11–16). The point is, however, that these efforts never achieved *traction* either in diplomatic forums or with a wider public in the way that the issue would thirty years later. The same point can also be made with respect to landmines, which, as early as the mid-1950s, were discussed in the secret committee established to implement the Tripartite Agreement between France, the United States, and Britain to restrict arms sales to the Middle East. However, in response to a French query as to whether APM exports should be restricted on "humanitarian grounds," the United States responded (and Britain concurred) that landmines were not "any more or less objectionable on humanitarian grounds than any other weapons" (Near East Arms Coordinating Committee, Minutes, November 14, 1954).

Reframing cluster munitions and landmines as immoral and inhumane was only made feasible with the advent of three interrelated factors: the mainstreaming of human security, the framing of intervention as humanitarian, and the construction of modern weapons as humane because of their greater capacity for precision. The mainstreaming of human security in the policy discourse of governments (however tokenistic in practice) created a facilitating environment in which the reconstruction of cluster munitions and landmines as threats to the human (understood as innocent civilians) could be undertaken. This was further enhanced by the representation of intervention as humanitarian and of precision weapons as instruments of a humane Western way of warfare undertaken to save strangers from "thugs who know little and care less about civilized behaviour" (Guthrie, cited in Coker 2001, 3). The combined effect was to create a legitimized discursive space into which campaigners could insert a re-representation of landmines and cluster munitions technology as inhumane.

The introduction of bans on cluster munitions and APMs is therefore a far more ambiguous achievement than is generally suggested in the mainstream literature. On the one hand, the legitimizing discourse of Western militaries and arms firms was turned against them in order to generate powerful taboos against particular categories of weapons— even in the face of opposition from these militaries. On the other hand, as I have argued elsewhere, "the same prohibitions can be understood as performative acts that simultaneously function to codify aspects of a new set of criteria for judging international respectability in a post–Cold War era, to reinforce the security framings of the era and to legitimize those categories of weapons successfully constructed as precise, discriminate and thus humane" (Cooper 2011, 145).

## Small Arms and Light Weapons

A similar, although less powerful and less complete process, has also occurred with respect to small arms. Even as late as 1990 Carr could note, "the standard response when arms transfer analysts discuss the trade in small arms is to dismiss the notion of control as both unworthy of their time and unworkable" (Carr 1990, 24). In the post–Cold War era, however, small arms have been successfully reframed as problem weapons that require detailed scrutiny by analysts and policymakers. Consequently, they are now discussed as "weapons of individual destruction" (Stohl et al. 2007, 11), a threat to "millions of human lives," and a category of arms that have "a significant impact on human security" (Stohl and Grillot

2009). This is not to underestimate the terrible impact small arms can have on conflicts. However, rather like the issue of landmines, this is a form of military technology that has become particularly problematized in the post–Cold War era. Indeed, as Goldring has noted, it is now "conventional wisdom . . . that light weapons are the dominant and generally the sole weapons used in current conflicts" (Goldring 2006, 89). Thus, for the UN forty-seven out of forty-nine conflicts in the 1990s "were waged with small arms as the weapon of choice" (ibid.). This particular post–Cold War framing of small arms and light weapons is neatly reflected in the observation by the UK House of Commons Foreign Affairs Committee that "not all conventional weapons are equally lethal, with small arms and light weapons being particularly deadly" (House of Commons Foreign Affairs Committee 2009, 119 para. 299)—an observation unlikely to be made by NATO commanders at the height of the Cold War. Moreover, Goldring's research on civil conflicts that took place in 2004 suggests that the dominance of light weapons in civil conflict has been overstated—with both light weapons and major conventional weapons being used in twenty-two out of twenty-six conflicts (Goldring 2006, 90). If small arms were ignored in the Cold War, they have now been demonized to the point where the role of conventional weapons in civil conflicts has become almost invisible.

None of this is to deny the important role played by ethical framings and a concern with threats to the human in the construction of arms trade regulation and pariah weapons regulation generally. The point is, however, that the role of such ethical discourses is both more ambiguous and more complex than conventional narratives about the mine ban movement or the cluster munitions treaty usually allow. Moreover, as illustrated most clearly in the case of the 1890 Brussels Act, the presence of pariah weapons regulation is not necessarily a sign of a more general shift to the tighter regulation of the arms trade. Consequently, any consideration of the effects of pariah regulation on global and local peacebuilding also has to take into account the broader system of arms regulation in which it is located and the relationship that exists between pariah regulation and this broader system. The next two sections will offer some observations on these issues.

## The Post–Cold War Arms Trade Paradox

The approach adopted to the regulation of the arms trade in general does not simply reflect concerns about particular kinds of technology and their impact on power and interest, but also broader attitudes to political economy. For example, the dominance of mercantilism and the emphasis on autarky in the sixteenth century encouraged a more active approach to the regulation of arms transfers. Previously, exports had largely been restricted in order to guarantee domestic supply of scarce military material, a case in point being the writ issued by Henry V in 1414 prohibiting the export of gunpowder as part of his preparations for Agincourt (Barker 2005, 91). By the sixteenth century however, *surplus production* was also restricted. One example of this was the prohibition on the export of English guns imposed by Elizabeth I in 1574 owing to concern that such exports ensured "yor enemie is better fourneshed with them than our country ships ar" (Krause 1992, 41). Conversely, Elizabethan-era regulations notably extended earlier attempts to preserve English proficiency with the longbow by imposing a requirement on merchants to *"import* ten bowstaves for every tun of wine" (Strickland and Hardy 2011, 405).

In contrast, the shift in economic ideology from mercantilism to capitalism led to the more laissez-faire approach to the regulation of arms transfers in the late nineteenth century already noted above. For example, France passed legislation in 1885 reinstituting the private manufacture of arms and also repealed the law prohibiting exports (Kolodziej 1987, 15; Stohl and Grillot 2009, 14). Of course, belief in the beneficial effects of free trade nevertheless mingled with considerations of power, interest, and ethics to produce different coalitions of actors arguing for proscription or permission of the arms trade. However, these different positions were themselves rooted in common assumptions about the pacifying effects of trade and development. In one version of this, many nineteenth-century peace activists argued that while liberal economies would ultimately bring peace through trade and growth, it was necessary to help this process along by lifting the burdens of military spending and avoiding the interruptions to trade likely to occur from conflict among the major powers (Cortright 2008).

In another version, the nineteenth-century equivalent of the security-development nexus now so beloved of post–Cold War analysts of peace-building was deployed to argue in favor of the arms trade. In the context of the 1890 Brussels Act this was reflected in British arguments on the need for a provision permitting the transit of arms across the colonial territory of another state so that it could supply British settlers in the interior. Failure to adopt this provision, it was argued, would involve "the abandonment of . . . trading and missionary stations, germs of civilisation, to the mercy of surrounding savage tribes" (Lord Vivian, January 30, 1890). Similarly, for the Marquis of Salisbury, such a provision was necessary to advance "the strengthening of the civilizing element in Africa, the encouragement of its establishment in the interior and the consolidation of its power in contending with the brutalizing forces of the savage races" (Marquis of Salisbury to Lord Vivian, April 23, 1890). Although the language deployed was rather different, the rationale for both proscription and restriction of arms supplies in the era was, therefore, much the same as that deployed today in places like Afghanistan or Iraq: security for Western agents of civilization and their local allies needed to be guaranteed so that the benevolent effects of trade and development could work their pacifying magic on local populations.

Economic philosophy also shaped the discourse on the regulation of the arms trade in the aftermath of World War I. In particular, much of the criticism of the role played by arms merchants in the run-up to World War I focused on the way private arms traders had not only facilitated the build-up of weapons but had also encouraged it through the promotion of war. Instead, critics argued that nationalization of the arms industry would better ensure that weapons sales would serve the national interest. Indeed, from the perspective of the post–Cold War era, such critics evinced a touching faith in the idea that "a socialized arms industry was by definition a tribune of peace" (Kolodjie 1987, 28). However, the crisis of faith in private arms manufacturers came to a head in the 1930s as economic collapse prompted more general doubts about the viability of the capitalist system (Harkavy 1975, 36). One outcome was the creation of the Nye Committee in the United States and the Royal Commission on the Private Manufacture of and Trading in Arms in Britain, both of which examined the issue of greater state ownership of defense companies. The committees differed in their conclusions—the latter argued against it, the former in favor—but both symbolized a growing recognition of the need for government regulation and oversight of the industry. Although nationalization was avoided in most states, the 1930s did see the widespread adoption of national arms export licensing systems of the kind that would be recognizable today (Harkavy 1975, 222).

In the Cold War, a combination of national security considerations and the dominance of Keynesian approaches meant that domestic weapons procurement policies were characterized by a philosophy of welfare militarism in which the concern was not only to maintain security of supply but also to preserve jobs, stimulate economies, and preserve key technology sectors. Consequently, the defense sector was dominated by national champions (which in Europe were also increasingly transformed into state-owned companies) who were often awarded contracts without even any competition. On the one hand, the combination of welfare militarism and Cold War security concerns encouraged the further extension of government oversight of arms sales and also government's role in their promotion. At the same time, however, the overwhelming dominance of Cold War security logic meant that overseas arms sales were, at least until the late sixties, viewed more as instruments of geopolitical strategy than as commercial deals pursued purely for profit, as had been the case, for example, in the late nineteenth century.

The end of the Cold War coincided with (and reinforced) underlying shifts in conceptions of economy and security that influenced the debate on the arms industry and on arms transfer control. In terms of economy, the neoliberal agenda (understood here as an approach to political economy that emphasizes trade and financial liberalization, privatization, deregulation, and reductions of public sector employment and expenditures (see Smith and Verdeja, Introduction, this volume)) had already been thoroughly mainstreamed in the policy discourse of governments. Consequently, economic ideology reinforced other factors that, between them, have now led to a defense industry characterized less by state-owned companies and/or national champions and more by private multinational corporations with far more permeable national identities.

For example, BAE Systems, though nominally a British company, generated $17.3 billion in US sales in 2008 and $10.5 billion in other countries compared with $6.25 billion in Britain. The company's US sales made it the fourth largest contractor with the US Department of Defense, while its recent acquisition of an Australian company has also made it the largest arms producer in Australia (SIPRI 2010, 253). In this respect, today's multinational companies, with their subsidiaries in a wide range of countries and their coproduction deals with an even wider range of companies, more closely resemble the international networks established by the large defense companies, such as Vickers, in the early 1900s.

In terms of the approach to major arms transfers, the embrace of neoliberalism significantly reinforced the shift to a more commercial attitude that had been gradually evolving from the late 1960s onward. Indeed, as early as 1990 one commentator could wryly observe that decisions on arms sales had "passed from balance of power to balance of trade considerations" (Carr 1990, 24), and since then the role of economic considerations in arms transfer decisions has magnified. This trend has now become so pronounced that it has led some commentators to suggest that a defining feature of the post–Cold War arms trade system has been the erosion of supply-side controls on the export of major weapons (Spear, forthcoming).

This is not to deny that the post–Cold War era has also witnessed the proliferation of formal international agreements designed to regulate the arms trade (e.g., the EU Code, the Wassenaar Arrangement, the UN Program of Action on Small Arms, the UN Arms Register, etc). However, these developments merely highlight an (apparent) post–Cold War arms trade paradox: that the growth in formal international regulation has coincided with a relative decline in certain kinds of restraint, particularly with regard to the willingness of states to impose qualitative restrictions on the sale of highly advanced equipment (an issue explored in more detail later).

The growth in formal international regulation has also coincided with active efforts to reduce the regulatory restraints governing arms sales. For example, in 2000 the Clinton administration launched seventeen proposals under the Defense Trade Security Initiative aimed at streamlining the export licensing process (Stohl and Grillot 2009, 57); in 2007 the George W. Bush administration signed defense trade cooperation treaties (finally ratified by the US Senate in 2010) with Australia and Britain that permit license-free defense exports to approved end users in each state. More recently, the Obama administration has also committed itself to overhauling the US export control system to make it easier to export weapons to US allies and to emerging markets such as China (*Defense News* 2009). There are a number of initiatives associated with this reform, including a new license exception for the export of dual-use goods to NATO countries and other countries selected on the basis of their membership of multinational nonproliferation regimes. According to the administration, the effect of this reform will be to eliminate the need for export licenses in nearly three thousand types of transactions per year, affecting an estimated $1.4 billion in annual exports (Bureau of Industry and Security, 2011). Similar processes have been at work in other countries. For example, in 2002 Britain announced changes to its method of assessing license applications for components incorporated into military equipment for onward export, a reform generally interpreted as opening "a significant export licensing loophole" (Saferworld 2003, 9), while in 2007 France announced it would ease restrictions on products moving within the EU (Stohl and Grillot 2009, 69). In addition, in 2009 the EU adopted a directive on intracommunity transfers that aims to simplify export procedures for sales to member states by creating a system of either general or global licenses. The former, for example, permits transfers to certified recipients in member states without the need for an individual license for every transaction (Taylor 2011, 17–18). Many states already operate similar systems, so it is not clear what the exact impact of this reform will be, but the reforms are indicative of a broader trend toward relaxing licensing requirements for all but the most egregious of states.

Today then, sales of both major weapons systems and a range of dual-use items are primarily discussed (by exporters at least, if not by recipients and their neighbors) in the language of the technocrat and the banker—the language of jobs, financing terms, market share, and performance evaluation. In part this is a function of the shift to the neoliberal economic framework noted above. In part it is also a function of the shift to a human security-centered approach to conventional arms transfer regulation that has focused on pariah weapons deemed to have inhumane impacts, such as landmines and small arms. Indeed, both government and NGO concerns about the negative effects of the arms trade have bifurcated—with concern focused either on the problem of "weapons of mass destruction" (problematized primarily in terms of their potential acquisition by rogue state or nonstate actors) or, at the other end of the scale, on issues such as small arms (primarily problematized in terms of the illicit rather than the legal trade in such weapons).

### Arms and Security: From East-West to North-South Restraint

If neoliberalism has facilitated a more permissive approach to arms transfer regulation, then this raises the question of why any limits have been introduced at all. As noted above, one part of the answer is rooted in the relationship between legitimized and heroic weapons and those military technologies that lie outside the boundaries of the heroic and the legitimized; being the "other" of legitimized military technology facilitates successful problematization.

Additionally however, the architecture of global arms trade regulation has been transformed in the post–Cold War era along with the transformation in the objects of security that accompanied the transition from Cold War to post–Cold War. As noted above, the former era was characterized by the virtual absence of formal international regulation while Cold War security logic also justified the extensive provision of arms to allies. However, a notable exception to the absence of formal regulation was the COCOM regime (Coordinating Committee for Multilateral Export Controls) aimed at preventing the transfer of dual-use technology to the Soviet bloc, which was also supplemented by severe restrictions imposed by individual states on defense exports to the opposing ideological bloc. Consequently, one principal feature of the Cold War era was that the direction of national and international restrictions on arms sales traveled along the axis of East-West geostrategic security competition. Simultaneously, states were also concerned to manage the supply of arms to developing world allies. In part, such North-South restrictions simply extended the logic of East-West restraint to developing world actors perceived to be aligned with the wrong ideological bloc.

The same obsession with deterrence and the perceived effects of particular weapons systems on dyadic or regional security relations that dominated superpower thinking on nuclear arms control was also extended to thinking about conventional sales. This manifested itself not only in attempts to manage the volume of arms supplied but also efforts to calibrate the *quality* of weapons supplied to a particular country or region so as not to upset regional arms balances. Indeed, in a study in 1975, Harkavy concluded that suppliers in the Cold War era were relatively *less* likely to supply their most modern weapons compared with suppliers in the 1930s (Harkavy 1975, 93). Even the Soviet Union tended to be reluctant to supply its latest generation of equipment, and where it did it often provided a downgraded export model (Roberts 1983, 154–64). Only in the late sixties and early seventies did this begin to change as economic problems encouraged states to view sales in more commercial terms.

In other words, contrary to the picture often painted of the Cold War era arms trade, the primacy given to national security considerations meant that the realpolitik case for sales was often subject to important countervailing pressures for restraint grounded in exactly the same realist logic. Although there were notable exceptions, such as restrictions on sales to apartheid South Africa, arms trade regulation operated principally as an example of what Krause (2011) has described as a sovereign vision of arms control that concentrated on one type of violence (that perpetrated between states) and that aimed to triangulate between ideological discrimination, interstate/intraregion military balance, and maintenance of an armaments hierarchy by supplier states.

In the post–Cold War era the focus of regulation has turned to the management of North-South relations as the developing world has been reconstructed as the source of diverse security threats arising from weak and failed states (Cooper 2006b) and as humanitarian intervention has created a heightened imperative to establish order *inside* developing states as well as between them. As in the Cold War, then, one function of regulation has been to preserve a military hierarchy that both privileges the dominant powers in the global system and is a prerequisite for "successful" military interventions under the rubric of the liberal peace. In part this has been achieved through age-old strategies of technology denial.

In addition, however, as Beier has noted, the distinction at the heart of the pariah weapons agenda between illegitimate and legitimate technologies of killing has naturalized and valorized a larger constellation of claims to authority and thus contributed to the reproduction of the ideational bases of the new way of warfare adopted by Western countries such as the United States (Beier 2011, 170). Indeed, this particular set of distinctions represents a new variant of the "standard of civilization" mobilized not only to legitimize or delegitimize specific types of weapons and the modes of warfare associated with them, but also to reinforce oppositional identities as benign or barbarian. A further function of conventional arms trade regulation has been to facilitate the pacification of subjects of liberal peace intervention by reducing the availability of arms inside states, particularly to nonstate actors. In this sense, attempts, for example, to restrict small arms proliferation at the system level can be viewed both as intimately linked to broader postconflict liberal peace strategies of security sector reform and UN "disarmament, demobilization, and reintegration" efforts (DDR), and as descendants of the kind of measures envisaged in initiatives like the 1890 Brussels Act.

The campaign to promote an arms trade treaty may yet produce a more meaningful architecture of arms transfer control. However, the ATT negotiations are also notable for the way in which they echo interwar efforts to establish global agreements to regulate the arms trade, specifically the 1919 St. Germain Convention for the Control of the Trade in Arms and Ammunition and the 1925 Arms Traffic Convention. Although neither agreement received enough ratifications to enter into force, both mirrored the Brussels Act in that they sought, in the words of a skeptical US official writing about the St. Germain Convention, "to diminish the power of resistance of the natives to the spread and consolidation of the authority of certain powers" (Office of the Foreign Trade Adviser, April 7, 1922). Accordingly, the 1919 convention imposed far stricter limitations on sales to these areas as well as a ban on arms shipments to "any country which refuses to accept the tutelage under which it has been placed" (Stone 2000, 218). Indeed, although the convention never came into force, European powers nevertheless agreed informally to carry out its provisions in Africa and the Middle East (ibid.). The 1925 convention similarly imposed more severe restrictions on exports to special zones that covered most of Africa and parts of what had been the Ottoman Empire (Krause and MacDonald 1992, 717).

Thus, the post–Cold War regulation of the conventional arms trade is simultaneously characterized by a relatively more permissive approach to arms transfers in general but also a redirection of controls away from the governance of East-West relations and toward the governance of North-South relations. It has replaced the Cold War architecture of restraint with a *new* triangulation between efforts to discriminate against pariah state and nonstate actors, initiatives to underpin the bio-political goals of *intra-state* pacification, and the maintenance of military hierarchy. Moreover, rather than viewing initiatives such as the ATT or the landmines ban simply as a function of either the agenda setting preferences of particular NGOs or the specific advocacy strategies of human security activists, it is more accurate to suggest that they reflect the emergence of particular sets of relationships between power, interest, economy, security, and legitimized military technologies that in turn create the conditions of emergence for historically contingent architectures of global regulation.

### Conclusion: The Implications for Global Civil Society Action

The current architecture of conventional arms trade regulation can be summarized as aimed at the restriction of pariah technologies, the disciplining of pariah actors, the pacification of populations, and the maintenance of military hierarchy within an overall framework that is actually quite permissive. One consequence of this is that a loud ethical discourse around the restriction of landmines, cluster munitions, and small arms has gone hand-in-hand with recent rises in both global military expenditure and arms transfers. For example, between 2001 and 2009, US spending on defense rose 60 percent in real terms and now accounts for 43 percent of military global spending (SIPRI 2010, Table 5.2, 198). Overall, world defense expenditures are now estimated at $1,531 billion ($224 per person), an increase of 45 percent in real terms from 2000 to 2009 (ibid., 177). Similarly, global arms exports of major conventional weapons were 22 percent higher in real terms for the period 2005–2009 than for the preceding 2000–2004 period, with the United States, Russia, Germany, France, and Britain accounting for over two-thirds of exports (ibid., 285).

This raises some hard questions for campaigners. On the one hand, humanitarian arms control efforts have produced positive benefits for the security of the human, most notably via the relatively successful weapons taboo constructed around landmines. On the other hand, the framing of landmines and cluster munitions as problem weapons has been rooted in the same discourse that legitimizes military intervention in the post–Cold War era. Moreover, arms trade NGOs have largely neglected rises in defense expenditure in major weapons states such as the United States or intra-Northern trade in arms in favor of an agenda that conceives the South—and in particular pariah actors in sub-Saharan Africa—as the primary object of conventional arms trade regulation (Stavrianakis 2010). Indeed, international initiatives such as the EU Code or the Wassenaar Arrangement, national export regulations of the major weapons states, and the local initiatives of client states mostly combine to produce a cartography of prohibition that corresponds more closely with the disciplinary geographies advocated by the powerful rather than any global map of militarism and injustice. As one recent econometric analysis of major weapons transfers from the United States, Britain, France, and Germany concluded, despite much rhetoric about the need for a more ethical approach to arms sales from governments in all these countries:

> Neither human rights abuses nor autocratic polity would appear to reduce the likelihood of countries receiving Western arms, or reduce the relative share of a particular exporter's weapons they receive. In fact, human rights abusing countries are actually more likely to receive weapons from the United States, whilst autocratic regimes emerge as more likely recipients of weaponry from France and the UK (Perkins and Neumayer 2010, 254).

Of course, arms trade NGOs have often been the first to highlight such hypocrisies, and the work of most organizations include, to various degrees, elements of critique or advocacy that might be considered transformational. However, one of the principal features of recent arms trade activism is the extent to which NGOs have downgraded the radical critique of militarism in exchange for insider influence and government funding (Stavrianakis 2010). In part, this may be because of the political economy of both NGO funding from governments and charities that, to some extent at least, encourages work on topics that are either safer or more popular. For example, the big US foundations have moved away from a concern with national export controls (Stavrianakis 2010, 74). It may also reflect the political economy of that other currency crucial for NGOs: access to, and influence on, governments. As Carpenter (drawing on interviews with a range of arms trade NGOs) has noted, "mainstream human security organizations avoid issues that would be perceived to link them to the antiwar movement, as part of their credibility with states comes from a discourse that sees war as legitimate, within certain constraints" (Carpenter 2011, 97). Lastly, it may also be because many NGOs tend to focus on specific dimensions of the arms trade (such as human rights, development, small arms, landmines) rather than the overall morphology of regulation and its relationship to broader hierarchies of power.

Progress in one area of campaigning can thus more easily be perceived as a success for a bottom-up articulation of a human security agenda linked to specific arms trade issues. In contrast, it is more accurate to characterize the current humanitarian arms control agenda as, at best, *a form of arms control from below articulated within the logic of militarism from above*, a series of tactical reforms within an overarching economic and security paradigm that justifies intervention, regulation, and transformation of the South while (with the exception of token action on landmines) leaving the vast accumulation of Western armaments largely unproblematized.

To the extent that NGOs have followed this path they correspond better with Duffield's description of development NGOs, as actors who have been incorporated into the strategic complexes of the liberal peace (Duffield 2001), albeit perhaps as members operating more generally at the system level than within postconflict societies per se. This does not mean that an initiative such as the ATT should therefore be abandoned. It does mean that NGOs need to be acutely sensitive to the downside of such initiatives and attempt to mitigate them. It also means that far more priority should be given to supporting the lower profile but nevertheless important forms of "arms control from below" practiced by many local actors on the ground, whether through trade union action against problem arms shipments (Spiegel and Le Billon 2009), the creation of local weapons free zones, or, as in the African Great Lakes region, the creation of cross-border peace committees whose role includes monitoring small arms availability and misuse (Cooper 2006a, 130). In addition, NGOs need to prioritize campaigning on issues such as Western defense production and the gross armaments imbalances between the major weapons states and the rest of the world. These imbalances underpin hegemony and provide an incentive for the development of "weapons of mass destruction" as a means of offsetting such disparities.

Lastly, greater attention is needed on the problems posed by the trade in major conventional weapons and the way it facilitates the creation of substantial weapons arsenals. Such arsenals may not necessarily cause wars or be essential for the prosecution of mass violence, but they certainly help. Of course, given the role of Western defense arsenals in underpinning intervention and the hegemony of the liberal peace, Western countries are well positioned to determine who has the power to decide both the meaning of particular conflicts and the meanings ascribed to the weapons used to prosecute such conflicts. A prerequisite for any truly emancipatory program of arms regulation therefore is the need for continuous critical reflection on the role of regulation and taboo in underpinning hegemony, and the need for subversive projects that both reveal the interests behind dominant framings of particular weapons technologies and disturb them.

# 2

# Neoliberal Ethics, the Humanitarian International, and Practices of Peacebuilding

## Cecelia Lynch

In his pathbreaking book *Famine Crimes* (1997/2006), Alex de Waal created a name for a new social movement, the "humanitarian international."[1] In de Waal's critical treatment, however, this movement, comprised of "the cosmopolitan elite of relief workers, officials of donor agencies, consultant academics and the like, and the institutions for which they work," as well as "journalists and editors who faithfully propagate the humanitarian worldview," is not necessarily a cause for celebration. Rather, "the humanitarian international is avowedly dedicated to fighting famine, but does not in fact operate in a way that enables this to be achieved. There are 'successes' and 'failures' . . . but the unexpected consequences of humanitarian action are more significant" (3–4). De Waal argues that this humanitarianism all too often weakens the types of political accountability, or the "contract" between states and their peoples, that would prevent crises from occurring in the first place. Other observers have put forth similar arguments, although with varying culprits (Easterly 2006; Gibson et al. 2005; ICISS 2001; Terry 2002; Moyo 2010). Given that this movement shows

1. De Waal does not call this complex a social movement, however, but his description fits many scholars' definition of such movements.

47

no signs of abating, and instead appears to be proliferating at a significant rate, probing the movement and its effects on peacebuilding is warranted.

This book's critique of the role of neoliberalism and its relationship to structural inequities and structural violence provides a productive path for assessing current constraints and future possibilities for humanitarianism. I argued in 1998, before the Seattle anti-globalization protests, that social movements' weak responses to the alleged imperatives of market liberalism put movements in danger of "discursive demobilization" (Lynch 1998). After NAFTA and before the 1999 Seattle protests against the World Trade Organization ministerial meeting, many movements, including feminist, peace, environment, and others, appeared to avoid directly challenging structures of economic power, yet achieving their goals required reconfiguring capitalism. By not challenging forms of profitmaking that enabled and even encouraged discrimination, the arms trade, and environmental degradation, progressive social movements could only create change at the margins of social practice. In this chapter, however, I am especially concerned with the way in which neoliberal ideologies, mechanisms, and techniques promote particular ethics or sets of ideas about how humanitarian groups and the recipients of humanitarian aid should act and what they should accomplish. I assert that neoliberal discourses and ethics shape humanitarian practices, including those of NGOs, in ways that promote inequalities among peoples rather than their well-being. Neoliberal discourses, as a result, also threaten to increase the "discursive demobilization" of humanitarian NGOs.

As other chapters in this section point out, neoliberalism promotes and "fetishizes" particular terminologies and practices—read discourses—that underlie economic and political institutions and also shape the values and work of those seeking to enact various forms of cosmopolitanism (through human rights, human security, and humanitarianism). In the case of the transnational humanitarian social movement, we need to ask yet again how this result obtains and whether and what type of counterhegemonic ethics exist. This is necessary, I argue, because neoliberal ethics and practices also threaten long-term peacebuilding.

The "humanitarian international" social movement, like most social movements, is amorphous and covers a wide range of pragmatic goals and ethical possibilities. As many scholars have argued (Ferguson 1994 and 2006; Sending and Neumann 2006, 2010; Lynch 2009), the Foucauldian concept of "governmentality" (Foucault 1991; Burchell, Gordon, and Miller 1991; Rose, O'Malley, and Valverde 2006) captures the processes at work that intertwine NGO relief agencies, states, and multilateral organizations and agencies. The concept of "governmentality" allows us to see how issues that appear technical or economic are actually deeply political, and how ideologies that rely on their separation to solve problems—such as humanitarian coordination or economic development—are instead constitutive of particular forms of neoliberal power. In a related conceptualization, Jackie Smith and Dawn Wiest return to Weber's institutional "iron cages" to describe and analyze how "institutional logics" can lead to "organizational homogeneity, or isomorphism." As a result, "To be seen as a legitimate player in a given institutional context, one must accept particular organizational forms and practices, discourses, and standards of behavior" (Smith and Wiest, 2012, chapter 4).

Following these logics, we can see that the humanitarian international is part and parcel of neoliberal governance. Yet, as scholars have also pointed out (Klotz 1995; Keck and Sikkink 1998; Lynch 1999; Wapner 1996; Struett 2008; Smith 2010), social movements can also change the terms of debate, introduce new forms of action, and legitimize and delegitimize government and multilateral policies. In other words, social movements can at times act on the forms of power that shape their very existence. Whether these movements can reconfigure the power of neoliberalism in the present, however, is a major question of this book. I argue that we should be aware and wary of how the humanitarian international is constantly intertwined with the neoliberal project in both its broad vision and minute particulars, but that we also need to recognize the sites of resistance and reconceptualization from humanitarian groups that can reshape and possibly challenge neoliberal ethics. Recognizing sites of resistance and reconceptualization differs considerably from the liberal vision of social movement agency, requires attention to ethics and practices, and necessitates constant awareness and reflexivity.

In order to develop this argument, I first define the way I am using the term "humanitarian" (to include both emergency and development work), and then locate the humanitarian international in varying conceptualizations of cosmopolitan ethics. I then trace neoliberal pressures on humanitarians, focusing on the relationship between donor ideology and requirements and on practices by NGOs. Given these discursive pressures, which are both linguistic and material in nature, I discuss the development of NGO hierarchies, marketing pressures, and microfinance schemes as examples of neoliberal conditioning and ethical expectations. Each of these strategies is supposed to help remedy the underlying conditions of poverty that give rise (in part) to humanitarian crises. Challenges to neoliberalism certainly exist (some are discussed in this volume; I discuss others elsewhere), but I focus in the concluding section of this chapter on the conceptual issues that need to be acknowledged to redress discursive demobilization and foster social emancipation.

As a result, I delineate and examine both the cosmopolitan and the neoliberal ideological bases of the humanitarian/development international social movement, to understand better the effects of globalization on this movement and its prospects and limitations for peacebuilding. Studying the humanitarian/development international as a social movement is important because it recognizes the nexus of common goals in the midst of a range of groups and practices that make up the international. Studying this movement also privileges its construction as a complex of nonstate entities that interacts with both the state and international organizations yet also appeals and responds to diverse components within civil society. Finally, studying and understanding this movement is, I argue, critical for the further development of the literature on peacebuilding. This literature has arguably suffered from a liberal, if not technocratic or legalist, bias, as the editors make clear in the introduction to this book. Bringing questions of contestation and power more centrally into peacebuilding concepts and theory grounds them more firmly in actual global political processes.

## Defining Humanitarianism

The humanitarian social movement has a common normative foundation: (a) to relieve suffering in the midst of crises, and (b) to create a better life for people in the long-term. Increasingly, aid groups that previously specialized in emergency relief also work in development, and sometimes the inverse also obtains. As Barnett and Weiss (2008) point out, most "humanitarian" groups engage in a series of activities from providing forms of emergency aid (medical and food aid, clean water and shelter) to working in education, health, economic development, and reconstruction. Moreover, many groups engage in democracy promotion, election monitoring, money management, and programs to provide technological infrastructure. As a result, despite the fact that groups often try to separate emergency from development aid in policy debates, I assert that humanitarianism encompasses both short- and long-term aid and objectives.

It is by now a truism, however, that short- and long-term assistance can be at cross-purposes, leading to contradictory policies with implications for group objectives and ethics. This problem has led to a well-publicized debate between David Rieff, who argues that humanitarianism should stick with saving lives in the immediate sense, and Michael Ignatieff, who emphasizes the need for moving beyond emergencies to improve the "human condition" (Calhoun 2008). One of the difficulties of distinguishing between short- and long-term relief is the increasingly recognized complexity of humanitarian crises themselves. Crises that used to be thought of as "natural" or "unavoidable" are now understood as stemming from political and economic factors as well as environmental ones. The fact that humanitarian crises are most often human-made as well as natural, and the fact that emergency, reconstruction, development, and other agencies are almost always involved in generating responses to them, has resulted in the creation of the term "complex emergencies." This term connotes both the widespread acceptance of emergencies as part of global life and the difficulty of resolving them.

As a result, I bracket "emergency" relief work as something that has become a type of expectation about the regularity of crises in the international order. As articulated by Calhoun, the resulting "emergency imaginary" represents an idea that must be acted on as well as the cosmopolitan conscience that prompts action; most of all it reflects "growing global connections" (Calhoun 2008, 85). Because the cosmopolitan consciousness characterizing the "emergency imaginary" is troubled by the lack of order associated with conflicts and disasters, it tries to respond not only to the immediate but also to its understanding of what is necessary for human dignity and sustainability in the long-term. This connection between the immediate and the longer term, then, allows us to see how the humanitarian international reproduces itself as a necessary component of global order and continuity.

De Waal also notes the disconnect between short- and long-term humanitarian objectives, arguing that the goals and rhetoric of this movement often do not match events on the ground. In particular, he points out the strategies of fundraising and self-maintenance that thrive on the concepts of emergency and development and encourage new groups to join the fray. Thus, while Calhoun emphasizes the existence and ethics of the humanitarian's emergency imaginary as constitutive of globalization, de Waal also points to the economic motives promoting the international's need for self-maintenance. But while I, like de Waal, locate some of the problems of the movement in techniques that promote self-funding and self-maintenance over aiding others, I emphasize in this chapter the *globalized* ideological and material processes that shape these contradictory goals.

How do ethical constructs and processes of globalization intersect with this social movement? As Liisa Malkki (2009) asserts, humanitarians come with dual sensibilities, or "affective regimes": (1) a "'humanitarian sensibility' that hails a generalized suffering humanity, or, in another well-known formulation, the 'suffering stranger,'" and (2) an "unsentimental, consummate professionalism." In other words, humanitarians form part of a globalized cosmopolitan ideology of caring for those who suffer, while at the same time they also participate in a cosmopolitan professional class of social welfare providers: doctors, nurses, teachers, engineers.

The "humanitarian international social movement," in other words, is made up of people who share a strong affective sensibility as well as a set of types of professional training. They become part of a transnationalized "class" of aid workers, some institutionalized within states and international organizations, but the vast majority working for NGOs. Increasingly, this social movement comprises individuals and groups coming not only from the West, North, or developed world, but also those coming from the developing countries. Becoming an aid worker is now a major career goal of university students, nurses, teachers, and many others with a wide variety of types of expertise who seek gainful employment in both the global North and the global South.

Moreover, the relationship between NGOs, states, and multilateral organizations and agencies is one of overlapping institutional and identity boundaries. NGOs can be transnational (estimates of transnational NGOs range from 2,500 according to Barnett and Weiss 2008b, to 30,000 according to Beyer 2007) or local. They can be secular or faith-based. They can be more-or-less "non"governmental, as the terms "GONGO" (government NGO), "BONGO" (business NGO), and "RONGO" (royalty-sponsored NGO, for example in Jordan and elsewhere in the Middle East and Asia, as well as the United Kingdom and parts of northern Europe) attest. Not all aid groups and participating individuals are part of institutionalized structures—many local and transnational participants are temporary; others are long-term professionals. These features make the composite "movement" both fluid and capable of "sustained political or cultural contestation through recourse to institutional and extrainstitutional forms of action" (Escobar and Alvarez 1992, 321). Where groups are in fact NGOs, they are usually required to register with the state. This has positive components—the state knows who is operating within its territory and can attempt to control unscrupulous groups, and negative ones—corrupt and/or autocratic states can try to prevent activities that may be beneficial to society but work against excessive governmental power. State and multilateral control are also exercised through donor relationships.

Globalized donor relationships also shape the humanitarian international's increasingly hierarchical and sophisticated use of market-based tools. These include techniques of accountability, evaluation, and innovation that can never completely deliver and that also lead to the promotion of silver-bullet development schemes. For example, microfinance is touted as an essential means to ensure sustainability of aid programs over the long-term as well as one of the primary solutions to poverty. Globalized market ideologies, then, become necessary components of sustaining humanitarian work, and they also encourage groups to blur the lines between short- and long-term as well as profit and nonprofit forms of assistance.

## Humanitarianism and Cosmopolitanism

The very existence of the humanitarian international social movement, then, is a product of intersecting strands of globalization, resulting in a range of overlapping "globalizing projects" (as defined in the Introduction of this volume). Each of these strands deserves more dissection, however, in order to understand the multiple workings of globalizing processes. First, the cosmopolitan sensibility of the humanitarian international is one that has difficulty approaching the Platonic ideal of altruism, in the sense of selfless service to others with no strings attached, especially in ways that do not impose externally generated moral views or institutional practices. This is because the "humanitarian imagination" is always a situated one, and reflects phenomenological or experiential limitations. The humanitarian imagination is motivated at least in part by the desire to redress the victimization and suffering of others, and these perceptions of victimization and suffering are of necessity constructed out of partial information and affective response.

As a result, a serious question is whether cosmopolitanism itself is always compromised, never able to achieve its nonnative pretensions. The definition and content of cosmopolitanism are much debated today. Nevertheless, "the nebulous core shared by all cosmopolitan views is the idea that all human beings, regardless of their political affiliation, do (or at least can) belong to a single community, and that this community should be cultivated. Different versions of cosmopolitanism envision this community in different ways, some focusing on political institutions, others on moral norms or relationships, and still others on shared markets or forms of cultural expression" (*Stanford Encyclopedia of Philosophy*, 2006). The reason for cultivating a cosmopolitan sensibility, for most of its advocates, is to overcome various forms of exclusivity that hinder peaceful relations among peoples of different identity commitments

(Sen 2006). Some conceptualize cosmopolitanism as enabling dialogue among difference rather than erasing these identity commitments altogether (Appiah 2006). Still others recognize that cosmopolitanism has never been adequately conceptualized, let alone realized, and argue that the "minority cosmopolitans," the migrants, refugees, and exiled, require cosmopolitanism to "give way to the plurality of modes and histories— not necessarily shared in degree or in concept regionally, nationally, or internationally." They propose instead that "cosmopolitanism be considered in the plural, as cosmopolitanisms" (Pollock, Bhabha, Breckenridge, and Chakrabarty 2002, 8).

Some scholars trace humanitarian cosmopolitanism, the work of "going elsewhere" (Lynch 2000) to redress the suffering of others, to the founding of the ICRC by Henri Dunant during the Crimean War in the mid-nineteenth century. As a result, Erica Bornstein and Peter Redfield consider the humanitarian sensibility to be a phenomenon specific to contemporary modernity (Redfield 2008; Barnett and Weiss 2008b). I assert, however, that missionary work prior to the nineteenth century also embodied the humanitarian cosmopolitan goals of improving the welfare of distant populations. While the ICRC was perhaps the first major manifestation of a secular humanitarian sensibility, it arguably represents the same type of cosmopolitan ideals of caring for strangers. It may also come with similar expectations regarding how best to help those who are culturally and experientially different. The cosmopolitan imagination is, like its internationalist political expression, rooted in its own cultural specificities (Ishay 1995; Lynch 1998).

As Pollock, Bhabha, Breckenridge, and Chakrabarty (2002, 8) point out, decentering the Western cosmopolitan heritage "to avoid the imposition of practices and histories that do not necessarily fit interpretations devised for historical situations elsewhere," including misplaced assumptions about race, gender, and class, is critical if the cosmopolitan promise is to be fulfilled. But how well does the humanitarian international social movement negotiate this historical and geographic terrain? In the next section, I examine the ways in which neoliberal discourses shape short-term notions of "emergency" and longer-term aid practices on the ground, as well as how these discourses blur the lines between marketized and nonprofit forms of assistance.

## Humanitarianism and Neoliberalism

If debates about the desirability of globalized cosmopolitanism versus other identity commitments infuse the humanitarian international social movement, what is the role of globalized neoliberal discourses and practices on this movement? Neoliberalism has become a much-criticized trope among theorists of global civil society and movements working for social justice, because it is seen to privilege goals of privatization, property rights, individual achievement, and (especially financial) efficiency and success over social justice goals such as health, education, and safe havens for all.[2] Yet the tremendous growth and impact of the humanitarian international social movement also results from the strength of neoliberal discourse and practices from the 1980s to the post–Cold War era. Specifically, Western governments retreated from social welfare guarantees and institutions at the same time as they encouraged NGOs to take over, often using them to channel government aid at home and especially abroad (Ferguson 1994, 2006; Lynch 1998). Groups that organized to relieve suffering in the short-term are still in existence generations later, and numerous new groups have joined them. As a result, many areas of the global South are inundated with NGOs—especially areas where recent conflicts or natural disasters have occurred, but as the current wave of critiques indicates, it is unclear that either the expansion or reorganization of aid has resulted in lasting improvements in human welfare. As Broad and Cavanagh point out in their critique of Jeffrey Sach's book, *The End of Poverty*, the massive expansion of aid and the proliferation of new organizations have not generated the improvements in human security and welfare promised by the

2. Marshall and Keough, *Finding Global Balance*, describes one set of ongoing discussions to attempt to resolve tensions within the faith community over neoliberal policies. I do not hold them responsible, however, for my emphasis on the importance of neoliberal policies in this chapter!

neoliberal globalizing project (Broad and Cavanagh 2006). The proliferation of NGOs, as a result, breeds both expectations and cynicism on the part of many people in developing countries. As someone from the global North, I am frequently asked when I travel to other parts of the world whether I am part of an NGO (or know an NGO) that can help with health, education, or social welfare issues; I am also treated to numerous critiques of NGOs by people I encounter in service sector jobs such as (nonluxury) hotels, buses, trains, taxis, markets, and restaurants.

State governments remain significant actors vis-à-vis NGOs, but primarily in the capacity of lender of first resort. As Janice Gross Stein has argued, "States have withdrawn from 'service delivery' and have become 'donors,' either directly through national development agencies that fund their 'own' nationally headquartered nongovernmental agencies or through their funding of international agencies that, in turn, support humanitarian organizations. . . . As states have retreated, however, and contracted out the delivery of emergency assistance, they have increased their monitoring and regulation of nationally headquartered humanitarian nongovernmental organizations" (Stein 2008, 127). While bilateral aid or official development assistance (ODA) remains the major type of assistance given to developing nations (Fearon 2008), my concern in this section is with the relationship between humanitarian NGOs, states, and multilateral agencies, or Ferguson's "transnational apparatus of governmentality" (Ferguson 2006). The donor community that is so critical to the work of the humanitarian international social movement is comprised of state and regional agencies such as USAID, the EU, and aid agencies in countries such as Norway, Sweden, Ireland, Denmark, Canada, and to a lesser extent Britain, Germany, and other (especially European) countries, along with the World Bank. While these donor agencies differ somewhat in their aid requirements and RFPs (Request for Proposals), NGO interviews, websites, and brochures in Europe, the United States, Africa, and the Middle East indicate that common neoliberal orientations shape much of their outlook and funding practices, including pressures to demonstrate metrics of success and results. This donor-NGO relationship is part of a broader phenomenon that often marginalizes states in the South (Ferguson 2006), replacing state governance with what might be called "nongovernmental governance." Ironically, this type of externally led governance most often hinders the institutional building blocks of stable, *localized* control that peacebuilding strategies rely on.

One manifestation of these orientations is the globalized discourse that is used by almost all actors in the humanitarian international social movement. In other work, I have highlighted some of the most often-used terms in this discourse, including "training," "capacity-building," and "partnership" (Lynch 2009). Here, I note that the first two of these terms, especially, suggest a hierarchical relationship—providing knowledge and technical expertise to those in developing societies so that they can better manage their own affairs. These terms also imply a faith that these societies can indeed be trained and their capacity built. As a pastor said in his sermon at a church service I attended in Accra, Ghana, in August 2009, people in the First World use the term "developing countries" "when they want to make us feel good." The third term suggests a more egalitarian "partnership" between transnational and local societies, and for peacebuilding work also indicates the need for collaboration with governments. Yet the term "partnership" also indicates the necessity of bringing in for-profit corporate and financial organizations into nonprofit humanitarian work.[3]

What has developed over the past two decades is a hierarchical system of NGOs in which the larger and better-connected transnational organizations have considerable decision-making power vis-à-vis smaller, often more localized groups. The problem of listening to indigenous NGOs, let alone other social groups, has been noted by many observers in a number of contexts, including discussions among some of the larger NGOs in the International Council of Voluntary Agencies, based in Geneva (Thompson 2008). Here I wish to note not only the question of who gets included in official deliberations about how to resolve humanitarian crises in the short- and long-term, but also the issue of the "rationalization,"

3. For example, in the November/December 2007 issue of the Heifer International *World Ark,* Bobby Shriver enthused about the involvement of American Express in the (RED) campaign: "American Express is a bank, right? And they printed on their card, think about it, . . . they said that they're going to eliminate AIDS in Africa" (17).

in a Weberian sense, of the channels of programmatic development and financial access. The larger groups that have developed strong relationships with donors have also become experts in employing "NGO-speak" and tailoring their proposals to meet goals of numbers of people trained, for example. They then become the conduits for information and knowledge about smaller, start-up groups to donors. Moreover, criteria for demonstrating worthiness as a local NGO partner revolves in part around the ability to employ effectively the terminology promoted by donors and to provide reasonable assurances of rapid results measurable according to accepted metrics of success.

The ability of some groups to influence and find funding for local groups can be positive: for example, Oxfam Great Britain, the Mennonite Central Committee, and the Anglican Development Desk cofounded PeaceNet Kenya in the early 1990s. While Oxfam and other groups still act as major donors, the network has created space for Kenyan groups to work together, foster dialogue, and resolve conflicts in areas of the Rift Valley. During the violence following the December 2007 presidential elections, PeaceNet Kenya and the Nairobi Peace Initiative-Africa (NPI-Africa) formed important networks working across the country to stem the conflicts (Lynch 2011b). These efforts, then, provide an example of how larger, transnational NGOs can work with local groups to identify a need and then provide funding and support for local groups to tackle it. Yet my interviews also indicated considerable disaffection among other NGOs that have not been able to convince larger, transnational groups of their legitimacy. For example, interviewees in Nairobi (in June 2007) described a situation in which transnational NGOs determined which groups working in Somalia were legitimate and which were "brief case NGOs," a term created to denote "foreign or domestic front groups led by unscrupulous entrepreneurs who pocket donor money without enacting promised projects" (Lynch 2011a). The transnational aid groups had strong relationships with major donor countries and were in the position of being able to fund smaller (and frequently indigenous) NGOs. Their ability to make decisions about the legitimacy of other groups, and for those views to affect others' capacity to raise money for their work, therefore, caused resentment among the more localized organizations.

The increasingly hierarchical relationship among NGOs also reflects the need to rationalize how humanitarian products are marketed. Smaller NGOs that can assist in demonstrating the reach and success of donors and intermediate groups in serving vulnerable populations are more likely to be featured as local partners on websites and brochures. Local partners, in turn, frequently adopt the language disseminated by donor agencies to demonstrate results. I do not dispute the necessity of training and capacity building in many instances. But these concepts do rely on a particular type of cosmopolitan assumption grounded in the Western/ Northern imaginary that replicates modernization discourses from previous eras. Even though the end result of training and capacity building are conceived to be rising standards of health, education, and life, the need for the organizations providing these services to raise funds and demonstrate success in order to maintain their own existence, in combination with the type of cosmopolitan imaginary that sustains them, are both constitutive components of privatized global welfare that lies at the heart of neoliberal ideology.

When techniques for short-term success fall short over a period of time, new techniques are devised. The drive to demonstrate short-term success is both an ideological and a material imperative in neoliberal discourse. Ideologically, success for the humanitarian international is supposed to solve problems (poverty, disease, illiteracy, and by extension, conflict and war); materially, it works to increase donor confidence and funding. Ironically, this drive employs marketing strategies derived for the short-term to try to resolve long-term problems and structural inequities.

Oxfam America is one of the larger groups that has done the most to accommodate its public message (on its website and in its annual report) to neoliberal strategies. Its 2006 Annual Report opens with the following:

> New ideas for a better world.
>
> Innovation. Thinking big. Thinking strategically. This is what underpins successful entrepreneurial endeavors. Profit-making ventures like start-up companies have long fostered edgy, creative innovators, while development organizations were supposedly home to good-hearted, earnest workhorses.

We think it's time to raise the bar and update some stereotypes. Time for new ideas. That said, we are not attracted to innovation for the sake of novelty. We're interested in getting bigger and better outcomes. We like clever ideas as much as the next person, but what we're really after are the ideas that lead to social change.

We intend to draw on our own strengths and on those of partners and colleagues around the world because we've set our sights high. Building the proverbial better mousetrap is one thing. We're in it to build a better world.

The combination of the terms "innovation," "bigger and better outcomes," and "successful entrepreneurial endeavors" suggests that if development is strategically rebranded, with new and innovative ideas in place, then substantial results can be obtained. The search for the new entrepreneurial solution is, then, very much part of the "cutting edge" of the humanitarian international social movement.

Paul David Hewson, better known as Bono of the rock band U2, who has done as much as, if not more than, anyone in drawing attention to humanitarian needs in Africa, expresses similar sentiments. In a July 2009 *New York Times* Op-Ed piece, he argues that Africa should be "rebranded," for example as "the birthplace of cool." Such a rebranding could challenge the constant images of Africans as victims, although it would also risk romanticizing and homogenizing aspects of "culture." However, Bono instead follows the lead of gurus such as Jeffrey Sachs in lamenting the corruption that "stalks Africa's reformers" and arguing in favor of investment, development, and transparency (Bono 2009). Corruption indeed stalks many regimes on the continent, but we might also ask how, given the economic meltdown of 2009, we can criticize corruption on the part of some African leaders without acknowledging its endemic nature in Western financial institutions and even legal systems. The cozy and corrupt relationships between Western banks and corporate interests, African leaders, and US government officials and regulators raises serious questions about the ability of foreign investment to engender the kind of development that Bono and other sympathetic activists desire.

Both ideologically and materially, the drive for short-term results and the belief in market innovation hinder principles of locally led peacebuilding strategies in favor of externally imposed ideas, ethics, and practices. These drives also lead, perhaps ironically, to faith in homogenized solutions that are supposed to deliver quick results and that muddy the boundaries of what it means to be nonprofit for the humanitarian international social movement. Oxfam's annual report, cited above, explicitly compares stodgy humanitarianism with edgy, innovative, "profit-making" companies. However, perhaps the most interesting not-quite nonprofit activity of the humanitarian international social movement is microfinance. Almost all humanitarian and development groups now have a microfinance program. These programs are extremely popular because they are supposed to lift the poorest of the poor (especially women) out of poverty by providing the means for them to become self-sufficient. Poverty, in turn, is seen to be one, if not the, major factor inciting violence in many parts of the world. Microfinance, therefore, is increasingly portrayed as a one-size-fits-all technique to equalize gender relations and solve the problem of the feminization of poverty (Roy 2010). Moreover, as Crystal Murphy points out in her studies of Juba, South Sudan, microfinance is also used as a significant component of broader postconflict strategies for generating economic institutions and growth, and hence "peacebuilding" (Murphy 2011; see also Ohanyan 2008). NGOs that provide microloans are proud that these loans do not give mere handouts or charity, but instead provide the means for empowerment of the poor by making them small business entrepreneurs. According to neoliberal ethical assumptions, assistance that causes dependency is bad; assistance that allows recipients to become entrepreneurs in their own right is good.

Microfinance initiatives have increasingly been criticized, however, for muddying the waters between for-profit and not-for-profit activity. Loans frequently come with interest rates of between 15 to 50 percent or more, and ethnographers are finding that these rates can be crippling for recipients, making the loans something less than the panacea to end poverty that they are often made out to be. One of the major microfinance organizations, Results Educational Fund, acknowledges some of these problems in its State of the Microcredit Campaign Report (2009), even while it continues to advocate these loans as the best way to end global poverty. The report uses individual success stories to highlight "the profound agony of poverty and the inexpressible joy and triumph that can be unleashed through a series of microloans" (1). But it also addresses criticisms of microloans: "Critics have questioned profit-minded MFIs' [microfinance institutions] commitment to serving the world's poorest people, noting that many have not passed on cost-savings to clients through lower interest rates. . . . Conversely, others worry that MFIs are not commercial enough, saying that their commitment to social justice keeps them from maximizing their potential profitability. . . ." This debate occurs in a context in which MFIs provide "an estimated US $15–25 billion in loans" out of "an estimated $300 billion demand for services." The report asserts, however, that the choice between nonprofit and for-profit is "a false dichotomy" (10). It proposes instead that microfinance be viewed as a "platform" for distributing a variety of financial services, rather than a single product that is supposed to serve both social justice and financial (i.e., nonprofit and for-profit) goals.

While this report and other studies consistently find that recipients of microloans are good credit risks, resulting in extremely high loan repayment rates, the success of microfinance in lifting large numbers of people out of poverty is less measurable. Consequently, NGOs rely on demonstrating numbers of loans given, repayment rates, and individual stories of happiness and success. The overall narrative is one in which the market can fulfill its function of doing good without sacrifice and with only benefits to all. This narrative, of course, supports neoliberal ideals of bootstrap assistance, return on investment, and success, even though the question of success for whom has not been answered adequately.[4]

These and other examples indicate that many components of the humanitarian international social movement act within (and frequently help to reproduce) neoliberal forms of organizational ethos and bureaucratic accountability. The term "philanthrocapitalism" (Edwards 2008) denotes the increasing adoption of market models by NGOs. This term points to the ways in which philanthropy is deeply intertwined with

---

4. The report also partially excuses unscrupulous lenders by suggesting that the poor cannot make wise decisions about which lenders best suit their needs.

neoliberal modes of governance, or the techniques of governmentality articulated by Foucault to describe how institutions of governance are put in the service of neoliberal mechanisms of power (Foucalt 1991; Ferguson 2006; Sending and Neumann 2006, 2010; Rose, O'Malley, and Valverde 2006; Lynch 2009). It also describes a situation in which the "voluntary" and nonprofit nature of NGOs is increasingly compromised. For some time, market terminology and metrics of success have been applied to nonprofit humanitarian "products." But increasingly, the lines between profit-seeking and nonprofit activity are also becoming blurred in the developmentalist discourse of humanitarianism.

### Cosmopolitan Ethics and Implications for Peacebuilding

Certainly lives do get saved and livelihoods improved in many instances, despite the arguments of Moyo, Easterly, and others that the humanitarian international social movement does a disservice to long-term social welfare and peacebuilding as much if not more than it aids individual people. Aid workers put in long hours, suffer emotional traumas, and agonize over difficult choices, and many of the relationships they forge and programs they create and maintain are critical for people's day-to-day survival. My concern in this chapter, however, is with the types of lenses through which many humanitarians organize themselves, advertise their good deeds, and structure their programs, and how these lenses affect continuing humanitarian practices and ethics, including those of peacebuilding. As Lederach, Neufeldt, and Culbertson (2007) assert, "Peacebuilders must find creative strategies to be effective in the moment of crisis, and, at the same time, consider changes across decades, all within tight project timelines and limited funding" (2).

Yet Jackie Smith has shown that studies of peacebuilding, even when critical of liberal market assumptions that peace, democracy, and economic liberalization go hand-in-hand, advocate slowing down the introduction of market forces rather than questioning their utility for conflict resolution in the long term (Smith 2010). Her work challenges more directly the ongoing construction of neoliberalism at the core of many peacebuilding assumptions and practices, arguing instead that power, including economic power, needs to be addressed as a central component of peacebuilding. This task is critical because "asymmetries of power can mask structural sources of conflicts that can resurface over time" (248).

The attention to gender and poverty in microfinance programs, disease eradication goals, and long-term social stability is positive, but even their advocates cannot measure the success of the techniques and institutions through which these concerns are promoted. Although I question the long-term helpfulness of neoliberal institutions and the ethical assumptions on which they are based, other aspects of globalization can assist peacebuilding. If globalization is the ability to cross borders—national, ethnic, religious, linguistic—through numerous means, including technological and ideological openness, then it can promote knowledge dissemination and intercultural awareness. Recognizing multiple practices, organizational sensibilities, and paths to peace can, if embraced and developed, create additional peacebuilding possibilities.

This is perhaps not a new conclusion, and others have certainly put forth pragmatic ways to enact such possibilities on the ground. For example, Lederach, Neufeldt, and Culbertson (2007) cite the difficulty of measuring peace, advocating instead "evaluation as learning, rather than evaluation as measuring." This reframes the necessity to demonstrate "results" into reflection about ongoing *process*. Others advocate pragmatic and theoretical change in the assumptions underlying the relationship between democratization, elections, the global economy, and international law (Mgbeoji 2003).

For the purposes of this chapter, however, we need to return to the ideological homogenization desires of traditional understandings of cosmopolitanism. Is it possible to get out of a "partial" cosmopolitanism that relies on the imposed construct of the idealized, individualistic entrepreneurial subject? Is it possible also to transcend neocolonial assumptions about non-Western peoples and cultures that underlie neoliberal modernizing projects? Is it possible, in other words, to widen our sensibilities to acknowledge the importance of "cosmopolitanisms" that draw on multiple, locally derived emancipatory projects (rather than "empowered" subjects, as Smith and Verdeja point out in the Introduction to this volume)? For comprehensive peacebuilding, such an acknowledgement requires,

I assert, sustained attention to the mechanisms promoted by neoliberal assumptions and techniques that push NGOs into the rush for magic (and homogenized) solutions and quick results in ways that pass over rather than embody multiple cosmopolitanisms. This type of sustained attention should avoid disciplining postconflict subjects into deserving and well-behaved postcolonial members of the global market economy as one of its primary goals.

Resistances to neoliberal techniques do exist. In my interviews with faith-based NGOs, complaints frequently surfaced about the constant paperwork required to account for funds spent and to demonstrate success (numbers of local people—women, agricultural workers, nurses, etc.—trained; boreholes dug, water pipes installed, students taught), and sometimes about the narrowly conceived frameworks that metrics of accountability and success reflected. On the local and national levels, recipient partner groups also lament the constraints and agendas imposed by donor requirements. Dynamique Citoyenne, a Cameroonian civil society network created in 2005 to monitor human rights and corruption, cites in its brochure as one of five major motivations, "the unilateralism of donors in imposing conditions accompanying international assistance."[5] And a report on Kenyan NGOs states: "Without the ability to secure independent funding. . . . NGOs will never have the influence they should have on the country's development strategies. . . . This is because many NGOs are perceived as merely advocates of policies decided by donors."[6]

Even in emergency work, discourses that condemn creating dependency on the part of refugees and other vulnerable populations are beginning to be criticized. As Stein points out, "a concept such as 'dependency' often has no unambiguous empirical referents" (Stein 2008, 136). She also cites a review of the Humanitarian Policy Group, which states: "The persistence of the idea of a dependency syndrome says more about the

---

5. *Dynamique Citoyenne: National Network for Independent Monitoring of Public Policies and Cooperation Strategies* (Yaoundé, Cameroon, 2006), 2.

6. Samuel Lando, "For Kenya's NGOs, a Need to Cooperate," Devex Report, October 14, 2008.

attitudes of aid providers toward recipients than it does about the attitudes of the recipients themselves" (Stein 2008, 136, quoting Harvey and Lind 2005). In addition to incorporating these critiques of accountability and dependency discourses, humanitarians and peacebuilders need to take on board proposals for new forms of cosmopolitanism as central components of their strategies. These are sometimes conceptual, as in the project of Pollock, Bhabha, Breckenridge, and Chakrabarty (2002) to decenter the Western core and its assumptions of cosmopolitan consciousness, which is also similar to the earlier project that Ngũgĩ wa Thiong'o articulated in his 1993 treatise, *Moving the Centre,* or the project of "humanism" promoted by Edward Said (see Duvall and Varadarajan 2007) to question the construction of "otherness" in neocolonial civilizing or development missions. These debates are also at times procedural, as in the articulation of "feminist social criticism" by Brooke Ackerly (2000). Feminist social criticism assumes that feminist "cosmopolitans," including Western activists (see Confortini 2010), have the capability to engage in critical self-reflection as an essential component of working toward their emancipatory goals. According to this framework, even Western feminists can begin their activism from the assumption that they are situated at the more privileged end of an unequal distribution of power, that silences that must be voiced ensue, and that social criticism is inseparable from self-criticism. Finally, these debates can also be institutional and ideological, as critics of neoliberal financial institutions at the World Social Forums demonstrate (Smith and Karides et al. 2007).

How do such conceptual and pragmatic projects challenge neoliberal humanitarian ethics? First, they do not begin from assumptions that aid recipients are dependent beings who need to be educated and socialized into individualist notions of autonomy and marketized ideas about profit making and economic success. Second, they recognize that these assumptions emanate from a particular time and geography, and as such represent one of a succession of failed modernization projects. Third, they understand that contemporary cosmopolitanism is tainted by its modernizing and globalizing pretensions. Fourth, however, they seek to envision and practice new forms of cosmopolitan ethics that prioritize learning and understanding from difference instead of imposing uniformity on it. This type of ethics also privileges economic redistribution and social and communal sustainability rather than innovation for profit to wean aid recipients from alleged dependencies.

Scholars and practitioners of peacebuilding can incorporate insights from these challenges to neoliberal humanitarian ethics by questioning the projects and techniques, of which microfinance is one, that link short-term relief to long-term stability. Incorporating feminist social criticism, for example, would lead to insistence on a more in-depth understanding of the lived experiences of female and male clients of neoliberal economic initiatives, rather than simply the ability of such initiatives to perpetuate themselves through market forces or repayment of loans. Incorporating the insights of World Social Forum critics of global financial institutions would lead to insistence on mechanisms for grants instead of loans—in addition to debt forgiveness. Incorporating race and class more centrally as categories of analysis would require attention to the neocolonial assumptions about Africans built into neoliberal modernizing projects. And understanding cosmopolitanism in the plural, as cosmopolitanisms that consciously "decolonize" thought processes and solutions to conflict and poverty, would engender collaborative conversations rather than imposed ideas about long-term well-being that view peace and economic justice as symbiotically related.

In sum, current activism and future scholarship needs to highlight and critique the problematic connection between our cosmopolitan affects and ideologies, on the one hand, and the economic relations of the humanitarian international social movement, on the other. Challenges to neoliberal humanitarian practices, in other words, must confront both "centering" cosmopolitan assumptions and their related market logics to avoid discursive demobilization. This is not an easy task. Such a confrontation requires constant awareness and reflexivity. It will likely always be partial at best. Finally, it requires constant discursive—both material and ethical—evaluations of the interconnected and very political nature of humanitarian action and ethics in both the short and the long-term.

# 3

# Laughing at the Enemy

*Rethinking Critiques of Communal*
*Political Violence in India*[1]

## Dia Da Costa

$F$ocusing on discursive representations of the structural forces enabling communal violence (i.e., violence among communities of politicized religion) in India, this essay critically analyzes the promise of grassroots cultural practices of peacebuilding in order to account for the success and limitations of everyday modes of sustaining just peace. Specifically, this essay focuses on a particular cultural action by citizens of the political Left as a primary means of critiquing violence. I examine three plays on communal violence by Janam—a theater group—that reject both neoliberal and cultural nationalist solutions to capitalist and communal violence in India. Janam's critique thereby transcends the charge leveled

1. I am indebted to the generosity, intellect, and commitment of members of Janam, in particular Sudhanva Deshpande, Komita Dhanda, Moloyashree Hashmi, and Sarita Sharma. I gratefully acknowledge funding received from the Senate Advisory Research Committee at Queen's University and from the Social Sciences and Humanities Research Council of Canada, for making this research possible. This paper was first presented at a workshop at the Kroc Institute for International Peace Studies and the Center for the Study of Social Movements, University of Notre Dame. I am very grateful to Jackie Smith and Ernesto Verdeja for inviting me to participate and for their leadership in this project. Finally, I thank as well Nosheen Ali, Alexandre Da Costa, and Jayant Lele, who offered their insightful comments on earlier drafts of this paper.

against new social movements for neglecting analyses of market, capital accumulation, and class (Lynch 1998). As I will show, Janam's everyday political action counters conventional liberal explanations of violence that routinely misrepresent clashing civilizations as causes, view failed states as bounded spaces, and champion neoliberal institution building as conflict management solutions (Collier et. al 2003; Paris 2004; Huntington 1993). Janam's analysis joins the chorus of critical scholarship that has shown the ways in which neoliberal institution building exacerbates the global structural conditions of inequality, exploitation, and ethnic violence as norm rather than exception (Harvey 2003; Bernstein, Leys, and Panitch 2009).

In line with these broader academic trends, explanations of communal violence between Hindu and Muslim groups in India have wavered between culturalist explanations that imagine communities of essential difference at war with each other and structuralist explanations that recognize the role of state institutions, political party elites, and "elite revolts" in fomenting the conditions and occasions of communal violence (Thapar 1989; Basu and Roy 2007; Corbridge and Harriss 2000). Janam contributes to the structuralist school of thought by situating localized conflicts within broader global forces of persistent inequality, exclusion, and redistribution (Pugh, Cooper, and Turner 2008a; Mamdani 2004). Janam has played an invaluable role in publicly challenging the structural alliances between neoliberal globalization and cultural nationalism. Its contribution to peacebuilding thus takes the form of consciousness-raising based on the belief that making structural forces underlying violence apparent in everyday public thinking will result in thoughtful citizen action against the forces of violent conflict.

This essay does not set out to assert a causal relationship between Janam's political action and outcomes such as solidarity and peace. Rather, it sets out to analyze the promise, significance, and limitations of Janam's discursive forms of everyday peacebuilding, its truth claims, assumptions, and strengths. Despite its powerful contribution to public political action, I also argue that Janam's attempt at mobilizing democratic struggle is constrained by a narrow discourse that inadvertently simplifies the problem of communal violence. In part, this is because

Janam (a) laughs at cultural nationalism and presents it as something that "others" engage in for their instrumental purposes, (b) collapses religion and faith, (c) homogenizes working-class communities, and (d) neglects the role of middle classes in producing communal violence. These factors arguably dissuade crosscutting solidaristic ties, but Janam's weakness must not be viewed mechanically as a result of its affiliations with parties of the political Left. Rather, their weaknesses in mitigating ethnic strife are better explained by an unreflexive imaginary—one that could afflict state and social movement actors alike.

Recently, critical analyses have pressed for attention to the agency of actual perpetrators rather than externalizing analyses of violence onto abstract state or "structural forces" alone (Mathur 2008; Shani 2005). A reflexive imaginary combined with a global and relational analysis would enable us to go beyond the view that poor people are either fundamentally unlikely agents of violence or exceptionally susceptible to violent action. Thus, I argue that in addition to demystifying structural forces of violence as a strategy of bottom-up approaches to political and social emancipation (Santos 2007b), building just peace is emboldened by recognizing that a range of actors, and not just factors, help perpetrate forms of violence. That is, as we foreground structural forces of violence, we must also recognize why people in varied socioeconomic positions are persuaded by, or otherwise contest, such forces.

Moreover, progressive actors who tend to place themselves outside the structural factors causing violence, upon closer scrutiny can turn out to be (inadvertently) complicit with the privileges, actions, and views that perpetuate violence. A crucial ingredient of building a just peace therefore ought to be to counter the unreflexive assumption that violence is that which only the desperate engage in because "they" (unlike "us") need scapegoats and enemies to blame for their marginality. A critical reflexive imaginary therefore involves a threefold process of recognizing, historicizing, and problematizing agency rather than merely enacting or celebrating it. Ultimately a reflexive imaginary can be nurtured when institutional, social movements, and everyday actors who attempt to construct just peace by demystifying structural violence and inequality equally consciously fight the temptation to place themselves outside of the structural and historical forces of violence that they seek to battle. By a reflexive imaginary I mean to place anticapitalist struggles for social emancipation and their structural and symbolic explanations of violence *within* the historical formation of class and communalized society. This call is not original. Yet it bears repeating since the optimism of alternative or transformative visions and epistemologies have historically numbed alertness to the fact that alternatives are projections of difference that emerge as relational outcomes of structural violence.

I make these interrelated arguments in four sections. In the first section, I introduce Janam within its social context as a way to highlight the blurred space between state and social movement politics that Janam occupies. In the second section, I introduce the context of Indian communal politics within which Janam's plays intervene. In the third section, I describe the three plays and highlight their key contributions to critiquing the consolidation of communal violence and communalization of social life in India. In the fourth section, I return to the argument made in this introduction by highlighting the key dimensions of undermined potential for communal peacebuilding emerging from Janam's plays.

### Janam and the Blurred State

Janam was founded in the mid-1970s. Since then, Janam has worked actively as the cultural wing of the Communist Party of India (Marxist), or CPM, and has been doing street theater in Delhi for the past thirty-five years. Performing in working-class neighborhoods, university campuses, factories, and election campaigns, Janam uses Brechtian theater methods to complement offstage mobilizations by trade unions, women's groups, and political parties of the Left. They have combated the everyday privatization of social life, means of communication, and the idea within neoliberalism that there is no alternative (Deshpande 2007).

Janam's onstage and offstage political action navigates electoral competition for the political Left and democratic politics of the social Left. Janam is unabashed about its party affiliation and participates in election campaigns for the CPM. It is also engaged in a host of other democratic struggles that have touched the Delhi region since the 1970s—from

inflation to violence against women, from industrial workers' strikes to
child abuse. Janam has generated a vast body of plays and maintained
a remarkably regular schedule of performances. The plays are scripted
through discussion among actors (who need not be CPM members) about
the issue at hand. Rehearsals and discussions lead to the formation of a
play, while the ultimate selection process is subject to choices made by the
director and around important struggles in any given period.

As the cultural wing of a party with minimal political clout in north
India, Janam is part of a thoroughly marginal leftist movement in this
region.[2] This bolsters Janam's identity and claim as a leftist cultural and
political movement rather than as "the state" in this region, even if the
political party it works for is a persistent competitor for electoral and parliamentary power. While red flags conspicuously inform political agendas
in performances and discourses, Janam's membership is not limited to
card-carrying members of the CPM, nor do individual participants have
to declare allegiance to a leftist political platform. Nor are audiences limited to their natural allies or political constituencies. If plays support a
party line, they also push CPM-affiliated trade union members to attend
to issues conventionally neglected by them. Yet, as Janam performers,
participants do enact a party line, especially for election campaign plays,
whether enactments match individual convictions or not. Although I have
discerned no homogenous politics within Janam, I was once in a conversation with a Janam member who asserted that legitimate definitions of
being part of the Left hinge on political party affiliation. To be "Left" one
had to be part of the organized, political Left. These examples show that
Janam actors must be simultaneously understood to be seeing like "the
state" and beyond it, depending on the context.

Sometimes Janam finds itself defending the idea of its work as oppositional politics. For example, one evening in the summer of 2005 when
Janam made its way through a busy market area to find an adequate spot

---

2. The reasons for the Left's political weakness in Delhi are complex, highly under-
studied, and beyond the scope of analysis here. However, it is important to bear in mind as
we consider the political framework for Janam's work.

to perform, a middle-aged man seated on a pushcart called out, "You don't get to critique the government any more. You *are* the government." The comment visibly annoyed one of the theater troupe leaders. She said in response, "Why don't you all understand that we are not the government? We are merely supporting them from the outside." The man was referring to the 2004 national election, at which the CPM took the unprecedented step of supporting a rival center-right political party—the Indian National Congress—which had dominated electoral politics from 1947 until the 1990s.

In 1998, a notable coalition government came into power as an alternative to hegemonic congress rule in India. The coalition was led by the Hindu rightwing party, the Bharatiya Janata Party (BJP), which stayed in power until 2004. The BJP ruthlessly pursued its communalization, militarization, and liberalization agenda, supported largely by urban and middle- and upper-class voters in India. In 2004, the Congress Party returned to power by leading the United Progressive Alliance (UPA), comprised of allies with significant outside support provided by the CPM. This parliamentary alliance disabled the BJP from returning to power and brought back poverty alleviation, hunger, and employment to the central government agenda. Notwithstanding the political Left's rationale for providing "outside" support to the UPA, as bearers of CPM flags the middle-aged onlooker was questioning Janam's legitimacy in critiquing the state, since it was now viewed as part of the state apparatus. It seemed that the parliamentary alliance disqualified the possibility of a critical stance. These examples show that state-society lines are constantly blurred by Janam and in public political life in India more generally. Yet these lines are also indispensable means of claim making about legitimate politics and disciplining political belonging and commitment.

Keeping these complexities in mind, I evade the task of defining Janam in definitive terms as a cultural wing of the state or as a social movement. Such categorization imprisons Janam within social scientific categories that it often exceeds (Smith and Kutz-Flamenbaum 2010). Instead, I draw on a perspective of state-society relations that accepts that "the state is a unified symbol of an actual disunity" (Abrams 1988, 79). I view this statement to be as applicable to political movements that struggle *for* state power as it is to the "newest" forms of social struggle that do not, because neither is outside structures of capitalist power relations.

## Demystifying the Interlinked Structures of "Unholy Alliance"

Achin Vanaik has recently called communalism "the paradigmatic form of violence in India" (Vanaik 2009, 143) defining it as "intolerance and tensions between religious communities" (141). Vanaik is joined by numerous social scientists who have characterized the communalization of Indian politics as "elite revolts" (Corbridge and Harriss 2000), which map a transition from development nationalism to cultural nationalism (Desai 2004; Sarkar 2008). According to Sumit Sarkar, in its formative years in the 1920s, while every other nationalist political ideology was preoccupied with the problem of mass poverty, this concern was decisively absent in Hindu communal thought—just as it is today. Sarkar's point is that it is not surprising that the cultural nationalism of the Hindu political Right fits well with contemporary neoliberalism's equally political disregard for mass poverty. This kind of critical scholarship refuses to see communal violence as a localized conflict, but rather views it in relation to the political economic history of global capitalism and its attendant forms of struggle.

Janam's plays contribute to this kind of analysis of communal violence by publicizing the "unholy alliance" of capitalism, imperialism, and religious fundamentalism (Afzal-Khan 2001). I borrow Fawzia Afzal-Khan's term for the Pakistani context to characterize Janam's tremendous work, which consistently exposes the fact that ethnic *forms* of violence in India hide "unholy alliances" among industrialists, divisive party politicians, communal leadership, and US imperialist interests. Janam's method follows the Brechtian aesthetic of enabling audiences to enjoy a play enough to choose sides just like spectators who would enthusiastically choose sides in a boxing match (Brecht 1977, 6–8). In addition to demystification, Janam's plays also advertize the historic strength and continuing significance and potential of working-class solidarity, brotherhood, and national unity to combat communalized politics.

The unholy alliance identified in the first play, *Weapons*, is among industrialists, hired criminals, and Congress Party politicians. This play is set in the context of the 1978 riots in the northern Indian city of Aligarh—home to a historic lock industry where Hindus and Muslims worked together, which nonetheless became the site of highly orchestrated violence. The second play, *The Abduction of Brotherhood*, was written in the 1980s when ethnic strife—from rising right-wing Hindu fundamentalism, to separatist movements in Kashmir, among Sikhs, by Tamils in Sri Lanka, and in the northeastern provinces of India—threatened to unravel Indian territorial unity. Janam focused on publicizing the unholy alliances among Hindu, Muslim, and Sikh leaders and their dependence on American arms and dollars.

In the third play, *This Heart Desires More, Guruji* (Anonymous 2002), Janam highlights the unholy alliance among the Hindu political Right and the military-media-consumer-capitalist complex as it emerged in India in the 1990s with the liberalization of the Indian economy. This play responds to political economic changes and violent events in the aftermath of the BJP's electoral victory in 1998. In its first term, the BJP conducted a nuclear test in Pokhran, which helped construct the discourse of the Hindu bomb. In the summer of 1999, India fought Pakistan in the Kargil War, responding to Pakistani infiltration beyond their designated place along the Line of Control. Kargil justified an increased military budget in India, expanded the importation of weapons from Israel, and resulted in a massive surge in popular patriotism and war films by the Indian film industry. Along with the mass mobilizations of Hindu pride through religious processions and rewritten history textbooks, the new media of television and film were key modes of constructing the Indian public as Hindu in the 1990s (A. Rajagopal 2001; Sarkar 2002).

Janam's plays thus identify instances of "unholy alliance," marking shifts in the reinvented Indian polity and public sphere flagging the interlinkages among structures of military-industrial, neoliberal, consumer-capitalist, and cultural nationalist relations of violence. Viewing capitalist domination, exploitation, and violence as dividing and recruiting people—either for the Left or for fascism by the Right—Janam's plays encourage people to understand the violence of capitalism and to "vote" for the Left in the ideological battle between Left and Right.

## Three Plays by Janam

*Communal Violence as Weapon*

*Weapons* was written in the immediate aftermath of the 1978 riots in Aligarh. The proximate cause for the 1978 riot was a wrestling match between Hindu and Muslim teams in which a Hindu wrestler was stabbed by some Muslims. Intervening in culturalist narratives about Hindu-Muslim riots as spontaneous resurgences of age-old differences, Janam's play depicts these riots as instigated through the collaboration of industrialists, Congress politicians, and their hired criminals. Each in this unholy alliance has an interest. The industrialist wants to disrupt the interdependent division of labor that binds Hindu and Muslim communities through the small-scale lock industry. The big industrialists are described as "wolves hungry for human blood [who] want to ruin the workshops and appropriate and enslave the local skill for their own profit" (Janam 2002, 55).[3] The Congress politicians support the industrialist's plan of displacing small industry for the greater good of the "national economy," and the hired criminals, skilled at destruction, are only too happy to be paid to tear Aligarh apart. The criminals in the play are unmarked in ethnic terms, but recruited as weapons for serving the larger political-economic motives of fuelling communal divisions. In scene after scene, actors playing the politician switch roles to play the industrialist, and the criminal switches roles to play the police, emphasizing that the faces of criminality and justice, as well as political and economic interests, are indistinguishable.

Despite numerous efforts to incite workers into violence, Sadiq and Ramkishan, Harkishan and Rafiq (representing two generations of Hindu-Muslim friends) refuse to nurture ethnic differences since they have lived, worked, and played together for years. Even when Sadiq and Ramkishan die and the opposing religious community is blamed for stabbings actually done by hired criminals, the fathers of the slain sons are

3. All translations from Hindi are by the author.

not stirred to draw their swords against the communal other. The message in the play is stark. Quintessential Hindu-Muslim brotherhood and working-class solidarity is being actively torn asunder by Hindu nationalists and (Indian National Congress) politicians who rhetorically invoke Gandhian principles of communal peace while hiring criminals to perpetrate violence for electoral and monetary profit.

Janam's play reverses essentialized narratives of Hindu-Muslim enmity with an essentialized view of intercommunal solidarity founded in working-class solidarity while drawing attention to the political economic interests *really* responsible for ethnic violence. While seeing the structural enemy in these terms, Janam's play betrays some key silences. First, it assumes an a priori working-class and communal solidarity in Aligarh, viewing it as an outcome of relations of production, working lives, and neighborhood histories tied to the lock-manufacturing industry. This unity of Aligarh's working population is exaggerated. In the lock industry, traders and suppliers have been Hindu (Varshney 2002), while the locksmiths have been mostly Muslim until recently (Laskar 2000, 510). Thus, while there is division of labor and interdependence between the ethnic communities, Muslim labor has historically relied on Hindu control over capital, credit, and trade (Varshney 2002, 128). The division of labor therefore manifests both interdependence and inequality between Hindus and Muslims.

Second, Janam's play neglects to address the role of the growing Muslim middle class. Ashutosh Varshney argues that the formation of the Muslim middle class in the 1970s produced a critical complication in Aligarh's communal relations (Varshney 2002, 136–41). When Muslim class mobility became possible without reliance on Hindu traders or capital, Hindu-Muslim working-class interdependence unraveled. Until 1969, communal riots in Aligarh centered on the political history of the Aligarh Muslim University (AMU), which fortified Muslim pride, marked the educational modernization of the Muslim landed aristocracy, and became a central force of separatist politics that led to the formation of Pakistan in 1947 (ibid., 136–38). While AMU was both a site of Muslim cultural pride and marked class disparity *among* Muslims in Aligarh—differentiating the landed aristocracy from those in the lock industry—class disparity was underplayed by Muslim separatists and Hindu nationalists alike (ibid., 152–57).

The riots in the 1970s were a consequence of a growing, previously nonexistent Muslim middle class. This middle class gained from migrating to the Middle East after the 1973 Gulf oil boom. Bridging the historic disparity between the Muslim elite and working population, the repatriated workers now had the "muscle and financial capacity to take Hindu nationalists on" for the first time (ibid., 159). Janam's play treats this case of communal violence as an outcome of the machinations of the ethnically unmarked industrialists, politicians, and mercenaries who make victims out of ethnically marked workers. Instead, Janam's account might have better addressed "structural violence" through a complex account of middle-class agency by exposing how rationales for mercenary violence, class interests, and ethnic ties intersect and feed one another.

In sum, the exaggeration of solidarity (in a simplistic displacement of the "clash of civilizations" view) and the neglect of intersectional class and ethnic formation of the Muslim middle class allow Janam to extricate complexity from relevant "structural" and "political economic" forces that lead to the Aligarh riot. Janam's analysis privileges and successfully identifies an external enemy in the anonymous *lumpen* duped into the machinations of conniving politicians and industrialists.

### The Ringmaster of Indian Insurgency

If the first play focused on communal violence as a weapon for Indian politicians and bourgeoisie, the second play, *The Abduction of Brotherhood*, written in the 1980s, focuses primarily on Hindu, Muslim, and Sikh community leaders (the few bad apples) who ally with the United States for arms and financial support to perpetuate insurgency and ethnic violence in India. In this play, the seemingly localized conflict among ethnic groups in India is connected to broader forces of capitalism and the US military-industrial complex.

In *The Abduction of Brotherhood*, the United States comes to India as the ringmaster of The Great American Circus in order to feed and train the animal known as communal violence. A street performer and his pet monkey are in search of Brotherhood, who was reportedly kidnapped. In the course of the search, the monkey is waylaid by the American ringmaster, who needs help locating simmering ethnic tensions. The monkey tells the ringmaster that "communal violence" is the most dangerous animal in India, first introduced by the British, and now reproducing uncontrollably. Delighted, the ringmaster asks for the whereabouts of such violence. Since communal violence was declared the national animal and "our prime minister takes great care of wild animals too" (Janam 2002, 68), the monkey informs him that government permission is necessary.

Denied help from the government, the ringmaster covertly finds, feeds, and trains the leaders of Hindu, Sikh, and Muslim communities who promise to transform the map of India in exchange for dollars and arms. Here, unlike the first play, the few bad criminals who perpetuate violence are not unmarked in ethnic terms but are recognizable leaders of separatist politics in India from the 1980s. While the communal disharmony is music to the ringmaster's ears, Brotherhood calls for solidarity, since the disharmony is traumatic for him. Brotherhood's call invites beatings and leads to his capture by Hindu, Sikh, and Muslim private armies.

The play ends with the street performer calling on his audience to help set Brotherhood free and stop the fragmentation of the country. A poem about Brotherhood's birth centuries ago, his fight for Indian independence, and his current role in ensuring that India does not descend into civil war seals the message. Janam's play reinforces hope that the unity of the anticolonial nationalist movement can be resuscitated for present struggles, while situating ethnic conflict and armed insurgencies in the 1980s within a broader global military-industrial complex. Here, Janam's class analysis decisively shifts to the arena of international relations with little attention to the class politics *within* the ethnic communities engaged in tumultuous violence. As such, this play still deifies and reifies Brotherhood rather than examines conditions of solidarity in light of the complex rationales for actually perpetrating violence. The abstraction of "Brotherhood" is subject to enemy attack by imperial and communal forces. Differentiations among communally and economically marginal classes and aspiring middle classes remain invisible in their analysis. Scholarship has shown that minority separatism and communal violence became rational options for the working and middle classes in the 1980s (Das 1990). Assuming that a few bad apples are at work to undermine an essential brotherhood is, in such cases, wishful thinking rather than effective consciousness-raising for social emancipation. As we see below, the redundancy of this "Brotherhood" narrative became all too clear by 2002.

*Neoliberal Hindu India*

In 2002, fifty-nine Hindu pilgrims returning by train from Ayodhya were killed as train compartments were mysteriously set on fire near Godhra, in the province of Gujarat. Projecting assumptions about the perpetrators being Muslim, a state-orchestrated ethnic cleansing of Muslims in Gujarat followed, which was publicly justified as revenge. The explosive violence in Gujarat was shocking even though communal violence had become routine in India. In response, Janam organized a conference in Delhi inviting cultural activists and intelligentsia across India to reflect on, analyze, and condemn the events in Gujarat. They were intent on understanding the failures and future work for the Left.[4] Disrupting the normalization of state-sanctioned violence against minorities, Janam's organized response democratized the public discourse on Gujarat. They called Gujarat an orchestrated pogrom and genocide not a spontaneous riot, they identified differences between majoritarian and minority communalisms, and highlighted the significant economic dimension where calculated harm was intended to strike Muslim businesses in places like Ahmedabad (Karat 2002). They publicly assessed the spread of the BJP in other provinces, argued that "art alone will not do" in the fight against fascism (Tanvir 2002; Achuth 2002; Saiwal 2002), and reinforced the message "organize, or perish" (Ahmad 2002, 61).

4. The talks and interviews with various artists as well as select artistic productions were consolidated into a special issue of Janam's bilingual literary magazine *Nukkad* (2002) and later published in a special issue of *Seagull Theatre Quarterly* (2002). These gatherings and publications enabled the cultural and political Left in Delhi to publicly reflect on the spread of communal violence across India.

Most significant for this essay, at Janam's conference, the narrative of assumed brotherhood was deemed inadequate in a reflexive critique by the Left. Ashish Chatterjee said, for example, that plays of the past such as *The Abduction of Brotherhood,* still performed in West Bengal, are not enough because "brotherhood is not enough" (Chatterjee 2002, 129). People wondered how Ahmedabad city, Gandhi's city of peacebuilding and educational institutions, could be torn apart so completely. Some Dalit writers such as Joseph MacWan (2002) roundly refused this Gujarati claim to exceptional nonviolence, arguing that structural violence is the norm. Others claim that communal harmony has disintegrated over the years. Contributing to the latter view, Ashutosh Varshney provides one explanation centered on the active destruction and neglect of intercommunal associations in Ahmedabad by the late 1960s—from educational institutions and Gandhi ashrams, to business associations, the Congress Party, and trade unions of the Left—to explain how Gujarat 2002 could have come to pass (Varshney 2002, 219–61). Others argue that Gujarat had become a laboratory for communal hatred, largely enabled by a shift in Ahmedabad's class and caste politics confronting rising unemployment due to closed textile mills, the politics of reservations, and the transition to an aggressive industrial class with ties to a rich peasantry (Shani 2005; Sud 2007; Suhrud 2002, 100–101). Yet identifying broader external forces does not explain the persuasive appeal of participating in violence. Indeed, as Shubh Mathur puts it, "it is the displacement of responsibility from individual action to 'vast social forces' that produces modern genocide" (Mathur 2008, 47; see also Chaturvedi 2011)

The genocide in 2002 was orchestrated by the Hindu fundamentalist government, and the Hindu middle class participated enthusiastically in premeditated arson, looting, and killing of Muslims (Suhrud 2002). However, what stands out is that Dalits[5] and Adivasis[6] also participated in

5. "Dalits" literally means downtrodden and is the term used by groups formerly known as untouchables within the Hindu caste system.

6. "Adivasis" literally means original dwellers and is the self-designated term for indigenous populations of India.

perpetrating violence against Muslims (Suhrud 2002; Lobo 2002; Mathur 2008; Shani 2005). The Hindu rightwing led by upper-caste conceptions of Hinduism had done the seemingly impossible. Rather than assuming brotherhood as an a priori formation (as Janam did in its plays), they constructed a notion of "brotherhood" and a representation of the enemy among populations historically oppressed by upper-caste Hindus. Groups historically marginalized within Hinduism were willing to kill in the name of an ethnic supremacy, difference, and pride that did not seem to reflect their own ascriptive ties or political economic place. But as Shubh Mathur has argued, participating in communal violence promised Dalits and Adivasis the possibility of symbolically defending and thereby rising in status within Hindu society (Mathur 2008, 126). Ornit Shani provides a concrete analysis of this claim by viewing the 2002 Gujarat riots in light of riots in the 1980s. She argues that what is commonly viewed as communal (Hindu-Muslim) rivalry and violence actually began as intracommunity (Hindu) caste conflict founded in upper-caste/class Hindu anger against the Gujarat government's reservation policies in the 1980s (Shani 2005). In the context of textile mill closures, the Hindu Right mobilized among a diversity of unemployed caste and community groups. In particular, "Hindu organizations captured and fulfilled both the need for a politics of redistribution and the need for pride and acceptance" through relief work in Dalit neighborhoods and by hosting Hindu festivals in which, for the first time in the 1980s in Gujarat, Dalits were allowed to participate (Shani 2005, 890). Gujarat makes it difficult to know the enemy in categorical communal, caste, or class terms because of the conflation of these designations and dynamics in politics and social transformation.

To what extent did Gujarat push Janam to reconfigure its narrative about the enemy? In the aftermath of Gujarat, Janam wrote and performed the play *This Heart Desires More, Guruji*. This title was recognizable across the Indian public sphere as the popular jingle featuring Indian celebrities advertising Pepsi in 1998. This line was then used as Captain Vikram Batra's battle cry in the Kargil War between India and Pakistan in 1999 when the Indian army was belatedly deployed to stall Pakistani infiltration into Indian territory. Subsequently, it became the title of a Bollywood film. Like the two earlier plays analyzed above, this play identifies and publicizes an unholy alliance—this time, between violent Hindu nationalism, military power, and icons of global consumer capitalism. Significantly, Janam brings the question of the middle class via consumerism into its depiction of structures of violence. Critiquing urban middle-class capitulation to Hindutva, which brought BJP to power following the liberalization policies of 1992, Janam satirizes the endless thirst for the foreign Pepsi by those who claim to be thirsty for a pure Hindu nation.

Of the three plays analyzed I have only had the opportunity to see this one performed. Without doubt, it made me laugh about things that puzzle and pain those diasporic middle-class Indians whose political coming-of-age was marked by anger about India's transition to cultural nationalism. At a time of despair, Janam's play asserts the power of laughter to signal human resilience in the face of the absurd efficacy and persuasions of fascist violence and consumer capitalism.

Replete with slapstick and satire, this play rests on the central characters—Guru, Brain, and Brawn—mirroring the organizational structure of the Hindu family of organizations on the political Right—with the Rashtriya SwayamSevak Sangh (RSS) as the ideological think tank, the BJP as the political wing, and the militant Bajrang Dal (BD) ready for armed struggle. The Brain (representing the RSS) has accomplished the absurd, peddling ideas that the Hindu nation will be modeled on "our ancestors two million years ago, in the golden age of dinosaurs," who have been proven to be Hindu (Janam 2002, 117). Brain has also accomplished the impossible, controlling information broadcast on all forms of popular media from newspapers to television, radio, and textbooks. The national anthem now celebrates the Hindu bomb instead of Indian unity. Anyone who does not follow the principles laid out by the Guru (RSS) and Brain (BJP) is subject to the brainless Brawn's (BD) indiscriminate violence. Women are required to have strong sons and pregnant mothers are encouraged to watch WWF championships or Bollywood films that glorify the Indian military. Brain claims that the Hindu bomb was given by the Sun God to Indians, but Brawn foolishly disrupts the idea of the Hindu bomb when he reads the writing on the bomb "With Love, from America" (Janam 2002, 119). The Guru has a ready explanation for the discrepancy, explaining that those foreigners who help accomplish our goal of a pure nation are real Indians too. Here, the aspirations and guilt of the middle-class diaspora who left for better opportunities, their reinvented sense of belonging articulated in part through fuelling long-distance Hindu nationalism via the World Hindu Council, is incorporated into Janam's epic satire. Brawn finally understands that the purity of the Hindu nation not only has endless desires but is also able to Hinduize everything from dinosaurs to the cell phone, from Coca Cola to the Taj Mahal.

While the two earlier plays highlighted solidarities and common vulnerabilities of Hindus and Muslims, the third play moves away from humanism and claims about working-class solidarity. Instead, it focuses on satirizing the BJP's hypocritical cultural nationalism that depends on neoliberal consumer capitalism and the Indian diaspora. While Janam makes significant advances in highlighting the seductions and aspirations in consumer culture that captivates Indians, the play primarily constructs this as the machinations and hypocrisy of BJP and its followers. Rather than use this as occasion to insert a critical and reflexive account of what makes consumer capitalism and cultural nationalism so persuasive for middle-class Indians more generally, Janam resorts to its formulaic search for the external enemy.

In an effort to go beyond analyses that treat people as spontaneously and magically manipulated into communal violence by political elites, Tania Li has called for shifting focus from the working classes to the "actual and aspiring middle-classes" because these classes often lead acts of violence as a result of being excluded from opportunities and professional advancement (2009, 171–72). This is precisely Ornit Shani's explanation for how some Dalits came to unite as Hindus against Muslim others in Gujarat (2005). While the middle class is not absent from Janam's plays, the working class, the capitalist, state, and communalist leaders dominate the narrative. Yet it is their lack of attention to the ways in which communal and caste boundaries intersect with and reformulate class identity and politics that results in linear accounts of what counts as structural forces underlying communal violence.

It bears repeating that Janam does essential work in highlighting unholy alliances in the public space, since to many these appear as the distinct spheres of religion versus capitalism, tradition versus modernity, national versus global politics. Part of the goal of this edited volume is precisely to disabuse analyses of violence and peacebuilding of such categorical and scalar separations. However, understanding violence and rebuilding peace ultimately requires a more complex discussion of how unholy alliances intersect with ethnic and class formations, while displacing the logic and possibility of class solidarity. Laughing at the enemy does not do the equally important work of nurturing a reflexive imaginary that would place the political Left and middle classes *within* the political history of capitalism, religion, and cultural nationalism.

This is not unprecedented criticism as evident from the post-Gujarat discussions among Janam supporters and well-wishers. Yet, as I show below, this reflexive critique does not make an adequate mark in Janam's most recent play on the subject.

## Vanishing Interruptions of Reflexive Critique

In this section, I use the term "interruption" to indicate a Brechtian editorial style of choppy disruptions that cut up the seamless flow of a plot by juxtaposing *seemingly* disconnected forms of storytelling and disparate events in the presentation of a play. The purpose of such interruption is to dissuade easy emotional empathy with characters and nurture critical thinking by situating particular events within a larger canvas of epic historical analysis. I use the term "interruptions of reflexive critique" to mean onstage and offstage critique that challenges easy ideological empathy and explanation of violence by highlighting ambiguity, complexity, and complicity as germane to experiences of violence. As I show below, these interruptions of reflexive critique vanish in the sense that they make no dent on reimagining epic accounts or resist the ways in which neat explanations of violence serve to "normalize the violence" (Mathur 2008, 170). In what follows, I identify instances of reflexive critique in an interview with the playwright, CPM member, and professor G. P. Deshpande, and in the play *This Heart Desires More, Guruji,* in order to then highlight the fact that these fleeting instances of reflexivity fail to make a lasting mark on Janam's analysis.

In an interview in 2002, G. P. Deshpande addressed three issues of concern for street theater practitioners mobilizing in regions of India where the political Left is historically insignificant. First, he asserts the inadequacy of repeating a script devised twenty-five years ago in which the message was that a few bad apples from each ethnic community are responsible for "provoking people into the wrong courses and wrong positions" (Deshpande 2002, 43). As evident in each of the plays analyzed above, Janam's enemy consists of the corrupt, powerful minority with little attention to what persuades the marginalized majority to consent to structural violence. Second, Deshpande argues that the leftist cultural movement must monitor and comment on mainstream cultural productions, without which audiences are free to subscribe to the seductive simplicity of fascist messages.

Third, and most important, Deshpande argues that while street theater has predictably celebrated brotherhood and critiqued violence and capitalism, it has not examined the fundamental problem of "why is it that a given ideology creates the kind of audience that it does in a given society." *This Heart Desires More, Guruji* makes us laugh at archetypal Hindu buffoons with their irrational and childish cultural nationalism, divisive politics, and violent goals of purity. Yet the play fails to help its audience understand why the Guru has any disciples at all. Deshpande suggests that there is an enemy within leftist cultural activism. That is, a leftist inability to take seriously the human need for ethical thinking, which is increasingly monopolized by communal thinking. Deshpande does not elaborate how this is to be addressed even as he candidly acknowledges that the Left's negativity toward religious consciousness and disregard for the cultural efficacy of violence has turned out to be the enemy within. Janam plays have the capacity to make us angry about communal violence and laugh at cultural nationalism, but, as Deshpande has astutely observed, "You can laugh at a given notion of cultural nationalism. You cannot laugh at cultural nationalism *per se*" (Deshpande 2002, 44).

Although Janam identifies the irrationality of cultural nationalism and the hypocritical enemy who practices it, it makes the significant error of placing itself outside of cultural nationalism *itself*. Excluding itself from the problem of ethical thinking (that is, practices that adjudicate between and enable us to act on "right" and "wrong"), the political Left and its cultural forms secure the privilege of standing outside the categories of "problem" and "enemy." As Aditya Nigam puts it, politically, "there is no Archimedean space" from which critiques of and claims to cultural nationalism and secular imaginaries are proposed and understood (Nigam 2005, 289). There is little room in Janam's high modernist vision for the agency and the "indeterminacies of the self" that produce and persuade cultural nationalism (Bharucha 2006, 477). While they were busy laughing at the enemy, the Indian Left might instead have recognized that the joke is actually on "us," not "them," considering that it is the ethic of class solidarity that appears utterly undermined in contemporary constructions of political agency and solidarity.

In the rest of this essay, I highlight missed opportunities for reflexive critique where Janam might have combined a critique of manipulating religion with recognition of the complexity of lived religion and piety for piety's sake. In foreclosing piety and faith as politicized religion, Janam succumbs to instrumentalizing religion to construct its critique of the Hindu Right's instrumental use of religion. Arguably, building solidaristic ties might require a reflexive imaginary in which Janam rethinks its own ideology on and relation to faith as a source of ethical thinking.

The only interruptions in mocking the enemy's ideology are two of the three poems that highlight that, perhaps, we cannot know who the enemy is since we are all complicit. The first poem follows a dead silent display of placards with images of Gujarat's business capital, Ahmedabad city, burning in 2002 with statistics of what was destroyed. After this quantified display of destruction, two actors stay onstage to recite a poem entitled "The Journey of a Burning City," written by Vimal Kumar. The poem welcomes people "to this burning city of slowly melting glass/ You are welcome to this city that begs for water before dying" (Janam 2002, 116). The poem goes from being hospitable to almost mocking the listener/viewer/visitor:

> What a nice thing!
> You have come to see a city of broken dreams
> You have come to wipe the tears of innocent children
> And silence the weeping women
> You have come to place flowers upon this execution ground

In addition to drawing attention to the violence experienced in the city, the poem expresses the ambivalence and anger, the violence of and the human need to pay respect by placing flowers "upon this execution ground." Kumar's poem represents the "surplus of meaning" fundamental to experiences of violence, which exceeds explanations and strategies for peacebuilding (Mathur 2008, 48). It asks the reader to consider, "Is it inadequate that you came to see the heaped ashes?" And answers,

> In these modern times
> You have come to witness deep insecurity and uncertain futures
> Because all of this is now meant to be displayed

In the play, the poem performs the function of a quintessential Brechtian "interruption" that pulls the audience out of grieving about the statistics on placards they have just seen to critically think about why grief looks as it does at a particular historical moment (Brecht 1978). In welcoming the audience to a burning city it refuses the audience's pity. In implicating the audience as tourist it reminds us of our sullied political location—the audience's complicity, everyone's complicity—before we are introduced to and begin to judge the three buffoons of the Hindu Right. The poem is critical of a historical conjuncture that has made witnessing the spectacle of "deep insecurity and uncertain futures" a source of tourism revenue (Kumar, cited in Janam 2002, 116).

Consider the second poem, which is another reflexive interruption that emphasizes the ambiguity of categories of "us" and "them" presented with certainty in the rest of the play. This poem is entitled "The Dead Witness from Gujarat," by Manglesh Dabral. In it, a working-class man in Ahmedabad talks about his daily struggle: "Earlier too, perhaps I died bit by bit/My childhood was about living a little and dying a little" (Dabral, cited in Janam 2002, 119). And he talks about his daily work:

> I repaired broken bits and pieces of things
> I used to make colorful batons for the *garba* dance
> I made little cycles out of aluminum wire
> For children

In a startling description of communal violence, the poem continues,

> And I was killed as if a number of people were being killed through me
> There wasn't much purpose to my life
> But I was killed as if there was an enormous purpose to my death
>
> And when I was asked, "who are you?"
> Have you hidden an enemy's name within?
> A religion, an amulet?
> I couldn't say anything, I was empty
> Just a painter, a carpenter, a craftsman, an artist
> A laborer
> When I was repairing the broken bits
> Inside myself
> When the tiny tyres of the aluminum-wired cycles
> Circled inside me
> That's when a flaming rock fell upon me
> I raised my hands in my last prayer
> And realized that a slave never receives a reply

Concurrent with a general leftist emphasis on worker identity over religious consciousness, this poem portrays a worker who is so much more a worker though he is also shaped by the habit of prayer. This worker realizes in his last hour that a "slave never receives a reply" for prayers—another denial of faith as a possible source of ethical thinking, action, solution, and solidarity (Dabral, cited in Janam 2002, 119). We know too from the previous verse that a communalized death gives this man's life its purpose, showing that religion only has meaning and consequence as violence in this worker's life. *And yet*, the dead witness wonders in conclusion whether the killers encounter their own fragile humanity as they face the dead.

> Now that I am merely the wiped out trace
> Of a human form,
> A dead name
> You now look at me with a bit of amazement, a bit of fear

Are you trying to recognize me?
Searching in me a relative perhaps?
Some friend or acquaintance?
Or even perhaps yourself?
Do you see someone else returning to your own face?

Do the killers see the enemy within as they encounter the face of their dead victim? Notwithstanding the focus on worker identity over religious consciousness, when it comes to the question of ethical thinking itself, Dabral's poem interrupts the flow of the play because it does not rely on the narrative of brotherhood to absolve anyone or any category (class, community, ethnicity, or political affiliation) from the problem of ethical thinking.

In contrast to the profoundly reflexive interruptions of these two poems, the concluding poem reinforces the dominant message of mocking the pathetic Hindutva ideologues for ultimately failing to construct the pure Hindu nation. Despite the extensive killing, it notes "the poor things were still not able to construct their Hindu nation" (Janam 2002, 122). It mocks the "global tender for building the Hindu nation," highlighting for the last time the utter hypocrisy of the enemy's cultural nationalism and its strategic reliance on global forces, and abandoning the message of complicity, complexity, and possibility in the two earlier poetic interruptions.

With a concluding message such as this one, there is little room for eschewing instrumental uses of religion *and* instrumental critiques of religion as equally cold comfort for the worker. Janam's consideration of piety for piety's sake as the everyday social life of religion need not exclude critique or recognition of less-than-benign uses of religion, or religion's relation to modernity/rationality/capitalism.[7] Grappling with piety would rather imply recognizing the conditions under which those who are receptive to the Hindu Right's message that "all you need is faith" become successful. Indeed, instrumental critiques of religion by the political Left might be one condition under which the political Right's manipulative

---

7. I am grateful for conversations with Jayant Lele, which have helped me articulate this point.

celebration of noninstrumental faith gains persuasive efficacy. The Hindu right *misrepresents* its politically instrumental claim about the noninstrumentality of faith as power. But this misrepresentation may be persuasive and becomes powerful ideology because people place value on ethical thinking as a form of noninstrumental thinking in the first place. This manipulation by the Hindu Right is surely worth publicizing, but in response, the political Left has to do much more than laugh, even though laughter as a sign of resilience in the face of violence is a powerful tactic. Seeing a worker as fundamentally betrayed by faith, prayer, and religion ultimately treats religion instrumentally and disregards the value of faith as source of ethical thinking, and the fact of people's myriad paths to noninstrumental ethical thinking.

## Conclusion

I have argued that since the 1970s, Janam has done the invaluable work of tracing the unholy structural alliances that benefited from and exacerbated India's transition from development nationalism to cultural nationalism. I highlighted the shifting formations of India's "paradigmatic form of violence" as they are captured in discursive representations of the cultural and political Left. Janam counters the hegemonic commonsense of communal violence as an emblematic outcome of cultural difference by revealing the structural interests of collaborations between capital and communal consciousness. It celebrates peace and solidarity by remembering historic working-class and nationalist solidarity. Yet, as I argued, Janam's plays exaggerate working-class solidarity, neglecting divisions among the working class and the role of middle-class aspirations and privilege. While revealing the political-economic conditions of cultural nationalism, they pay inadequate attention to the complexity of class formation in particular historical contexts. In so doing, perpetrators of communal violence are constructed in the plays as extraordinary enemies and fools, fundamentally different persons from the political and cultural self that narrates and analyzes communal violence in the plays.

My goal in identifying the promise and limitations of Janam's work is not to pretend that their discursive representations bear direct causal connections to the success or failure of the political Left in constructing solidaristic ties for peace. As I hope secondary sources here have shown, the structural causes and agential persuasions behind given events of communal violence are far more complex than the motivations of any isolated political force. Likewise, I don't pretend to provide a definitive solution to some of the limitations in the agenda of the political Left. However, I have argued that apart from marrying structural accounts of global causes and conditions with analyses of complexities of agency, a reflexive imaginary that rethinks the way in which the political Left instrumentalizes critiques of religion in response to the Hindu Right's instrumental use of religion might be a significant step forward. Taking faith and piety seriously as sources of ethical thinking is an important correction to conflating politicized religion with faith itself in analyses of communal violence, because it eschews the political Left's alienating analysis on questions, persuasions, and personhoods of faith. This more empathetic approach to understanding faith and piety as ordinary sources of ethical thinking that are, *under certain conditions,* politically manipulated into instrumental use precisely by posturing as nonpolitical and noninstrumental, I argue, is crucial because it alerts the audience to the political Left's ability to discern the value of faith in everyday life. This approach might hold promise in persuading citizens to rethink the displacement of class conflict and solidarity in the everyday contemporary imaginary, thereby renewing foundations for structures of peace.

# Part Two

# Global Models and Local Conflicts

4

# Toward Human Security and Gender Justice

*Reflections on Afghanistan and Iraq*

## Valentine M. Moghadam

More than a decade ago, the United States under the administration of George W. Bush invaded and occupied Afghanistan and Iraq, generating what became both international wars and civil conflicts. The costs have been tremendous—especially to ordinary citizens in Afghanistan and Iraq—but there also have been spillover effects on neighboring countries, along with many debates in the United States about the human toll, ethics, and financial costs of the wars. The conflicts showed no signs of letting up, even after the United States (and the British government) announced plans to withdraw its military from both countries. In Iraq, for example, the March 2010 elections were followed by a spate of bloody killings that continued over the subsequent two years. The resurgence of the Taliban in Afghanistan, and an insurgency in neighboring Pakistan, was met with renewed military commitment on the part of the Obama administration, but the Taliban persisted. Meanwhile, the conflicts became the subject of numerous discussions and debates on globalization, the economics of war, the new imperialism, international security, and the prospects for peacebuilding in a world marred by all manner of inequalities and injustices.

An examination of the conflicts in Afghanistan and Iraq offers an opportunity to pose a number of questions about the relationships among conflict, hegemony, and inequalities. How are the conflicts connected to globalization? What does it mean to build peace, stability, and security in societies torn apart by invasions and foreign occupations as well as by their own social divisions? How have social movements and networks responded to the challenges of war making? And what are appropriate strategies for conflict resolution, reconstruction, and development that might prevent future violence while also guaranteeing gender justice?

Drawing on insights and concepts from the literatures on the world-system, feminist international relations, and the economics of war, and demonstrating the interconnections among the concepts and realities of *need, greed, creed, gender,* and *hegemony,* I argue that the conflicts in Afghanistan and Iraq should be seen as key elements in the building of a post–Cold War world order predicated on the (re)assertion of US hegemony and the global spread of (neo)liberal democracy, and justified by the so-called global war on terror; and I argue that the conflicts unveil the injurious effects of hegemonic or hypermasculinities, whether on the part of the occupiers or the insurgents. I propose that the focus thus far on privatization, US national security, and military escalation has been morally flawed and a foreign policy failure. What is needed instead is a focus on human security, human development, and women's rights achieved through regional cooperation, social protection, and gender justice. Without attention to the broad, world-systemic sources of the "structural violence" that underlie insurgencies, rebellions, and conflicts, and without recognition of the gendered nature and impacts of conflict, peacebuilding will remain a sideshow to the broader global processes of neoliberal expansion, hegemonic rivalries, and economic, social, and environmental crises.

### Conflict, War, and Structural Violence in the World-System

Debates on the sources and origins of conflicts and wars typically have emphasized the role of grievance, ideology, or—especially since Paul Collier's work on the economics of war—greed. In analyzing the conflicts in Afghanistan and Iraq, however, which are both international wars and civil conflicts, I propose that we begin with the world-system and with the pervasiveness of gender, and then move on to examine what may be distilled as "need, greed, and creed."

World-system theory posits the existence of a single capitalist world economy comprised of the economic zones of core, periphery, and semiperiphery, along with an unequal interstate system whereby the core countries—led by a hegemon—wield economic, political, technological, and military power. Theorists associate wars with hegemonic rise and decline, changes to and challenges within the interstate system, and upswings and downswings in long-term historical patterns of economic expansion and contraction (known as Kondratieff waves, or K-waves), including changes in world economic growth and activity. Christopher Chase-Dunn (1998) identifies three structural roles played by (world) wars: (1) they represent struggles for control or dominance over the entire interstate system; (2) they may be used to facilitate the upward or downward mobility of individual states and the creation of a new power structure by key actors; (3) they may be used to restructure relations between core states and the periphery. For some time there has been evidence that the United States—the world-system's hegemon since the end of World War II—has been in historic decline. On the other hand, following the invasion of Afghanistan in late 2001 and the routing of the Taliban, and for at least one year after the 2003 invasion of Iraq, it appeared that the neoconservative Project for the New American Century was being successfully implemented. Some argued that the resurgence of US militarism represented "the new imperialism" (Harvey 2005), while others maintained that it was in fact evidence of hegemonic overreach, decline, and transition (Wallerstein 2003). The essential point here is that a strategy for effective peacebuilding must account for how a particular country is embedded in the world-system, and it should find alternatives to the often unjust "peace" agreements driven by hegemonic or (neo)liberal interests.

Gender injustice is pervasive in "normal times"; it is especially rampant during conflict.[1] Invaders, occupiers, and officials who decide to

---

1. The "peace" agreements of the early 1990s that followed the withdrawal of Soviet troops from Afghanistan and were brokered by the United Nations under US pressure, by Pakistan as the US proxy, and by the Islamic Republic of Iran, ignored the misogyny of the tribal Islamist rebels, who were grouped around seven parties known as the Mujahideen.

wage war or begin a conflict are almost invariably men. This is because of gender socialization patterns and because economic, political, and military power remains in male hands. Characteristics associated with conflict and war—competition, rivalry, swagger, aggressiveness, violence—are also associated with what we may call hegemonic or hyper- or even heroic forms of masculinity. Conflict and war are damaging to women and men, young and old, but for women there are distinctive risks and consequences ranging from new or heightened controls on women's dress, conduct, and mobility to sexualized violence such as kidnapping and rape. The "humiliation" that Peter Uvin (2003) includes in his definition of the term "structural violence" (which, along with inequality and social exclusion, results in various forms of "acute violence") is felt most often by men and visited most often on women, whether they be women in the family, women in the community, or women of a rival ethnic group. The counterpart to men's humiliation, as well as to male domination, is therefore women's bodily insecurity. As feminist scholarship has shown, constructions of masculinity and femininity have tended to "normalize" and "naturalize" violence against women (Breines, Connell, and Eide 2000). What is more, governments may seek to placate challengers by passing laws restricting women's rights within the family. Too often, women's participation and rights are ignored in conflict resolution processes, and at times they are sacrificed on the altar of expediency and "peace" deals. Gender justice—defined in this chapter as the recognition of women's rights to redress and to equality—is essential to postconflict peace and security.[2]

---

There was no justice for women under Mujahideen rule and even worse after the Taliban came to power in 1996. For details see Moghadam 2003, chap. 7; and Moghadam 2002.

2. Discussions of gender justice derive from at least three sources—political philosophy concepts of human agency, autonomy, rights, and capabilities (e.g., Susan Okin; Martha Nussbaum; Iris Young); political science theories of democratization, citizenship, and constitutionalism (Ann Phillips; Ruth Lister; Georgina Waylen); and legal scholarship on gender equality, judicial reform, and access to justice (Catherine MacKinnon; Joanne Sandler and Anne-Marie Goetz; Lamia Shehadeh; Lynn Welchman).

If world-systemic processes and the social relations of gender shape conflict and war, other more proximate factors also play roles. We now turn to "need, creed, and greed," with examples from Afghanistan and Iraq.

Insurgencies may be driven by legitimate grievances, especially about poverty, government corruption, basic needs, and basic rights. Emphasizing the role played by "the joint occurrence of high inequality, social exclusion, and the humiliation characteristic of symbolic violence," Uvin (2003, 149) notes that this generates "the loss of social capital" (158) as well as feelings of desperation and anger that lead to violent outcomes, including civil war and communal violence. Mohammad Hafez asserts, in his book on "why Muslims rebel," that those who adhere to the worldview of political Islam are reacting against "predatory state repression" (Hafez 2003). Ordinary citizens may attach themselves to insurgents—or they may try to migrate—because of the same issues or because of infrastructural damage, the loss of livelihoods, and other grievances concerning both the occupying armies and the insurgents. For example, Iraqis have seen their standard of living deteriorate since the early 1990s—as a result of the punitive UN sanctions regime—and especially since the US/UK invasion of 2003. Afghans still suffer from underdevelopment as well as from the results of US aerial bombings. Grievances and need must be taken into account in strategies for peacebuilding and rights-based development.

The role of ideology, or politicized religion, in fomenting or perpetrating conflict may be found among the insurgents, the government, and the occupiers. Under the Bush administration in particular, the US "war on terror" was accompanied by the goal of establishing a market economy and a political system of electoral democracy. In Afghanistan, the Taliban were motivated at least in part by Islamic fervor, while Hamid Karzai's government sought to placate a vocal Shia minority through a highly controversial family law restricting women's mobility and requiring that they have sex with their husbands at least once every four days![3] In Iraq,

---

3. See Boone 2009a. The law permits Shia men to deny their wives food or sustenance if they refuse to obey their husbands' sexual demands. This came four months after the law

Sunni-Shia competition and violence heightened after 2004. Nouri al-Maliki's government was seen by Sunnis as favoring the Shia, a sentiment that helped to perpetuate the civil conflict.

Conflict also can be driven by economic self-interest, or greed; insurgents, government officials, and external powers may be interested in the acquisition of wealth through the control of natural resources or geostrategic waterways. In Iraq, the country's oil wealth was a source of interest for the Bush administration and for US corporations such as Halliburton and Bechtel; considerable wealth was amassed by all manner of US contractors, including highly questionable security firms such as Blackwater (Scahill 2008; Klare 2008; Klein 2007). In Afghanistan, the insurgents control the country's lucrative narcotics trade, although some government officials and warlords have been implicated as well. Aid to Afghanistan has been largely diverted to private contractors or corrupt officials. Such greed tends to instigate or perpetuate conflict. Ending the dependence on aid and natural resources and laying the groundwork for a balanced and diversified economy should be a key objective of a postconflict agenda for reconstruction and development.

Chase-Dunn, Collier, and Uvin may be said to agree on the importance of "economic" factors in the causes of conflicts and wars.[4] The emphasis on global inequalities, trade dependence, unequal exchange, and maldistribution of wealth found in world-system analyses is also found in Chase-Dunn's (1998) discussion of K-waves and competition for

---

was first proposed and met with international condemnation. The Shia comprise about 20 percent of the Afghan population. On the other hand, the government has placed restrictions on the importation of schoolbooks from Iran, on the grounds that they represent a Shia worldview and as such are inappropriate to predominantly Sunni Afghanistan. Personal communication, December 2009, Carol Mann, FemAid. See also http://www.femaid .org/ for Dr. Mann's reports and photos.

4. I recognize that Chase-Dunn, in keeping with a Marxian perspective, disputes the separation of the economic from the political, and he spends some time in *Global Formation* (1998) discussing this. However, for the sake of convenience and generalization, we can assert that his framework emphasizes the role of economic resources, and in this regard bears some (superficial) similarities to that of Collier.

surplus in the emergence of international wars. Collier and his colleagues (2008, 4) mention "three underlying economic characteristics which make a country particularly prone to conflict: low income, low growth rate and a substantial contribution to the economy of primary commodities exports. In addition, small countries, those with many ethnic divisions, those which are mountainous, and those with a high proportion of youth have increased risks." While Uvin integrates elements of social psychology in his framework, he stresses the interdependence of peacebuilding and international development, noting that "global society is stunningly inegalitarian" (Uvin 2003, 154). A key difference among the three frameworks, however, is that Collier does not acknowledge the role of class or class interests. What is more, nowhere in his analysis is there room for "external" causes of conflict, which is where the concept of "structural violence" is useful, especially when elucidated by world-system theorizing. Within such a framework, a particular conflict would be examined in terms of features of the international state system, including economic zone location and the relationship to the hegemon, along with internal social divisions. Even this framework, however, is lacking acknowledgment of the role played by gender in fomenting or perpetuating conflict. In fact, gender is a key explanatory factor in violence, conflict, and war. Addressing gender inequalities and injurious forms of masculinity must be included in conceptual frameworks, movement critiques and strategies, and policies and mechanisms to minimize rivalries, crisis, and conflict.

## On Hypermasculinities, Conflict, and Women

The feminist critique of militarism, patriarchal state systems, and international relations is a longstanding one, and has been augmented by recent studies of masculinities (Enloe 1990, 2007; Eisenstein 2004; Marchand and Runyan 2000; Tickner 1992). Armed conflict has dire effects on all citizens, but women face specific risks. Preexisting patriarchal concepts and practices can exacerbate the vulnerability of women during conflict. Wars, and especially occupations by foreign powers, often are accompanied by crises of masculinity that lead to restrictions on women's mobility and increases in violence against women (Enloe 1990). Women become the symbols or markers of contending ideologies or competing cultures, and gender morphs into an "ethno-marker" (Meznaric 1994). Observing conflicts and wars through a feminist lens helps one determine that a culture of "hegemonic masculinity" prevails among the major political actors, be they the occupiers, the resistance, or the state.

"Hegemonic masculinity" has become a key concept in gender analysis since Robert Connell (1998) identified it as a particular culture's standard and ideal of real manhood, at a particular time in history. In countries such as the United States and Australia, Connell explained, hegemonic masculinity is defined by physical strength and bravado, exclusive heterosexuality, suppression of "vulnerable emotions" such as remorse and uncertainty, economic independence, authority over women and other men, and intense interest in "sexual conquest." What Connell defined as "emphasized femininity" is constructed around adaptation to male power and acquiescence to male authority. Its central feature is attractiveness to men, which includes physical appearance, ego massaging, suppression of "power" emotions such as anger, nurturance of children, exclusive heterosexuality, sexual availability without sexual assertiveness, and sociability. Both standards and ideals may be observed in many cultures, albeit with variations on the sexual element. In Muslim cultures, for example, female modesty is valued far more than sexual availability. And rather than intense interest in sexual conquest, hegemonic masculinity in a typical Middle Eastern context might consist in the capacity to "protect" family or personal honor by controlling the comportment of the women in the family and sometimes in the community. Cross-cultural specificities notwithstanding, hegemonic masculinity is reproduced in various social institutions, notably the family, religion, the sports arena, the media, the military, and even in many peace agreements. The masculinist institution par excellence is the military, but hypermasculinity is also a defining feature of the corporate domain—with its risk takers, rogue traders, reckless speculators, and manipulative financiers—who in fact may become part of a postconflict "peacebuilding" or reconstruction project. Indeed, feminist scholars have noted how neoliberal globalization, with its attack on the welfare state, has contributed to a kind of "masculinization" of the state (Marchand and Runyan 2000; Peterson 2003; Peterson and Runyan 2010; Moghadam 2005).

"Global militarism" (Enloe 2007) is driven in part by corporate and state interests but it also reflects and perpetuates hypermasculinity.

In a similar analysis, Lauren Langman and Daniel Morris (2004) discuss "heroic masculinity," although they tie it more to militarism than is the case in Connell's analysis. They point out that civilizations and cultures based on conquest or expansion, societies where politics and militarism are fused, or countries where the military is a central and valorized institution, all exhibit discourses, images, and practices of heroic masculinity. In considering American society and the role of its military in both capitalist accumulation and expansion of US power, and in considering the foundational narratives of heroic masculinity in Islam, one can easily imagine a "clash of heroic masculinities" (as Langman and Morris put it), between the American security state and Islamist rebel groups.

Contemporary rivalries in hegemonic or heroic masculinities mirror the intercapitalist rivalries of the early part of the twentieth century—which, as world-system analysts have noted, led to World War I and World War II. Rival masculinities were at play in the showdown between Saddam Hussein and the George W. Bush and Tony Blair governments in 2002 and 2003. Rival masculinities underlie, too, many of the factors that have been attributed to what Mary Kaldor and others have called the "new wars" of the post–Cold War era, such as the emergence of a global weapons market, the decreasing capacity of states to uphold the monopoly of violence (Kaldor 1999; Kaldor and Luckham 2001), interethnic competition (Chua 2003), and what Benjamin Barber famously termed "Jihad vs. McWorld" (Barber 1995). Indeed, it would appear that rival masculinities constitute a key factor in the conflicts that emerge over natural resources, such as oil or diamonds; in aggressive nationalism and ethnic rivalries; and in politicized religious projects (Moghadam 2010). From a feminist perspective, hegemonic or heroic or hypermasculinity is a causal factor in war, as well as in women's oppression. It also is injurious to men (in terms of loss of life and livelihood, and forced migration) and to soldiers, especially those drafted against their will or who come to suffer from post-traumatic stress disorder (cf. Peterson and Runyan 2010, 163–66).

If hegemonic/hyper/heroic masculinities can trigger war, the reverse is also true. As noted, wars, and especially occupations by foreign powers, are often accompanied by feelings of humiliation and crises of masculinity that lead to restrictions on women's mobility and increases in violence against women, both at home and on the streets. In areas where honor is all-important, such as in many Muslim-majority societies, concepts of hegemonic masculinity and emphasized femininity may be heightened, and the protection of women and girls may become an exaggerated feature of the society, with increases in honor killings or veiling or the reassertion or strengthening of traditional gender ideology and its legal frameworks. In societies where the issue of women and the public space is already fraught with the legacy of guardianship and segregation, women may be compelled to remain at home, or to venture outdoors only when fully veiled or accompanied by a male relative. Governments may be complicit in these forms of "disciplining" women, or they may be too weak to exercise control and protect women's rights, including their autonomy.

In times of conflict, therefore, women are caught between weak states, occupying powers, armed opposition movements, and patriarchal gender arrangements. Some may be co-opted into carrying out questionable acts of resistance, such as the case of young women in Iraq being recruited by al-Qaeda as suicide bombers (Steele 2008). In postconflict reconstruction, politics often remains masculine and male-dominated, with women largely excluded from political decision-making (Moghadam 2007). Despite the adoption of UN Security Council resolutions 1325 (2000) and 1820 (2008) on women, peace, and security, we continue to see the sidelining of both women actors and gender issues in many contemporary conflicts, peacekeeping initiatives, and reconstruction efforts.[5] Peacebuilding efforts that ignore issues of social and gender inequality

5. SCR 1325 and 1820 are framed in at least two ways. One is by representing women as victims of sexualized violence and other forms of human rights violations, and reiterating the responsibility of states to protect women; the other is by representing women as key players in peacebuilding and reconstruction, and depicting sexualized violence as an obstacle to peace and security. For a discussion of these and other instruments pertaining to women, conflict, peace, and security, see Yakin Erturk, "The Quest for Gender-Just Peace: From Impunity to Accountability": http://www.opendemocracy.net/5050/yakin-erturk/quest-for-gender-just-peace-from-impunity-to-accountability.

can only reproduce the hierarchies and structural violence of the world-system that are at the root of civil and international conflicts.

## Afghanistan and Iraq: War and the Hegemon

It is almost a banality to note that armed conflict destroys resources and lives and sets back socioeconomic development, but it is worth repeating some of the details here for the two countries under consideration. Afghanistan and Iraq have seen more than three decades of conflict, starting at roughly the same time; both countries have experienced invasions and occupation by foreign troops; and both are beset by ethnic, communal, and sectarian divisions.

The Democratic Republic of Afghanistan (DRA) came into being in 1978 with the Saur (April) Revolution. A revolutionary program was announced, to include land reform, formal rights for the various nationalities, women's rights, and compulsory schooling. A tribal-Islamist uprising emerged in the latter part of 1978; covert US military support for the insurgency began in the summer of 1979, six months before the intervention of the Soviet army, which had been requested by the Kabul government. During the Reagan administration, US military support through its proxy, Pakistan, drew the Soviet military into a protracted international war. What should be underscored is that the United States backed an Islamist rebellion opposed to girls' schooling, while the Soviet Union supported the modernizing, leftwing government dedicated to women's emancipation and social development in the impoverished country. The US involvement in Afghanistan in the 1980s would have long-term and very adverse effects.

After the departure of the Soviet army in February 1989, the conflict raged until April 1992, when the government of Mohammad Najibullah fell to the Mujahideen, the seven-party alliance of insurgents. The consequences were the collapse of a modernizing state, a civil war among the Mujahideen (1992–1994), the decline of Afghan women's participation and rights, and the rise and victory of the Taliban in 1996. The Taliban instituted a medieval-like regime and what international feminists called "gender apartheid." In addition, the Taliban offered hospitality to the likes of Osama bin Laden. Following the attacks on the World Trade Center on September 11, 2001, Afghanistan was invaded by American troops in concert with former Mujahideen commanders, now known as the Northern Alliance. The Taliban were removed from power later that year.[6]

For a while, the so-called Bonn process for Afghanistan—which involved assistance from the United States, the European Union, and NATO—was considered a success story of international intervention and postconflict reconstruction through development aid, even though the first *Afghanistan Human Development Report* (UNDP 2004) emphasized the continued risks and threats.[7] Donors made much of the introduction of elections; of the "restoration of women's rights" and the introduction of a 25 percent gender quota; of the building of schools, especially for girls; and of the start of an array of businesses.

But conditions began to stagnate and then to deteriorate, especially after the Taliban resurgence, with an upsurge of all manner of gender injustices. In April 2006, the Taliban attacked a primary school in Asadabad, killing seven children and injuring thirty-five. In Kandahar, the base of the Taliban resurgence, killings of women leaders and acid attacks on schoolgirls followed. Assassinations of women leaders since 2006 include those of Safia Amajan, head of the women's rights department in Kandahar, and Malalai Kakar, a well-known policewoman in the same city. Sitara Achakzai was shot dead after leaving a provincial council meeting; the Taliban claimed responsibility. In November 2008, teenaged schoolgirls attending Mirwais Mena School were attacked by men on motorcycles (Filkins 2009). The 2010 elections saw a valiant effort by women to run for parliament, but five of Fauzia Gilani's campaign workers were murdered while other women candidates were "inundated with threatening phone calls" (Boone 2010). Throughout, women leaders blamed the government for the absence of security and for the existence of a culture of

6. For more details on Afghan political history, see Cordovez and Harrison 1995; Moghadam 2003, chap. 7; Rubin 1995.

7. The Bonn agreement was signed on December 5, 2001, under UN auspices, outlining the terms of the re-creation of the new Afghan state.

impunity (Joya 2009). A consistent criticism—which has emanated largely from the women's rights community and especially from bold women leaders and members of parliament such as Malalai Joya—concerns the sinecures given to former Mujahideen commanders guilty of war crimes, including sexualized violence against women.[8] Injustices against women continued, including mutilation of those charged with spurious infractions in Taliban-controlled areas (Baker 2010).

In 2009, President Obama authorized an additional 17,000 troops to Afghanistan for a total of 57,000 US troops (and 37,000 from its allies, notably Britain), which became known as the "Afghan surge" (Baker 2009). This was accompanied by the arrival of thousands of more contractors, bringing the total, according to one account, to anywhere from 130,000 to 160,000 (Pincus 2009). By 2010, however, and in the wake of a disputed presidential election in Afghanistan, it was clear that the experiment had failed. Apart from the Taliban resurgence, Afghanistan is among the poorest countries in the world, ranking 172 out of 187 countries on the UNDP 2011 human development index. A large percentage of the population suffers from shortages of housing, clean water, and electricity, and cannot afford the rising cost of food. Afghan women face the highest rates of illiteracy and maternal mortality in the world. Educated youth have few job prospects, and male youth in particular are likely to attempt illegal migration to Europe, often under hazardous conditions.

Afghanistan's reconstruction enterprise rested on neoliberal principles. The country was said in 2012 to have an economic growth rate that averaged 9 percent per annum since 2002. However, much of that growth was attributed to foreign aid, opium poppy cultivation, a construction boom in a few cities, and cottage services such as restaurants

8. At a meeting in Jakarta of members of the Women's Learning Partnership for Rights, Development, and Peace (April 10–11, 2010), Afghan women's rights activist Sakina Yaqoobi emphasized the complicity of the Karzai government with warlords and their joint responsibility, along with US aerial raids, for destruction and continued insecurity. This is a common sentiment expressed by women leaders in Afghanistan, including Malalai Joya and various spokespersons of the Revolutionary Association of Women of Afghanistan (RAWA).

catering to international workers and the small business elite. What is more, the government's liberal economic policies allowed for the importation of cheap Chinese shoes that threatened to put domestic cobblers out of business (Constable 2009). The Bush administration focused on generating quick "success stories" and a "leave-it-to-the-hands-of-the-private-sector" approach rather than the arduous and long-term task of building a viable and self-sustaining economy through carefully planned public-private partnerships (Chandrasekaran 2009a, 45). Private US firms such as Chemonics profited from their contracts in Afghanistan but had little to show for their USAID-financed work. As one analyst noted, within USAID, there were few agronomists or agricultural experts left following the budget cuts of the 1980s and 1990s. When a proposal was made to USAID to subsidize Afghan farmers and wean them away from poppy to cotton production, the agency rejected it; the free market model made farm subsidies anathema. A proposal to counter poppy production in southern Afghanistan through agricultural credit and price supports also was rejected. As the analyst put it: "The aid program has been driven at the operating level by people who are very ideologically private-sector, by people who have an antipathy toward government programs to assist farmers" (Chandrasekaran 2009b). The result was continued poppy cultivation, US-led aerial destruction, and rural discontent. In some cases, farmers agreed with government officials to switch from the lucrative poppy cultivation to wheat production in exchange for roads and water, but corruption and complacency within the Karzai government failed to deliver the promised infrastructural development.

International aid levels to Afghanistan remained low and consistently lagged behind stated requirements. Critics maintained that what was delivered tended to be supply-driven and to reflect donor preferences rather than addressing the population's real needs. The highly critical March 2008 OXFAM/ACBAR report on aid effectiveness stated that only $15 billion of the $39 billion originally pledged was disbursed. Out of that, a "staggering" 40 percent of the aid was returned to donor countries through company profits and consultants' salaries. According to one account, more than half the international aid promised to Afghanistan "is bound by national procurement rules that require resources and services be purchased from the donor country" (Kaldor and Theros 2008, 2). Much of the balance was lost through Afghan corruption.

Small wonder, then, that the main source of wealth was the drug economy. This has been of considerable concern to Afghanistan's neighbor Iran, which suffers from very high levels of drug addiction, resulting largely from the illicit cross-border drugs trade (Christensen 2011). By 2007, Afghanistan supplied 93 percent of the world's opium. What is more, the drug economy funded more than one-third of Taliban operations (citing a UN report, Kaldor and Theros 2008, 2). Indeed, poppy cultivation and the drug trade became the single largest source of revenue for warlords, insurgents, and criminal organizations, as well as government officials including police. As noted, efforts to eradicate poppy production were neither successful nor popular. The United States favored aerial spraying—although the UN, NATO, and the Afghan government opposed it, concerned that it alienated farmers and drove them to support the Taliban. Without real options for alternative livelihoods, peasant farmers saw poppy production as the only means to guarantee their family's welfare. Even so, they received less than 20 percent of drug revenue while the rest went to "a nexus of traffickers, traders, corrupt government officials, and factional commanders" (Kaldor and Theros 2008, 3). President Karzai's brother, Ahmed Wali Karzai, who was based in Kandahar until his assassination in July 2011, was implicated in the opium trade (Klein 2008). Citing a report by Human Rights Watch as well as comments by an advocate in the Afghanistan Human Rights Organization, one analyst referred to Afghanistan's "criminal state" (Baker 2009, 40); another commentator noted that Afghan police have reputations for torture and blackmail (Filkins 2009). Thus over a decade after the fall of the Taliban and despite billions of dollars of foreign aid, there was little tangible change in the lives of millions of Afghans.

The conflict in Afghanistan originated in world-systemic processes—the rivalries of the Cold War era and the core-periphery hierarchy—as well as in the hypermasculinity of the contending forces. The problems were compounded by the pervasive nature of corruption and the greed of insurgents, warlords, and international contractors. In turn, the corruption and impunity of government officials and warlords, along with the aerial bombings, eroded public confidence and trust. As Uvin (2003) would point out, this feeds the desperation and anger that leads men to join the insurgency. Assaults on government and NATO sites have continued through the present.

Turning now to Iraq, Saddam Hussein became the Iraqi leader in 1978, and in 1979 faced a belligerent neighbor in the form of the new revolutionary government of the Islamic Republic of Iran. Thinking that the Arab residents of southern Iran would join his war effort, Saddam invaded the Iranian province of Khuzestan in September 1980. What followed was a long and bloody war that lasted until 1988. In addition to the loss of military and civilian lives, both countries saw infrastructural damage, including military attacks on their respective oil fields. Subsequently, Saddam's government declared that Kuwait was part of Iraq and invaded the country in December 1990, launching an international war that pitted Iraq against the United States and its allies Saudi Arabia and Egypt. After the Iraqi army was defeated, a punitive sanctions regime was installed under the auspices of the United Nations. The sanctions led to considerable civilian hardships and setbacks to the social development that had characterized Iraqi modernization in the 1970s (Al-Jawaheri 2008). Iraq was invaded and occupied by American and British troops in April 2003.

The end of the Cold War spawned international discussions about the "peace dividend," whereby budgets previously devoted to military spending and the nuclear arms race would be reallocated to social and economic development. But the collapse of the Soviet Union left the United States in a position of unparalleled military predominance, and the ruling elite began using this strategic asset in the 1990s to redraw the geopolitical map of the world, first in the Gulf War after Saddam Hussein's invasion of Kuwait and then in the Yugoslav wars of Bosnia and Kosovo, followed by the invasions of Afghanistan and Iraq. The focus on "the greater Middle East" was connected to the continued demand for oil. Rather than developing alternative sources of energy, the Bush administration's national energy policy backed the continued production and consumption of oil—even though, or perhaps because, the Chinese government had decided to make car production and ownership a pillar of the Chinese economy (Klare 2008). Controlling Afghanistan and Iraq was thus a way to guarantee oil supplies to the United States. It certainly reflected the Bush/Cheney administration's "commitment to the perpetuation of the Petroleum Age by any means and at any cost" (Klare 2008, 39). But it also unleashed legitimate resistance to American imperialistic designs in Iraq—invasion, occupation, control over the country's oil resources and privatization of the security apparatus, designs that David Harvey (2005) has aptly called "accumulation by dispossession." The resistance to the new imperialism was both local and transnational, and it was fierce.

The Bush administration may have expected the invasions of Afghanistan and Iraq to be easy military accomplishments, but in fact both military adventures have served to underscore the limits of US power. In Iraq, the invasion and occupation destroyed the state apparatus, including the national police, military, and political/ideological institutions, resulting in lawlessness and predation. It also released longstanding ethnic rivalries and unleashed sectarian violence, some of it over control of oil resources in Kirkuk and Basra. Despite declarations to the contrary, the US military was not able to secure a military victory in Iraq, much less create the conditions for peacebuilding, stability, and security. Nor did the introduction of electoral democracy satisfy the population's desire for security and social welfare. What is more, China and other states appeared to be obtaining a piece of the Iraqi (oil) pie that some US officials and corporate leaders (e.g., T. Boone Pickens) expected to be an exclusively American entitlement. All along, the United States sought to implement a privatization plan for Iraq, although some of its proxies in the Iraqi government had qualms about a rapid transition from state-led to market-led development and growth. The privatization legislation that the Bush administration was keen to see quickly enacted became stuck in parliament awaiting ratification; the minister of industry and minerals was quoted as saying that he did not expect any state industry stake sales until at least 2012.[9] As of early 2013 there was still a fierce debate over the terms of a national oil law, in particular over the role of the government as the sole guarantor

9. "Privatization in Iraq Taking off Slowly," Gulf Research Center and Reuters, July 29, 2009, http://corp.gulfinthemedia.com/gulf_media.

of deals with foreign companies, including those of Russia and China as well as Europe and the United States.[10]

What is more, there has been considerable corruption on the part of both Iraqi officials and US contractors. A July 2004 US Government Accountability Office report found that under Paul Bremer's Coalition Provisional Authority, about $8.8 billion intended for Iraqi reconstruction had gone missing or was unaccounted for (Harriman 2005). Instead of healthy economic reconstruction, Iraq's "war economy" had generated predatory smuggling networks: "people and goods flow unregulated into Iraq while capital and resources flow out" (Moore 2009, 23). It was commonly believed that US troops consumed a large portion of Jordan's exports to Iraq, particularly the large volume of foodstuff (Moore 2009, citing a 2007 Jordanian intelligence report). Meanwhile, US firms such as Blackwater, Halliburton, and its subsidiary Kellogg, Brown & Root, were permitted to overcharge the Pentagon for their contracting work in Iraq, and to make fortunes at the same time that the US economy was beginning to show signs of strain.

Here it is worth underscoring the relative economic weakness of the United States vis-à-vis other core countries and emerging markets such as Brazil, Russia, India, and especially China (collectively known as BRICs). For example, whereas Russia in 2006 had a foreign trade surplus of about $130 billion, the United States had a deficit of about $880 billion. Much of the US deficit came from importing about 13.6 million barrels of oil a day, at a cost of about $450 billion, including $10 billion worth of oil imported from Russia. In contrast, Russia was able to export 5.7 million barrels a day (Goldman 2008). China has huge cash reserves, holds US Treasury bonds, and makes loans to the United States. Yet the United States continues to spend far more than any other country on the military. According to the Stockholm International Peace Research Institute (SIPRI), the United States spent $607 billion in 2008, compared with China's $85

10. For historical details, see "Crude Diplomacy: Iraq, Iran, and the Politics of Oil," *The Economist*, February 20, 2010, 43. See also Macalister (2011), on the Iraqi government's special oil deal with BP and its Chinese partner CNPC.

billion; numbers three and four on the SIPRI list were France and Britain, with just over $65 billion each in military expenditures. These trends have continued, even as most US forces have left Iraq and prepare to leave Afghanistan. As Rees (2006) explains, it is the critical meeting point between overwhelming military strength and relative economic decline that explains the motivation of the Bush administration to rely on its military capacity to discipline both its allies and its competitors on the world stage. But militarism has proved costly in economic as well as human and moral terms. In neither Afghanistan nor Iraq has the United States been able to secure a military victory, and US troop casualties seemed to reach a threshold beyond which the American public could rebel. These unpleasant realities forced the decision to declare a timeframe for troop withdrawal from both countries.

Far worse is what Iraqis have experienced. Both the military occupation and the insurgency caused considerable damage, including the destruction of infrastructure and the loss of many lives. A recent book examines the "cultural cleansing" that took place through the looting of museums, the burning of libraries, and the murder of academics (Baker, Ismael, and Ismael 2010). The Iraqi government released estimates of about 85,000 dead between 2004 and 2008, but other reports place the casualties considerably higher. Iraq's human toll since 2003 is estimated to be as high as one million killed and 4.5 million displaced; one to two million widows and five million orphans (Tirman 2009). Iraq suffers from very high male unemployment, which followed the war and the restructuring of its economy by the occupying power. In addition to a ferocious conflict between disempowered Sunnis and ascendant Shiites, the small Christian minority was targeted. Many Iraqis sought asylum in Jordan and Syria; a relatively small number were allowed in the United States, though they reported being placed in miserable conditions, with little or no government support (Janega and Oliva, 2009).

The US military focus on "the greater Middle East" was no doubt related to the oil reserves in a region that has been of longstanding geostrategic importance—first to Great Britain and then to the United States. American hegemonic activity—which over the decades has been seen in other regions, too—began early in the Middle East, with the 1946

US-Soviet standoff over Iran's oil-rich Azerbaijan province, followed by
the 1953 CIA-sponsored coup d'état against Iran's Premier Mohammed
Mossadegh. Could it reach its end there, as a result of two misguided military adventures that have turned out to be a drain on US resources and a
blow to its international standing?

And what of the gendered effects of conflict and war in Afghanistan and Iraq? During the presidency of George W. Bush, officials liked
to point to regular elections and the 25 percent female parliamentary
quota as an achievement in both countries. But in Iraq, the results of the
2006 general elections showed that voting followed ethnic and sectarian
patterns. Women, meanwhile, were hardly empowered to take a right-
ful place in national decision-making, and their political participation
has tended to decline over the years. In late January 2009, Iraqis voted in
provincial elections, but frustrations abounded; the minister for women's
affairs resigned when her already small budget was slashed by 80 percent
(Sussman and Ahmed 2009). In the parliamentary elections of March 2010
Prime Minister Maliki lost his majority to the more secular Iraqiya political party, but after considerable delay he was able to form a government;
but again no women occupied influential posts beyond the guaranteed
seats in parliament.

The gendered effects of conflict and war go beyond the limits of the
electoral process and extend to all manner of gender-based injustices,
such as extrajudicial killings. In Afghanistan they include the destruction
of girls' schools by Taliban fighters and acid attacks on schoolgirls, assassinations of female leaders and rapes of young women, the persistence
of female illiteracy, and passage of a patriarchal Shia family law. In Iraq,
the destructive gendered effects since 2003 include the following: women
appearing in *hijab* in public, for fear of harassment or worse; a spike in
domestic violence, "honor killings," kidnappings, and rapes;[11] targeted

---

11. In 2007, a teenaged girl named Du'a Khalili was the victim of an "honor killing" by
her close male relatives because she, as a member of the Yezidi religio-ethnic community,
had fallen in love with a Muslim boy, converted to Islam, and eloped with him. In retalia-
tion for the killing of a "Muslim" girl, a mob attacked a busload of Yezidi men and killed

assassinations of women leaders; assaults by foreign soldiers and by the resistance; a drop in women's political participation, despite the electoral quota; ambiguities and contradictions in the Iraqi constitution, especially as regards women's rights in the family; and the use of young women as suicide bombers. Iraqi women are aware that their legal status and social conditions have deteriorated drastically since 2003. Afghan women's rights advocates fear for the future and say: "Afghan women need and require peace with justice. This is our request to the world and international communities" (cited in Khaleeli 2011, 30).

## Resistance and Alternative Visions: Toward Justice and Security for Women

The hierarchies, inequalities, and injustices of the world-system can produce at least three responses: (a) anger, resentment, frustration, and real or relative deprivation that can trigger resistance, civil war, or communal conflict; (b) crises of masculinity that can perpetuate violence against women; and (c) the formation of transnational networks and movements for justice, including gender justice. The cases of Afghanistan and Iraq illustrate the ways that the structural violence of the world-system and patriarchal gender relations alike can underpin international wars as well as civil conflicts. In this section I focus on the responses of social movements, and especially of transnational feminist networks.

The tragedies of Afghanistan and Iraq have motivated transnational mobilizations in addition to national-level resistances (Moghadam 2012). These include demonstrations against neoliberal globalization and war by what is called the Global Justice Movement (GJM), whether at the annual meetings of the World Social Forum (WSF) or in individual countries. The GJM has been extensively studied in recent years. Jackie Smith (2008) shows how the World Social Forum is an alternative arena for the

---

them all. For details on this and other examples of violence against women, see Susskind 2007 and Lattimer 2008.

cultivation of "skills, analyses, and identities that are essential to a democratic global polity" (224). Christopher Chase-Dunn and his students have examined the rise of a "global Left" comprised of transnational social movements that meet at the WSF as well as with a number of leftwing governments, currently concentrated in Latin America (Chase-Dunn et al. 2009). Positioning themselves against neoliberal capitalism and the new American imperialism alike, the "democratic globalizers" (Smith) and the "global Left" (Chase Dunn et. al.) exhibit the potential to form a counterhegemonic bloc in global politics. But if the bloc is to succeed, it will have to include transnational feminist networks, and its alternative frameworks will have to integrate feminist insights.

Mobilizations by transnational feminist networks (TFNs) in defense of women's human rights focus on the injurious effects of patriarchy, neoliberal globalization, and war. TFNs are among the key social movement organizations of the global feminist movement (Moghadam 2005, 2013). They are structures organized above the national level that unite women from three or more countries around a common agenda, such as women's human rights, reproductive health and rights, violence against women, peace and antimilitarism, or feminist economics. TFNs work with one another and with transnational advocacy networks to draw attention to the negative aspects of the world order, to try to influence policymaking, and to insert a feminist perspective in global advocacy and activism. TFNs generally evince a social-democratic outlook—notably support for public services and a woman-friendly welfare state that accompanies a critique of neoliberal globalization—but individuals among them, and some TFNs themselves, can be decidedly leftwing, and espouse anti-imperialist, ecofeminist, or socialist perspectives.

TFNs emerged in the mid-1980s and they continue to grow. Some formed to criticize neoliberal economic policies and their effects on women workers and the poor (e.g., MADRE, DAWN-Development Alternatives with Women for a New Era, and WIDE-Women in Development Europe), and others arose in response to the growth of fundamentalism and political Islam (notably, Women Living under Muslim Laws, or WLUML, and the Women's Learning Partnership, or WLP). These networks and older groups such as the Women's International League for Peace and Freedom

(WILPF) have been joined by new groups such as Code Pink and the Nobel Women's Initiative, criticizing US foreign policy, calling for an end to war and suffering in Iraq, and seeking a world characterized by equality and solidarity (See Tables 4.1 and 4.2). Combining a utopian vision for the world with a practical approach to women's issues, TFNs often work in partnership with local women's groups to raise awareness of gender issues, to influence legal and policy changes in favor of women's participation and rights, and to extend solidarity and support, which sometimes includes humanitarian assistance.

MADRE's work in Iraq dates back to the 1991 Gulf War, when it began collecting an assortment of needed supplies for Iraqi families, including milk and medicine. It continued this work throughout the 1990s, and frequently decried the detrimental effects on women and children of the sanctions regime. After the 2003 invasion and occupation of Iraq, MADRE partnered with UNICEF/Iraq and provided twenty-five thousand citizens with supplies and emergency aid, including essential drugs and medical supplies to those in need.[12] Working with its local feminist partner, the Organization of Women's Freedom in Iraq (OWFI), MADRE focused on the problem of honor killings and supported the creation of women's shelters for victims of domestic and community violence in the Iraqi cities of Baghdad, Kirkuk, Erbil, and Nasariyeh. The campaign gave rise to a web of shelters and an escape route for Iraqi women, known as the Underground Railroad for Iraqi Women and largely run by OWFI volunteers.[13] All this has been accompanied by a steady release of reports and publications denouncing the invasion and occupation of Iraq, especially for its effects on women and children.

CodePink's mission statement identifies itself as "a women-initiated grassroots peace and social justice movement working to end the war in Iraq, stop new wars, and redirect our resources into healthcare, education,

12. "Madre Programs in Iraq," *MADRE*, 28 November 2007, http://madre.org /programs/Iraq.html.

13. "Honor Crimes," *MADRE*, 28 November 2007, http://www.madre.org/articles /int/honorcrimes.html. This is also information from an interview I conducted with OWFI founder and leader Yanar Mohammad in Amsterdam, May 2005.

Table 4.1

Types of Transnational Feminist Networks

| Critique of Economic Policy | Website | Location/HQ |
| --- | --- | --- |
| Development Alternatives with Women for a New Era (DAWN) | http://www.dawnnet.org/index.php | Philippines |
| Marche Mondiale des Femmes | http://www.marchemondiale.org /index_html/fr | Canada, etc. |
| Network Women in Development Europe (WIDE)* | http://www.wide-network.org/ | Belgium, etc. |
| Women's Environment and Development Organization (WEDO) | http://www.wedo.org/ | United States |

| Advocacy for Women's Human Rights and Anti-Fundamentalism | Website | Location/HQ |
| --- | --- | --- |
| Arab Women's Solidarity Association (AWSA) | http://www.awsa.net/ | United States |
| Association for Women's Rights in Development (AWID) | http://www.awid.org/ | Canada |
| Equality Now | http://www.equalitynow.org/ | United States, Kenya |
| International Women's Tribune Center (IWTC) | http://www.iwtc.org/63/index.html | United States |
| MADRE | http://www.madre.org/index.html | United States |
| Women's Caucus for Gender Justice | http://www.iccwomen.org/ | Netherlands |
| Women's Human Rights Network (WHRNet) | http://www.whrnet.org/ | N/A |
| Women's Learning Partnership (WLP) | http://www.learningpartnership.org | United States |
| Women Living under Muslim Laws (WLUML) | http://www.wluml.org/ | Nigeria, Pakistan, United Kingdom |
| Women for Women International | www.womenforwomen.org | United States |

| Peace, Anti-Militarism, Conflict-Resolution | Website | Location/HQ |
| --- | --- | --- |
| Association of Women of the Mediterranean Region (AWMR)** | http://digilander.libero.it/awmr/int/ | United States, Cyprus |
| Code Pink | www.codepink4peace.org/ | United States |

Table 4.1 (*cont.*)
Types of Transnational Feminist Networks

| Peace, Anti-Militarism, Conflict-Resolution | Website | Location/HQ |
| --- | --- | --- |
| Grandmothers for Peace International | www.grandmothersforpeace.org | United States |
| MADRE | www.madre.org | United States |
| Marche Mondiale des Femmes | http://www.marchemondiale.org /index_html/fr | Canada, etc. |
| Medica Mondiale | http://www.medicamondiale.org/en /home/ | Germany |
| Women in Black | http://balkansnet.org/wib/ http://www.womeninblack.net/ | Various countries |
| Women's International League for Peace and Freedom (WILPF) | http://www.wilpf.org/ | Switzerland, United States |
| Women for Women International (WWI) | http://www.womenforwomen.org/ | United States |

*Since 2005 includes the Women's International Coalition for Economic Justice (WICEJ).
**Inactive

and other life-affirming activities."[14] Toward that end, it works with other feminist and social justice networks, including the National Organization for Women and United for Peace and Justice. CodePink has become famous (notorious, in rightwing corners) for its direct action tactics in confronting members of the US political elite over the war in Iraq. Its action repertoire also includes acts of feminist humanitarianism and international solidarity, as evidenced by visits to Baghdad to demonstrate opposition to war and solidarity with the Iraqi people. Founders Medea Benjamin and Jodie Evans, along with Sand Brim, travelled to Iraq in February and December 2003. In December 2004, CodePink coordinated the historic "Families for Peace Delegation" to Amman, Jordan, involving the three CodePink

14. "About Us," CodePink Web site, http://www.codepink4peace.org/article.php?list =type&type=3.

Table 4.2

Transnational Feminist Networks Working in Iraq and Afghanistan

| *Feminist Humanitarianism:* *Networks, Core Goals, and Activities* | | *Country Projects* | *Funds Disbursed* |
|---|---|---|---|
| MADRE (1983) United States | Gender, economic, and environmental justice; programs in peace building; women's health and freedom from violence; mobilizes resources for partner organizations to meet immediate needs of women and their families and develop long-term solutions to crises. www.madre.org/ | Sudan, Iraq, Nicaragua, Cuba, Haiti, Guatemala, Kenya, Peru, Colombia, Panama, Palestine | $22 million since 1983 |
| Women for Women International (1993) United States | Addresses the needs of women in conflict and postconflict environments; helps to effect transition from victims to active citizens; provides microcredits and business services. http:// www.womenforwomen.org/ | Afghanistan, Bosnia, Colombia, Iraq, Kosovo, Sudan, Nigeria, Rwanda, DR Congo | $33 million as of 2006 |
| Medica Mondiale (1999) Germany | Women's human rights and security; "We support traumatised women and girls in war and crisis zones"; medical assistance and counseling; safe houses. http://www.medi camondiale.org/_en/projekte /jugoslawien/ | Afghanistan, Albania, Bosnia, Cambodia, DR Congo, Aceh, Iraq, Kosovo, Liberia, Sudan, Uganda | N/A |
| Women's Learning Partnership (2000) USA | Women's human rights and leadership, especially in Muslim-majority countries. | Afghanistan, Bahrain, Iran, Jordan, Lebanon, Palestine, Morocco, Nigeria, Nicaragua, Zimbabwe, etc. | $60,000 to Lebanon following Israeli 2006 invasion, via Lebanese partner |
| Code Pink (2003) United States | Against war, militarism; United States out of Iraq; solidarity with Iraqi people; support US troops by bringing them home; provide medical supplies for Iraqis. www.codepink4peace.org/ | Iraq | N/A |

founders and a member of the antiwar group United for Peace and Justice (UFPJ), along with several relatives of fallen American soldiers and
families of September 11 victims. According to one report: "In an inspir-
ing act of humanity and generosity, they brought with them $650,000 in
medical supplies and other aid for the Fallujah refugees who were forced
from their homes when the Americans destroyed their city. Although the
American press failed to cover this unprecedented visit, the mission gar-
nered enormous attention from Al-Jazeera, Al-Arabiya, and Dubai and
Iranian television, who witnessed first-hand the depths of American com-
passion" (Milazzo 2005, 103; see also Brim 2003, 10–12).

CodePink has longed called for the withdrawal of US troops and
the increase of development funding.[15] In early October 2009, however,
a minor controversy erupted on the Left when Medea Benjamin traveled
to Afghanistan to meet with Afghan women leaders, including Masooda
Jalali, the minister of women's affairs. Following the meeting, and in def-
erence to the concerns expressed by the Afghan women leaders regarding
an early exit of US troops and a possible Taliban victory, Ms. Benjamin
said her group would be "more flexible about a timetable" for the exit
strategy (Mojumdar 2009). CodePink's statement reflected the dilemma
of women's groups in the context of a complex political situation whose
roots lie in US foreign policy spanning at least fifty years.[16] Still, CodePink
has consistently opposed military escalation, the "Afghan surge," and
the drone attacks, urging instead a reallocation of resources to women-
friendly development.

MADRE and CodePink—as well as other TFNs such as the Marche
Mondiale, DAWN, and WIDE—are part of the Global Justice Movement.
Their influence should be greater. Indeed, global feminism has much to
offer in the way of analysis of international relations as well as conflict,

15. See their stated position and petition, http://codepink.salsalabs.com/o/424/t/8834
/petition.jsp?petition_KEY=2125.

16. For a discussion of the diverse positions, see Michelle Goldberg, "A Feminist
Case for War?: Women's Rights Activists Are Conflicted over a Continued U.S. Presence
in Afghanistan," October 27, 2009, http://prospect.org/cs/articles?article=a_feminist_case
_for_war. See also Khaleeli 2011.

peace, and security. Catherine Eschle has discussed "globalized feminist movement democracy" created by "transversal feminist activism" (Eschle 2001, 279). Cynthia Enloe (2006) explains: "Focusing our attention on the military-industrial complex, oil and empire isn't enough. If we dismiss the politics of femininity and masculinity, we will never get to the bottom of what fuels militarization. We will never roll it back because we won't know what propels it forward" (30). Christa Wichterich, a WIDE scholar-activist, argues that feminists have to go beyond the legitimate liberal perspective of gender equality and women's human rights to push for "interventionist reform in favor of poor people, social justice and gender equality on the one hand, and on the other hand fight against the overexploitation of human and natural resources, against the commodification and privatization of everything, the destruction of livelihoods and alternative economic arrangements" (cited in WIDE 2007, 30). Ann Tickner aptly put it thus: "the achievement of peace, economic justice, and ecological sustainability is inseparable from overcoming social relations of domination and subordination; genuine security requires not only the absence of war but also the elimination of unjust social relations" (Tickner 1992, 193). It is not difficult to interpret such discourses, as well as the practices of many TFNs, as a kind of feminist counterhegemony.

Although the conflicts in Afghanistan and Iraq are rooted in world-systemic processes, including the restructuring of the international state system under US hegemony, prospects for their resolution differ because of the respective histories and social forces. While in neither case will the United States prevail or militarily withdraw with a sense of mission accomplished, the conflict in Afghanistan and its problems appear to be more intractable. Iraq has a larger middle class, a longer experience with development and state building, and a key natural resource that can generate revenue and finance economic and social development. Afghanistan, however, lacks the necessary institutional, infrastructural, and human resources. To this observer, the defeat of the government of Najibullah in 1992 marked the end of a valiant attempt to centralize power, implement long-term economic and social development, and modernize the country. Since then, neither the Mujahideen nor the Taliban nor the Karzai government has been able to unite the country and embark upon economic and social development. And since the Taliban resurgence, the international community has been faced with the question of how to address the insurgency. The decision by President Barack Obama to escalate the US military mission and extend its presence in Afghanistan was taken presumably because of the weak nature of the Afghan state as well as the spread of the Taliban to Pakistan. The surge, however, proved futile. According to many in the feminist and global justice movements, ending the conflict begins with the withdrawal of US troops and a concerted international effort toward reconstruction and development, while preventing future conflicts depends on the fundamental reordering of international priorities and power relations.

### Gendering Human Security

This chapter began with a conceptual framework drawing on world-system and feminist insights and a critique of the greed and hypermasculinity of both the hegemon and the insurgents. Here I turn to a policy framework for reconstruction and development, which rests on concepts of human security, human development, and human rights. The short-term (and apparently elusive) goals of winning battles against the insurgents—whether in Afghanistan or Iraq—should be replaced by a longer-term strategy for the establishment of *human security* and *women's security* through international and regional cooperation and financing devoid of neoliberal conditionalities.

The end of the Cold War saw the introduction of new concepts, notably *human development* and *human security,* with the UNDP's *Human Development Reports* of 1990, 1994, and 2000 largely responsible for both concepts. In these reports and other documents, the concept of "security" was broadened from its traditional associations with state sovereignty, military preparedness, and balance of power to encompass economic, health, environmental, personal, community, and political securities. Personal security, water and food security, rights to healthcare and political participation, and economic security came to be considered fundamental to and inseparable from human development, and the foundation for human rights policies and practice. Efforts were made, therefore, to connect human security with human rights, and establish links among security, rights, and participation toward a holistic goal of the empowerment of people and communities.

The UN Development Programme's (UNDP) Human Development Report Office first offered a conceptualization of human security in its 1994 report for discussion at the World Summit on Social Development, which took place in Copenhagen in March 1995. The report's assertion that "the search for human security lies in development, not in arms" should have been heeded in the early 1990s, but was not, because it was sidelined by the new discourse of "humanitarian intervention," followed by the "war on terror." It should have been immediately applied to Afghanistan, but was not. The 1994 report also argued that the attainment of human security was in the interest of not only the global South but also the rich countries of the North. And it called for "a new world social order" through a 20/20 compact for human development that would allocate 20 percent of donor aid to social development and 20 percent of government budgeting to the social sector (UNDP 1994).[17]

In this alternative policy framework, security, development, and rights are understood to be applicable to all and not only to the most powerful. Recall that in the wake of September 11, 2001, the United States was concerned with its own national security (as well as with the reassertion of its international power and the success of its private-sector contractors). When the United States chose to bomb Afghanistan in 2001 and Iraq in 2003 in the name of national security, it was denying security to the citizens of those countries. Quite apart from the fact that the US mission backfired in both countries, one may well ask if the attainment of security by one country can legitimately and morally come at the expense

---

17. See in particular UNDP, *Human Development Report 1994* and *Human Development Report 2000*. It should be noted that the UNDP's broad definition and understanding of human security is not shared by all analysts.

of the security of another. A question may be raised, too, concerning the attempted imposition of a neoliberal model predicated on denationalization and privatization. Was this not an alien economic model that ran counter to citizens' expectations of government action and social protection, especially in Iraq? And when the very presence of US troops in both countries instigated insurgencies, the result was continued insecurity for ordinary citizens and stalled economic and social development. In what sense, then, can the military option be said to have brought anything close to security, development, and rights for women and men?

The global war on terror, the emphasis on national security through militarization, and the spread of neoliberal globalization have offered diminishing returns for "human security" as a concept or program. To date, the concept has yet to find its way into conventions and norms, though it has been the subject of many UN and academic discussions and publications.[18] Michael Pugh and his colleagues refer to the concept's "emancipatory potential in its emphasis on rights."[19] Certainly the concept has captured the attention of intellectuals and academics in countries suffering from stalled development or unending conflict.

As noted, the first *Human Development Report on Afghanistan* was published in 2004, with a focus on human security. More recently, human security was the subject of the *Arab Human Development Report 2009.* The Arab Report addresses human security through attention to pressures on environmental and natural resources; the efficacy of the state and prospects for human security; the insecurity of vulnerable groups; economic vulnerability, poverty, and unemployment; food security and nutrition; health and human security; and occupation and foreign military intervention. To its credit, this report includes attention to gender inequality and women's participation and rights. Gender, however, is seen mainly

18. See, for example, *Human Security Now,* the final report of the United Nations Commission on Human Security (2003) and Human Security Center (2005). See also, publications on the website of the Department of Foreign Affairs and International Trade Canada: http://www.humansecurity.gc.ca/whatsnew_publications-en.asp.

19. Pugh, Cooper, and Turner 2008c, 393.

as a variable rather than a fundamental building block of society that shapes and indeed can predict attitudes and behaviors, whether on the part of individuals or collectivities. Forms of gender socialization that entail notions of male privilege and female subordination—when combined with patriarchal governance and external interventions—can lead to the highly damaging forms of violence against women that we have come to observe across the globe. The implications are clear, if profound: a genuinely emancipatory notion of human security requires new forms of gender socialization. It also demands attention to women's security and to gender justice, especially for women victims of sexualized and other forms of violence.

The country foci of this chapter are Afghanistan and Iraq, but another example of the urgent need for gender justice and women's security comes from Palestine, where women have faced violence from male relatives as well as Israeli soldiers and settlers. The Women's Center for Legal Aid Counseling (WCLAC) is an important Palestinian and feminist institution working on reforming the personal status laws, combating violence against women, and increasing women's political participation. It faces many obstacles, however, from both Palestinian society (conservative forces) and the Israeli occupation. The Israeli house demolition policy and other human rights violations perpetrated by the Israeli occupation have had a terrible impact on health, education, adequate standard of living, work, and family life. The frustrations and indignities of everyday life contribute to violence against women by male kin—who unfortunately enjoy impunity for their actions. As WCLAC leader Maha Abu-Dayyeh states: "The struggle for women's rights is formidable under ideal circumstances, but in a situation of a militarized conflict the task becomes overwhelmingly difficult" (Rought-Brooks, Duaibis, and Hussein 2010: 141). WCLAC continues to document violations of Palestinian women's human rights, with a view toward eventual gender justice as well as national liberation. In the meantime, however, the structural violence of the world-system and the hierarchies present in the Middle East prevent redress, much less equality.

The sources of contemporary conflicts, and the problems of peace-building, inhere in the capitalist world-system, with its hierarchies, inequalities, and injustices. Clearly the demands of transnational peace and justice movements for a restructuring of global power relations are legitimate and necessary. But how do we get there, and what of responsibilities and actions in the short-term? I suggest that we focus on practical as well as strategic needs, with a vision that is at once utopian and pragmatic. This is, after all, the preferred modus operandi of transnational feminist networks (Moghadam 2005), and it is also an approach of some groups within the Global Justice Movement.

Since at least the 1995 UN World Summit on Social Development (Social Summit), groups within the Global Justice Movement, and especially ATTAC, have been advocating the so-called Tobin tax, which would impose a tax on financial speculation in the interest of preventing volatility in financial markets. Recently, a "Robin Hood tax" on banks has been promoted and debated.[20] Governments rejected the proposed Tobin tax at the 1995 Social Summit, but it is significant that the International Monetary Fund (IMF), while detested in many progressive quarters, was spurred by the global financial crisis of 2008 to consider a tax on banks, which would raise funds to pay for any future financial crisis caused by banking malfeasance. In particular, a tax on financial activity would serve at least two purposes: a disincentive to the kind of reckless speculation that led to the Asian crises of 1997–1998 and the 2008 financial crisis, and a source of funding for development, employment generation, social welfare, and human rights. With the proper oversight, it would enable governments to put in place policies and programs that could reduce the inequalities and social exclusion that often lead to violence and conflict. It would help bring about social justice and gender justice by allocating the necessary resources for those purposes.

With respect to Afghanistan and Iraq, governments and international partners need to work in cooperation with women's groups, human rights agencies, and labor groups. To realize gender justice, they need to ensure that women's policy agencies have adequate budgets so

20. See Oxfam, UK, http://www.oxfam.org.uk/get_involved/campaign/actions/robin hood.html. See also ATTAC, http://www.attac.org.

that these agencies can address the problems suffered by war widows, implement or supervise income-generating projects for women in the provinces, work with the judiciary to ensure justice for victims of sexualized violence, and help implement international instruments pertaining to women's rights. To bring about social justice, governments and donors, again in concert with civil society organizations, need to develop and implement plans for economic, infrastructural, and social development. Farmers need subsidies and other government support. In many developing countries, food supply policies are part of a social contract based on state provision of essential needs in exchange for the people's loyalty. Such an approach could prove highly effective in Afghanistan, where more than 80 percent of working-age men are small farmers, and where concerted efforts also should be directed toward incentivizing the shift from the illicit narcotics trade to legal agricultural production for domestic consumption as well as for export. Alternatives for Afghan farmers could be wheat, pomegranates, pistachios, and dried fruits, as well as the legal production of opium for medicines such as codeine and morphine. In addition to serving local needs, these products generate considerable demand in rich countries.

Using a Robin Hood tax to help fund economic citizenship and gender justice programs—in a kind of "global social Keynesianism" that was the clarion call of some antiglobalization activists and intellectuals at the turn of the new century—can be complemented by a regional approach to problem solving. Economic, infrastructural, and social development—as well as border and national security—can be achieved through a regional approach to peacebuilding and cooperation. What is required for both Iraq and Afghanistan is a multilateral regional framework involving governments and civil societies from neighboring countries. This would serve not only Iraq and Afghanistan but also the neighboring countries, for several reasons. The conflicts in Afghanistan and Iraq have spread to neighboring countries, and client networks abound. The insurgency in Afghanistan, as well as the drugs trade, has affected Iran. As noted, there is now a Taliban in Pakistan, and porous borders allow easy access to Iran as well as Afghanistan. China and India share borders with Afghanistan. The United States, Syria, and Iran have been at odds over Iraq's direction, and Turkey has been nervous about an independent Kurdistan. Syria and Jordan have taken in the lion's share of Iraqi refugees (though the escalation of conflict in Syria in 2012 created more insecurity for Iraqi refugees). Thus all the neighboring countries have a stake in the stability and security of both Iraq and Afghanistan, even though there may be rogue elements within a state apparatus (e.g., Pakistan) that prefer to foment instability.[21]

In the positive scenario sketched here, Iran can offer much-needed development cooperation as well as assistance for social development, especially in the areas of education and health, and most urgently for Afghanistan. With respect to Iraq, even though the Iranian government has been satisfied with a Shia-dominated and friendly neighbor, it has an aversion to political challenges and uprisings; with the possibility of spillover effects from conflicts in the neighborhood, Iran surely would prefer that Iraqi divisions be resolved, al-Qaeda remnants be eliminated, and stability returned. The same may be said of Turkey. Both Iran and Turkey could play key roles in helping to resolve the conflicts in Iraq and Afghanistan.[22] The Iranian government would do well to end its nuclear folly and obsession with Israel and look to immediate problems across its borders. It could also help solve its own serious youth unemployment problem by dispatching graduates to teach in Afghanistan and undertake service learning in deprived areas in Iraq. To ensure security in Iraq and Afghanistan—given that the presence of US and Western troops in the two countries has hindered rather than helped bring about peacebuilding, much less reconstruction and development—the region could consider an international force drawn from neighboring countries. That force could work alongside local civilian leaders to understand and develop

21. An entirely new set of conflicts—outside the purview of the present paper but important as well as disturbing—involves Libya, Syria, and Yemen. The "humanitarian intervention" of NATO in Libya in 2011 seemed to be another imperial reenactment, while the violence in Syria and interference of US allies Turkey, Saudi Arabia, and Qatar undermined the human security of Iraqi refugees as well as Syrian sovereignty.

22. See "Turkey and the Middle East: Looking East and South," *The Economist*, October 31, 2009, 57–58.

localized security strategies and tactics—but only if women's participation and rights are valued, recognized, and integrated in the strategies.

## Conclusion

This chapter has addressed a number of questions about the relationships among conflict, hegemony, and inequalities. How are the conflicts connected to neoliberal globalization, the hegemonic transition, and patriarchy? How have social movements and networks responded to the challenges of war making? And what are appropriate strategies for conflict resolution, reconstruction, and development that would also help prevent future violence?

As I have argued, peacebuilding is elusive and illusory without attention to both the problem of the capitalist world-system and the problem of gender inequality. The conflicts in Afghanistan and Iraq have been driven by hegemonic imperatives and neoliberal interests, and they have been exacerbated by hypermasculinities and women's inequality. The causes that underlie the wars in Afghanistan and Iraq require a long-term strategy by social movements for the transformation of international relations in a more democratic and egalitarian direction, and a problem-solving approach involving activists and policymakers alike that would tackle the immediate problems that citizens and refugees face. A long-term strategy also is needed for legal reform and redress, new patterns of gender socialization, and educational mechanisms to promote respect for human rights and women's equality.

At the same time, a new human security approach within a multilateral regional framework that is stripped of its hegemonic underpinnings and is sensitive to gender issues could prioritize the protection of civilians in Afghanistan and Iraq as well as in neighboring states. Such an approach also would help the governments of both countries earn the trust of their populations and establish legitimacy through good government, programs for social development, and a commitment to citizen welfare and the rights of women. Were the Obama administration to consider supporting such an approach, US standing in the region could be enhanced.

But beyond the immediate, problem-solving approach, it is clear that a paradigm shift is needed, moving us from the neoliberal and hegemonic institutions and relations that obtain today to a global framework, and a counterhegemonic bloc, dedicated to redistribution, development cooperation, mutual understanding, human rights, and gender justice.

# 5

# Capitalism at Sea

*Piracy and "State Failure" in the Gulf of Aden*[1]

## Isaac Kamola

During 2008 and 2009 reports of Somali pirates captured the imagination of many in the United States and around the world. This made-for-TV spectacle reached a crowning height in April 2009 when US Navy snipers shot and killed three pirates holding captain Richard Phillips of the *Maersk Alabama* hostage. Journalists, academics, and policy researchers, however, have been quick to point out that piracy is not simply an oddly anachronistic spectacle, but rather a serious economic and security threat. According to the International Maritime Bureau, in 2008 pirates attacked more than one hundred ships off the coast of Somalia, making it "the greatest surge in piracy in modern times" (Montgomery 2008). Since then the number of pirate attacks and the range of these operations have

1. I would like to thank Jackie Smith, Ernesto Verdeja, and the Kroc Institute for International Peace Studies at Notre Dame for inviting me to participate in the Globalization, Social Movements, and Peacebuilding project. In addition, thanks to the participants of the Notre Dame workshop, as well as those at Dartmouth's International Relations/Foreign Policy workshop, for providing supportive feedback on this project. This paper owes considerable gratitude to Garnet Kindervater for his intellectual friendship, as well as to Stephen Brooks and Nelson Kasfir for their extensive comments. Also, a sincere thanks to the Department of Government at Dartmouth College for hosting me while I wrote this paper, and the generous funding of the ACLS New Faculty Fellows Program, which funded me while I completed the paper.

increased substantially (McDonald 2009). Some have expressed concern about a possible "piracy-terrorism nexus" in which pirated ships could be transformed into floating bombs, sunk in strategic shipping channels, used to "precipitate" an environmental disaster, or turned into a floating terrorist command center (Chalk 2008, 32; see also Luft and Korin 2004). In addition, piracy in the Gulf of Aden represents serious economic costs estimated at between $1 and $16 billion dollars annually (Chalk 2009), putting "the most important maritime route in the world into crisis" (Archibugi, quoted in Wander 2010).

The current academic and policy debates on piracy in the Gulf of Aden focuses almost exclusively on finding ways to solve the problem of piracy. Some commentators advocate decreasing the incentives for piracy by deploying military assets to combat and arrest suspected pirates. Many realize, however, that policing the Gulf of Aden represents a short-term fix and that a lasting solution to piracy requires addressing Somalia's failed state. However, both prominent policy suggestions— policing the oceans and statebuilding—fail to address the structural and economic conditions that make piracy a viable occupation. For example, while Kraska and Wilson recognize that the "threat of maritime piracy" results from "the desperate situation in Somalia and the devastated political economy along the coastline," their solutions focus not on addressing these economic conditions but instead on developing "legal and policy solutions" to curtail piracy through the deployment of international law and a coordinated military presence in the region (Kraska and Wilson 2009, 57, 66). Similarly, the US National Security Council argues that while "economic development"—along with establishing governance, law, and security—are "necessary to repress piracy fully," the only proposal that provides for addressing piracy is "reducing the vulnerability" of ships, using international law to disrupt piracy, and establishing a formal legal arena to prosecute pirates (National Security Council 2008, 6).

Those analysts who do recognize economic factors as a driving cause of piracy commonly offer the ahistorical argument that poverty stems from state failure. For example, Chalk and Smallman contend that because piracy is "a reflection of underlying socioeconomic conditions on land . . . the international community must confront the failed government in Somalia" (Chalk and Smallman 2009). As such, piracy is treated as a local problem—opportunistic individuals taking advantage of a failed state—to be solved through state building. In these accounts, piracy is treated as a problem to be solved rather than a symptom of larger, structural relations.[2] In adopting this problem-solving approach to piracy, most academics, journalists, and policy researchers have missed opportunities to use piracy in the Gulf of Aden as a moment for critical theory.[3] This chapter therefore examines piracy in the Gulf of Aden as an entry point to critically examine the emphasis on state building as the solution to violence. I argue that the focus on state building in Somalia obscures the ways in which *both* piracy and Somalia's "failed state" are symptoms of a century and a half of structural violence and

2. I take the distinction between the terms "problem-solving theory" and "critical theory" from Robert Cox, who argues that theory, and by extension political analysis, is "always *for* someone and *for* some purpose" (Cox 1986, 207). I argue that when analysts limit their analysis of piracy in the Gulf of Aden to a question of state failure they reinforce the ideological claim that acts of political violence (such as piracy) are the result of local and individual problems rather than symptomatic of the structural violence of capitalist production and circulation.

3. This article uses an Althusserian method I developed in my examination of the genocide in Rwanda (Kamola 2007). I argued that particular instances of violence are often wrongly conceptualized as local phenomena rather than symptoms of structural relations of production and reproduction. To make this argument I situated the genocide within the international economy of coffee production. This chapter similarly argues that piracy is not a local phenomenon caused by local factors (a failed state, opportunistic individuals, clan politics, etc.), but is instead a symptom of Somalia's forced integration into a highly unequal world capitalist system. My Althusserian analysis, however, highlights the ways in which instances of political violence can be both particular—piracy in some locations and genocide in others—but still structured. To make this argument I draw on the concept of over-determination. Althusser contends that the noneconomic regions of the superstructure—in this case, the state, individual actors, clan organizations, international institutions, etc.—also structure economic contradiction. As such, social production is not organized around a single, universal contradiction (i.e., between bourgeoisie and proletariat), but is the total-ity of different registers intervening on one another in kinetic and often contradictory ways. As such, everything from "local tradition to international circumstance" (Althusser 1970, 112) informs the particularity of a given contradiction.

economic dispossession brought about by the area's integration into the capitalist economy.

Piracy is particularly helpful in exploring the relationship between political violence and capitalist accumulation and circulation. While there exist many examples of "structural violence" resulting in "acute violence," most of these conflicts take the form of "violence between the underdogs" (Uvin 2003, 156). Most instances of political violence, such as ethnic conflicts, civil wars, and genocides, occur when individuals and groups that have suffered structural violence lash out at one another. Piracy in the Gulf of Aden, however, is fairly unique in that it does not target civilian populations and therefore remains distanced from gruesome tales of mass casualties and the corresponding moral outrage. Because piracy targets the circulation of capital itself, it actually highlights—in a dramatic and symbolic way—the relationship between political violence and capital. As such, the relatively charismatic figure of the pirate—as opposed to, for example, the *genocidaire* or the child-soldier—is particularly useful in bringing attention to the productive relationship between economic exclusion and political violence. Reducing piracy to a problem caused by state failure, however, forecloses the possibility of using this moment to critically examine the relationship between structural inequality and political violence.

This chapter contains three parts. The first examines how piracy is commonly understood as an effect of state failure in Somalia. The consensus solution of building a centralized Somali state, however, offers little more than an extension of regional geopolitical struggles that routinely undermine existing antipirate social groups in Somalia. The second section displaces the narrative of piracy as an effect of statelessness by situating the Horn of Africa within a century and a half of integration into a colonial and postcolonial capitalist economy. Instead of focusing on states and statelessness, therefore, I examine how the circulation of capital through the Gulf of Aden, from the building of the Suez Canal through the present legacy of toxic dumping and illegal fishing, not only weakens the Somali state but also makes piracy a reasonable response to economic dispossession. Today Somalia remains one of the poorest nation on earth; 75 percent of the population live on less than two dollars a day (Gilpin

2009, 4), while just off its shores 14 percent of world trade—including 26 percent of all oil exports—travel on route to (or from) the Suez Canal (Luxner 2004, 46). The final section argues that conflating peacebuilding with state building obscures the fact that building peace requires addressing the structural violence and economic inequality that produces both weak states and piracy.

Before proceeding, however, I should clarify some choices of terminology. First, I use the term *piracy in the Gulf of Aden* rather than *Somali piracy* intentionally. This discursive shift helps dislocate piracy from the particularities of politics on land and instead highlights piracy as a contestation over the circulation of capital—a struggle, in this instance, taking place primarily at sea. Second, I recognize that *piracy* is a contested term and, in many ways, reproduces the common assumptions that the capturing and ransoming of ships is simply an act of banditry. To complicate this story I often refer to these actors using the term they use to describe themselves, *badaadinta badah*—or "saviors of the sea." In problematizing the concept of piracy, however, it remains important to avoid too hastily treating *badaadinta badah* as "primitive rebels" (Hobsbawm 1959), proletarian heroes, or idealized Robin Hood characters. Instead, I argue that *badaadinta badah* is a symptom of, as well as a highly creative and deeply political response to, unequal relations of capitalist production and circulation. As such, my goal is not to identify heroes and villains but rather to argue that structural violence produces political violence in many forms. Therefore, while the violence of piracy is not beyond condemnation, neither is the structural violence and economic dispossession that shapes the Horn of Africa—and other parts of the world. As such, peacebuilding in Somalia (and elsewhere) requires taking seriously the structural violence generated by the exclusionary relations of capitalist production and circulation. The role of academics, journalists, and policy researchers therefore is twofold: first, to identify the ideological work being done when instances of political violence are reduced to a simple matter of statelessness, and, second, to begin advancing the arguments that a redistribution of wealth at a planetary scale is necessary to curb the spread of political violence. Efforts to build peace that do not tackle the maldistribution of wealth are little more than "global poor relief and riot control" (Cox 1995, 41).

## Piracy, State Failure, and Peacebuilding

United Nations Secretary-General Boutros-Ghali unveiled the policy of "post-conflict peacebuilding" in the 1992 "An Agenda for Peace" report, which laid out the United Nation's new emphasis on "rebuilding the institutions and infrastructures of nations torn by civil war and strife; and building bonds of peaceful mutual benefit among nations formerly at war" (UN 1992). The following year, facing a humanitarian crisis in Somalia, the United Nations passed Resolution 814 giving the UN Operation in Somalia (UNOSOM II) the "gargantuan task of peacebuilding" (Jan 2001, 65).[4] The UN mission, however, quickly proved incapable of carrying out this peacebuilding operation. Shortly after the death of US servicemen during a botched raid on Mohamed Farrah Aidid in Mogadishu, UNOSOM II left Somalia without having accomplished its objectives. In fact, "instead of helping to build peace, UNOSOM II bred further divisions among Somalis, strengthened those elements that were least likely to bring peace, and inhibited most local dynamics towards self-governance" (Jan 2001, 84). While UNOSOM II failed to bring peace, the United Nations and foreign governments never abandoned the objective of reestablishing a centralized Somali government. Starting in 1991 and continuing to the present, the United Nations and foreign countries have initiated more than sixteen unsuccessful efforts to unite Somalia under a single national government (Walls 2009, 372). Most notably, in 2000 the United Nations and the president of Djibouti helped broker a national peace conference in Arta establishing the Transitional National Government (TNG). However,

---

4. According to UN Resolution 814, UNOSOM II's duties included: "(a) assistance in the provision of relief and economic rehabilitation; (b) assistance in the repatriation of refugees and displaced persons; (c) assistance to promote the advance of political reconciliation through broad participation by all sectors of Somali society, and the re-establishment of national and regional institutions and civil administrations in the entire country; (d) assistance in the re-establishment of Somali police; (e) assistance in development of a coherent program for demining; (f) development of public information activities in support of UN activities in Somalia; and (g) creation of conditions for civil society participation in the political reconciliation process" (Jan 2001, 64).

despite being recognized by the UN General Assembly as the legitimate government of Somalia, the TNG possessed little domestic legitimacy and proved unable to extend sovereign control over Somalia. A 2004 conference in Nairobi replaced the TNG with the Transitional Federal Government (TFG), which similarly received diplomatic recognition, including seats in the United Nations, the African Union, and the Arab League (Bradbury 2008, 3). The TFG, however, largely "failed to develop any viable local" or "national administrative organization" and proves unable to curtail "the criminal activities of its warlord 'ministers' and assemblymen" (Lewis 2008, 85). In 2006, the governments of Ethiopia, the United States, and the African Union were even required to prop up the TFG during its fight against the Islamic Courts Union (ICU). In 2012 the TFG was succeeded by the Federal Government of Somalia (FGS), a similarly weak institution that has survived only through foreign military support.

For foreign powers, the focus on establishing an internationally recognized government in Somalia is motivated by the belief that both poverty and violence in Somalia stem from the absence of a functioning state. For example, Menkhaus argues:

> It is a truisim that state failure is ultimately at the root of many of the security threats and crises of underdevelopment both in south-central Somalia and in other zones of state collapse. To the extent that Somalia is exploited by local and international terrorists, the lack of an effective government provides them with safe haven beyond the reach of law enforcement. To the extent that economic development requires an effective government to provide a dependable legal and security environment for the private sector, obtain international development loans, provide essential public goods, and catalyze economic growth, the absence of a responsible Somali government directly contributes to the country's enduring underdevelopment, which in turn produces social environments conducive to crime, violence, and radicalism. (Menkhaus 2006/2007, 93–94)

Many academics, journalists, and policy researchers similarly point to statelessness as the cause of piracy, arguing that the absence of a centralized government allows individual opportunists to take advantage of state failure to achieve private gain (Walls 2009, 372).[5]

The argument that piracy stems from statelessness, however, largely ignores the fact that many statelike entities—"'organic' forms of public order and rule of law"—already exist in Somalia (Menkhaus 2006/2007, 74). Furthermore, many of these existing governmental forms are actually bulwarks against piracy. The semiautonomous region of Somaliland as well as the Islamic Courts Union have, for example, proven more capable of providing peace and security than the TFG, despite being excluded from the peacebuilding agenda. Somaliland, formed in 1991 when the guerilla organization Somali National Movement (SNM) created a truce with organizations loyal to the government, delinked itself from Mogadishu and, in the two decades of self-rule, has "held three consecutive competitive elections" and enjoys "a parliament controlled by opposition parties" and "a vibrant economy dominated by the private sector" (Kaplan 2008, 144). Today the Republic of Somaliland prints its own currency, levies its own taxes, funds a standing army, owns a national airlines, issues its own drivers licenses, license plates, and passports, and is symbolically represented by its own flag, national anthem, and national holidays (Kaplan 2008, 149; Bradbury 2008, 4–5). As such, Somaliland's "democratic credentials . . . rival any in the region" (Bradbury 2008, 1). Despite remaining unrecognized by foreign governments, Somaliland is a major player in the fight against piracy, having arrested and tried dozens of pirates and offering itself as a staging ground for international forces (Howden 2009).

The decision by foreign governments to not recognize Somaliland's juridical sovereignty, and instead treat the TFG and FGS as the only route

5. For example, Kaplan writes that "Somali pirates . . . have grown up in an atmosphere of anarchic violence. . . . The million-square-miles of the Indian Ocean where pirates roam might as well be an alley in Mogadishu" (Kaplan 2009). Somalia has been called "the very definition of a failed state" in which "pirates are simply more powerful (and wealthier) than the state" (Kraska and Wilson 2008/2009, 52). Somalia is "the prototype of a failed state" and is therefore attractive to "all manner of transnational criminals" from "al Qaeda-affiliated groups" to "small-boat pirates" (Borchgrave 2009).

to lasting peace in Somalia, has everything to do with geopolitical and strategic considerations.[6] For example, Ethiopia supports national unification in the hope that a centralized Somali state will cut down on the Islamist connections between Somali groups and groups in Ethiopian-administered Ogaden. Prior to the overthrow of President Hosni Mubarak, Egypt supported a unified Somalia as a strategic check against Ethiopia (Doornbos 2002, 105). Likewise, the Organization of African Unity (OAU), European Union, and United Nations "share a members only vision" and therefore can only "see the globe . . . as divided up into formally independent states that are recognized as members," a vision replicated in the OAU's successor, the African Union (AU) (Doornbos 2002, 106). And, finally, the prism of the "war on terrorism" drives American support for a unified Somali. In short, while both the United Nations and foreign countries advocate state building as the long-term solution to civil war, poverty, and piracy in Somali, their policy of supporting the Somali government as the domestic agent of state building is less about building functioning institutions to alleviate poverty and combat piracy than establishing a government that meets the geopolitical specifications of regional and international powers.

The Islamic Courts Union (ICU) also offered another form of domestic governance that proved capable of containing the threat of piracy. This Islamic group comprised of loosely affiliated religious leaders ousted the TFG from much of southern Somalia in 2006, introducing political stability enforced by sharia law. Under the ICU piracy was punishable by death and, during its brief rule, incidents of piracy lessened considerably (Raffaele 2007, 44). The ICU government, however, was "ousted six months later by the TFG backed by Ethiopian and US military forces" who accused the ICU of allying itself with terrorists (Bradbury 2008, 3). As a result of this invasion, Al-Shabab splintered from the ICU and gained considerable influence in the region. It appears that Al-Shabab later formed a "relationship of convenience" with some of the pirates providing "weapons,

---

6. For an excellent overview of the legal arguments for granting Somaliland political recognition see Carroll and Rajagopal (1993).

combat training and local protection" in exchange for a portion of the revenue generated from these operations (Bell 2009). In short, the policy of building peace by supporting the TFG as the only recognized source of legitimate state power effectively hindered the fight against piracy and opened up a new stage of civil war. When international powers claim that the TFG is the only legitimate actor, they do so based less on evidence of material capacity and domestic legitimacy than on the regional interests of foreign powers.

Despite the fact that most debates concerning how to end war and piracy in Somalia focus on building peace through establishing a central-ized Somali state, the absence of a strong foreign engagement in Somalia left the TFG and now FGS the rump domestic actor to serve as the agent of state building. As a consequence, not only are possible nonstate solutions marginalized (or actively undermined) by foreign powers, but the prob-lem of piracy becomes discursively constituted as an effect of the local condition of statelessness. The widely circulated claim that statelessness causes piracy, however, is seriously flawed. Not only do many countries with fairly strong national governments—such as Indonesia, Tanzania, Nigeria, and India[7]—experience piracy off their shores, but many Somali nonstate and quasi-state actors have also proven more capable of fight-ing piracy than the Somali government, which nonetheless still bears the mantel of the foreign-sponsored agent of state building. And, most important, the claim that piracy results from statelessness fails to criti-cally examine why Somalia's state failed in the first place.

Shortly after the collapse of Siyaad Barre's government in 1991, Abdi Samatar argued that "one of the casualties of the gruesome nightmare that is gripping Somalia has been the capacity to think historically and sys-temically about the nature of the malady" (1992, 625). Given the tendency to reduce conflict in Somalia to ahistorical accounts of traditional clan distinctions, Samatar argued that it is increasingly necessary to "unravel the dynamics of political and economic processes which condition the

---

7. The International Commercial Crime Services (CCS) hosts a live piracy map on its website documenting all reported instances of pirate attacks by year. See: www.icc-ccs.org.

structure of social relations" within Somalia (Samatar 1992, 626). Two decades later these words are no less true. However, journalists, academics, and policy researchers often blame piracy—as well as civil war and poverty—in Somalia on the monocause of state failure. As a result, state building in general, and the current Somali government in particular, become treated as the long-term solution to violence, poverty, and piracy. In the next section I provide a counternarrative, arguing instead that *both* piracy and state failure are structured by the integration of the Gulf of Aden into regimes of capitalist circulation.

## The Gulf of Aden and the Circulation of Capital

Many political analyses of Somalia start with the observation that Somalia—unlike most postcolonial African countries—enjoys a unified ethnic, linguistic, and national identity.[8] As such, the political violence in Somalia is often blamed not on ethnic or religious fragmentation, but on the long-term absence of a centralized state. Besteman, however, points out that Somalia was never a unified entity that simply fell apart when clan-based factions took advantage of the collapse of state power following the 1991 coup. Instead, Somali society has historically contained a number of contradictions, many dating back to the colonial era, such that the "dissolution of the Somali nation-state" was itself the result of a "political economy of class and regional dynamics" playing out "in an idiom of kinship" (Besteman 1996, 580). The production and expression of these class and regional contradictions are intimately tied to the circulation of capital through the

---

8. In her overview of the literature on Somalia, Besteman points out that: "Since I. M. Lewis's (1961) classic book on northern Somali pastoralist social organization first appeared, Somali society has usually been described in academic and popular literature as an egalitarian and ethnically homogenous population of nomadic pastoralists who shared an overarching genealogical system and a common language, culture, and religion" (Besteman 1999, 3–4). The argument of a single Somali nation not fragmented by ethnic, linguistic, and religious differences often finds its way into claims that what is needed is simply rebuilding a centralized state.

Gulf of Aden. The integration of Somalia into the capitalist economy created various political, economic, and cultural formations that, over time,
not only made piracy possible but also created the conditions for a persis-
tently weak state. In this section I argue that state failure in Somalia needs
to be contextualized within the history of the Gulf of Aden's integration
into the relations of capitalist circulation, which include the practices of
toxic dumping and overfishing which the *badaadinta badah* claim as justi-
fying their actions.

The area that constitutes present-day Somalia was part of a vibrant
regional economy prior to the arrival of colonial rule.[9] By the nineteenth
century, however, the rise of European industrial capitalism and expanded
colonial presence in the Far East made the Red Sea and the Gulf of Aden
increasingly important strategic points for European colonial powers.
For many European countries, imperial expansions and industrial production meant that more goods were being transported than ever before.
Raw materials sailed from the colonies to manufacturing centers in the
metropole and returned as commodities to be consumed in the colonies.
This quantitative shift corresponded to a qualitative transformation as
steamships replaced sailing vessels. In 1839, to facilitate steamer service
between India and Suez, the British developed a coaling station at the har-
bor city of Aden (present-day Yemen). To support this outpost, the British
imported meat and produce from the Somali coast (Laitin and Samatar

9. On the northern Somali coast, the towns of Berbera, Zeila, Bulbar, Meit, and Heis
connected the Gulf of Aden to the interior via caravans (Samatar, Salisbury, and Bascom
1988, 83). In fact, the "precolonial Somali pastoral economy was far from self-sufficient.
This society bartered pastoral products such as ghee, skins, and livestock as well as
products from the range such as gum, incense, ostrich feathers, and ivory for grain and
clothing. The trade between the pastoral society and the outside world moved in two
directions. Barter for grain was mainly westward with societies of eastern Ethiopia, while
the coast-bound trade involved the exchange of pastoral products for such commodities as
dates and clothes. . . . The Somali coast was known to the ancient Egyptians as the land of
incense, and Chinese and Arab traders noted the lively trade of the Somali coast" (Samatar
1987, 358).

1987, 48). This trading arrangement led to the creation of a small Somali coastal merchant class and local political structures that facilitated the transportation of cattle from the nomadic populations in the interior to the commercial centers on the coast. In this way, "Somaliland was introduced into a growing world market system long before it was colonized" (Samatar 1987, 359).

In 1859, Britain's colonial competitor, France, laid claim to the port of Obock and, over the course of the next few decades, developed the outpost of French Somaliland (present-day Djibouti). The French designed this outpost to secure its trading routes to colonial holdings in Madagascar and Indochina and to prevent Britain from monopolizing access to the Red Sea (Laitin and Samatar 1987, 49–51). In 1870 the Italian Raffaele Rubattino shipping company purchased Assab to use as its hub for shipping goods between the Red Sea and India. Italian holdings in the region expanded between 1882 and 1885, and the Italian government eventually consolidated control over present-day Eritrea (Lewis 2002, 44–45).

In 1869 a French company, Companie Universelle du Canal Maritime de Suez, completed the Suez Canal. This private enterprise not only proved immensely profitable for its European investors—in large part because of the "plundering [of] Egypt" (Piquet 2004, 109)—but also greatly expanded the flow of capital through the Gulf of Aden. The Canal not only halved the distance between Liverpool and Bombay, but also, unlike the Cape route, offered coaling stations at frequent intervals. This allowed ships to replace tonnage once reserved for coal with additional cargo, thereby rapidly increasing the volume of goods that flowed between Europe and the colonies (Fletcher 1958, 559). The rapid switch from sail to steam greatly benefited Britain, which already had an "abundance of capital and the availability of skilled manpower" necessary to make the transition (Fletcher 1958, 561–62). In the years following the Canal's opening, the fact that more than 70 percent of canal traffic was British only magnified the strategic importance of the Red Sea and the Gulf of Aden. In 1875, to secure this now essential trade route, the British government under Benjamin Disraeli bought a 44 percent ownership stake in the Canal Company (Obieta 1970, 8) and expanded its ownership to 56 percent by the early 1880s (Piquet 2004, 112). In 1882 the British landed troops to prevent the Egyptian government from seizing this now indispensable artery of the British Empire.[10]

In response to growing competition in the Red Sea and the Gulf of Aden, the British Empire annexed large portions of the Somali coast. During the 1880s Britain negotiated a number of treaties with various clans from northern Somalia as far south as present-day Kenya, securing access to the foodstuffs needed to support the military garrisons and coaling station at Aden (Laitin and Samatar 1987, 48–49; Lewis 2002, 46). These treaties granted British agents the right to operate along the Somali coast while preventing other powers from doing the same (Carroll and Rajagopal 1993, 658). In 1884 Britain officially established the Somali Protectorate, but treated this area as "a purely coastal colony" and refrained from intervening in the daily management of the colony; that is, as long as "caravan routes remained open" and traders brought goods to the coast (Samatar 1987, 360). Because Somaliland lacked "a promising source of primitive accumulation for metropolitan capital," the British Empire developed a "non-interventionist, undeveloped, and rudimentary state structure" administrated by the colonial government in Aden (Samatar and Samatar 1987, 676). Over the next seventy-five years Britain invested little in British Somaliland, the exception being during the first two decades of the twentieth century, when the empire spent considerable resources fighting Sayyid Mahammad's pan-Somali insurgency.

Since colonial infrastructure was never fully developed in this region, and since pastoralists often proved unwilling to trade the quantities of livestock required by the British, colonial agents designed methods to encourage pastoralists to bring their livestock to market. British merchants did so by introducing "novel commodities such as sugar, tea, rice, and cigarettes to soften the pre-capitalist fabric" (Samatar 1987, 360, 362) and, over time, the precapitalist pastoral economy became fully integrated into the economy of the British Empire (Samatar, Salisbury, and Bascom 1988, 83). As the northern coast of Somalia became an increasingly "integral part of

10. Britain remained in control of the Canal until 1954; Nasser nationalized the Canal two years later.

the global capitalist system," there developed significant rifts between the pastoralists and the growing merchant and state elite (Samatar 1992, 632). This conflict undermined the traditional social order, replacing it with "a new social order pregnant with a different kind of discord" in which "the competition for access to commodities, the consumption of objects beyond one's productive capabilities, and the accumulation of wealth in the urban centres were paramount" (Samatar 1992, 632–33).

The fragmentation of traditional governing structures was further compounded by Italy's colonization of southern Somalia. Starting in the 1880s, Italy began encroaching on the southern Somali coast, then nominally under British control. Italy established its presence by negotiating deals with local leaders and, over time, used these holdings to execute attacks on Ethiopia. In 1925, exhausted and overextended after a long fight against Sayyid Mahammad, Britain ceded large parts of its southern Somalia to Italy, which consolidated this territory into Italian Somaliland. Unlike the British, the Italians were relative latecomers to the colonial project and saw Italian Somaliland as a possible site to establish a settler colony. Starting in 1919, the Duke of the Abruzzi, supported by the fascist governorship of De Vecchi, began laying the foundations for a colonial export economy in Italian Somalia. Drawing on foreign investment, the duke established a private company, the Societa Agricola Italo-Somala, which received considerable land from the government and "rapidly developed into a highly efficient agricultural consortium producing cotton, sugar, bananas, oil and soap" (Lewis 2002, 93). However, the minimal economic gain yielded by this colonial experiment owed much to the use of plantation slavery and tariffs favoring the importation of Somali agricultural goods into Italy. In her study of southern Somalia, Besteman argues that the plantation economy in Italian Somaliland created a number of deep and lasting social stratifications such that "the dissolution of the Somali nation-state [in 1991] can be understood only by analyzing the turbulent history of race, class, and regional dynamics" created during this period (Besteman 1999, 4).

After World War II, Italy lost control of Italian Somaliland only to regain control in 1950 when the United Nations deemed the area a Trust Territory. In 1960 independence was granted to the British Somaliland

Protectorate and Italian Somalia. In a contested election the same year, these two former colonies voted to join together as the Republic of Somalia. The Act of Union, however, was highly contentious, given that Italian officials wrote the terms of the union, allowing northern politicians only marginal changes. As a sign of resentment, only one hundred thousand people in the former British colony turned out to vote—most rejecting the new constitution. In contrast, more than 1.8 million voted in former Italian Somalia (Carroll and Rajagopal 1993, 661). The continued regional differences formed during colonial rule continue to shape the legitimacy and long-term viability of a united Republic of Somalia, currently expressed in the secessionist aspirations of Somaliland and the semiautonomous status of Puntland.

The considerable political fragmentation undergirding the postcolonial Republic of Somalia was only exacerbated by the country's lack of economic viability. The state therefore became increasingly dependent on foreign sources of development and military aid. By refusing to align solely with the capitalist or Communist countries, Somalia was able to garner aid from both blocs, making it the largest per capita recipient of foreign aid—ninety dollars per person—in Africa (Laitin and Samatar 1987, 108). This, however, was a fairly unstable form of economic management, as various political factions struggled over positions within the government (Samatar 1992, 633). Nine years after independence, Siyad Barre overthrew this fragile government in a military coup and, siding with the Soviet Union, declared a policy of "scientific socialism." However, the Somali government remained impoverished during his reign. Because Somalia had almost no industrial base or mineral wealth, it imported nearly all its manufactured consumer goods (including oil), resulting in a large trade deficit. By 1980 its deficits reached $333.1 million, requiring an International Monetary Fund (IMF) bailout (Laitin and Samatar 1987, 125).

Livestock remained Somalia's most important resource and constituted more than 80 percent of the Republic of Somalia's exports during the 1970s and early 1980s. During this period Saudi Arabia, flush with oil money, purchased 95 percent of Somalia's livestock exports (Little 1992, 97–101). The sale of livestock to Saudi Arabia also expanded during this period as the number of Muslims completing the Haj dramatically increased.[11] The livestock industry, however, collapsed during the 1980s as Saudi oil wealth dried up and as Saudi Arabia stopped importing Somali livestock, claiming they were diseased and unsafe for consumption.[12] Between 1983 and 1989 the number of animals exported to Saudi Arabia plummeted from a high of approximately 160,000 in 1982 to around 10,000 in 1984 (Little 1992, 101). This drop was so severe that the Somali government took out a $32.6 million loan from the IMF to cover budgetary shortfalls (Laitin and Samatar 1987, 125).

The volatile export market, debt, and continued dependency on foreign funding necessitated a closer strategic alliance with Western powers. After the 1974 Communist revolution toppled Haile Selassie in Ethiopia, Somalia switched allegiances and became an important ally of the United States. In 1977 the economically weak government of Somalia launched an ill-advised attack on Ethiopia aimed at reuniting greater Somalia.[13] After the failed Ogaden War, the Siyaad regime remained considerably weakened and many clan-based and regional domestic factions began challenging its authority. During this period, the United States—still reeling from its expulsion from Iran and fearful of a growing Soviet influence in the region—looked to Somalia as a reliable site for military bases capable

---

11. Pilgrims to Mecca are expected to sacrifice a lamb. It is calculated that during this period, "50 percent of the Somali exports [of lambs] are for the Haj season" (Samatar, Salisbury, and Bascom 1988, 94).

12. Some have pointed out that embargos on Somali livestock correspond with Saudi investments in Australian ranches that profited from restrictions on Somalia imports. Regardless of the cause, the effect of import restrictions shook the Somali economy (Laitin and Samatar 1987, 125).

13. It is important to note that the name "Somalia" is often used as shorthand for the Republic of Somalia. For many, however, Somalia is a larger region that includes the former British Somaliland Protectorate, the former Italian Somalia, present-day Djibouti, the Ogaden region of eastern Ethiopia, and parts of northern Kenya. The five components of greater Somalia are represented in the five-pointed star on the Republic of Somalia's flag (Lewis 2008, 29). There have been a number of attempts to conceptually and physically unify these areas into a single entity. For example, in the beginning of the twentieth century Sayyid Mahammad organized a "pan-Somali resistance" against colonial occupation (Laitin and Samatar 1987, 58). The 1977 Ogaden War was another attempt to unify greater Somalia.

of securing the Persian Gulf (Besteman 1996, 581). Because of its strategic location, Somalia received considerable foreign development and military aid throughout the 1980s. Between 1980 and 1988 the United States established a number of military bases in Somalia and provided more than $500 million in economic aid (Besteman 1996, 581). Somalia's dependency on foreign powers for financial support in exchange for military positioning resulted in the country becoming awash in weapons. Between 1978 and 1988 the United States sent around $200 million in military aid, and between 1981 and 1990 Italy, the former colonial power, contributed more than $500 million to build a military arsenal. As his hold on power waned, Siyaad Barre released portions of this weapons stockpile to the civilian population (Peterson 2001, 13).

These severe political, military, and economic shocks meant that Siyaad was increasingly dependent on neighboring Arab countries, Western countries, the United States, the IMF, and the World Bank for support. These donors, however, all demanded that the regime liberalize the Somali economy, including privatizing the pastoral sector. This shift in policy, however, added "new kinks in relationships between the state and producers" and magnified existing regional differences (Samatar and Samatar 1987, 685). In the late 1980s, Siyaad sought both to tamp down regional political opposition in the north and to create a government-run livestock export economy. To achieve these ends he sought to "wrest control" of livestock exports and qat[14] sales, placing them under government control (Besteman 1996, 581). In 1988, in a challenge to "the economic and political strength of the Isaaq clan-family," Barre ordered the bombing of a number of northern towns, provoking even greater armed opposition (Besteman 1996, 581–82). The bombing of civilians, however, took place as the Cold War was winding down and received widespread condemnation by human rights groups. This pressure resulted in the United States and other donor governments drastically defunding the Somali regime (Besteman 1996, 581–82). Without international support and facing a civil war, the Siyaad regime proved no longer economically or politically

14. Qat is a leaf with narcotic-like qualities widely consumed in this region.

sustainable and finally collapsed. Since the early 1990s Somalia has lacked a centralized state. Today there remains considerable disagreement about whether Somalia should refashion a national government, establish a federal system giving the wealthier northern regions semiautonomy from the war-torn capital Mogadishu in the south, or whether the current autonomous regions of Somaliland and Puntland should break from the Republic of Somalia altogether.

Today many foreign powers prioritize securing a single, national Somalia. However, the existence of a strong Somali government has not always been the top priority for Western powers in the region. From the first colonial encounters through to the last years of the Cold War, foreign interest in Somalia focused almost exclusively on securing the Gulf of Aden as a commercial artery and geopolitical outpost. Under colonial rule there was interest in preventing the creation of a strong national Somalia, with Britain going to great lengths to combat Sayyid Mahammad's pan-Somali project. At the height of the Cold War, a strong national Somalia was prioritized only to the degree that it could be a reliable ally in an otherwise volatile region, a priority that shifted with the collapse of the Soviet Union. Given this history, it is not surprising that since independence in 1960 Somalia continues to suffer from weak state institutions, itself a symptom of the country's asymmetrical integration into the world economy. In many ways, the contemporary absence of a centralized Somali government is the logical conclusion for a state designed over multiple centuries by foreign powers whose engagement in Somalia centered on their own economic and strategic interests, *not* state building.

### The Gulf of Aden and the Political Economy of Piracy

Since the collapse of the central government in 1991, Somalia has not withdrawn from the capitalist economy. If anything it has become more integrated than ever before. Some areas enjoy a thriving cross-border cattle trade with Kenya and growing "service and hospitality" sectors (Leesen 2007, 701–3). A banking sector is developing as a result of remittances from overseas. Foreign companies—including Dole Fruit, General Motors-Kenya, and Total Oil Company—have invested in the area (ibid., 704–5). In

areas were piracy is the largest problem—the northeastern semiautonomous region of Puntland and parts of southern Somalia—subsistence and
commercial fishing has emerged as an important economic sector.

Since 1991, however, the absence of a centralized state made it possible
for foreign companies to plunder Somalia's marine life with an estimated
"700 foreign-owned vessels . . . engaged in unlicenced and unregulated
fishing in Somali waters, exploiting high value species such as tuna, shark,
lobster and deep-water shrimp" (HSTF 2006, 81), taking approximately
$300 million worth of marine life from Somali waters annually (Dagne
2009, 106; Editor 2009; Hari 2009). The presence of these ships has eviscer-
ated the local fishing industry that until recently supported many coastal
populations in Somalia. The Somali transitional legislator Mohamed Qanyare Afrah called this pillaging a more harmful form of piracy than the
hijacking of foreign ships.[15] In July 2008, the Special Envoy for the UN
Secretary-General for Somalia, Ahmedou Ould-Abdallah, blamed European and Asian countries for overfishing the coastal waters and held
them largely responsible for the upswing in piracy (Dagne 2009, 106).

In addition to overfishing, over the past fifteen years, European companies have used the Gulf of Aden as a dumping ground for toxic chemi-
cals. Brokered by mostly Swiss and Italian companies with alleged mafia
assistance (Carazzolo et al. 1998; Poaletta 1997), companies have disposed
of waste in the Gulf of Aden for an average of $2.50 per ton, consider-
ably less than the $250 per ton that is required to dispose of this waste in
Europe (UNEP 2005). After the 2004 Asian tsunami, toxic waste contain-
ers—some dropped as far as ten kilometers away—washed up on shore
(UNEP 2005; Dagne 2009, 106). The waste

> dumped along Somalia's coast comprised uranium radioactive waste,
> lead, cadmium, mercury, industrial, hospital, chemical, leather treat-
> ment and other toxic waste. Most of the waste was simply dumped on
> the beaches in containers and disposable leaking barrels . . . without

---

15. Mohamed Qanyare Afrah, "Somalia: Foreign Vessels in the Somali Waters Are
More Hazardous Than Pirates, Says Qanyare," October 19, 2009, http://www.somaliweyn
.org/pages/news/Oct_09/21Oct15.html.

regard to the health of the local population and any environmentally devastating impacts. (UNEP 2005, 134)

Both overfishing and toxic dumping—highly profitable enterprises for Asian and European companies—made it increasingly difficult for Somalis living along the coast to survive.

Piracy in the Gulf of Aden started initially as a source of wealth creation for those living in this highly impoverished area, and many of its participants justified their actions to domestic and international audiences as simply an organized response to the problems of over fishing and toxic dumping. Many fishermen from coastal villages began patrolling the immediate waters, referring to themselves as *badaadinta badah*, or the "saviours of the sea" (Bahadur 2009). In fact, the current bout of piracy in the Gulf of Aden started when groups with names like the Central Somalia Coast Guard, the National Volunteer Coast Guard, and the Somali Marines sought to tax passing ships (Gilpin 2009, 5). This practice evolved using Eyl and Garaad in Puntland and Hobyo and Harardhere in central Somalia as sites for organizing the hijacking of commercial ships that were both easier to capture and yielded larger ransoms than fishing vessels (ibid.). For example, Sugule Ali—a pirate who helped capture the *Faina*, a Ukrainian ship carrying military hardware to Sudan via Kenya—stated that his goal was "to stop illegal fishing and dumping in our waters" and that "we only want money so we can protect ourselves from hunger" (Gettleman 2008, 6). Mr. Ali argued that the actual "sea bandits" are "those who illegally fish in our seas and dump waste in our seas and carry weapons in our seas. We are simply patrolling our seas. Think of us like a coast guard" (Gettleman 2008, 6).

Economically speaking, piracy has brought considerable wealth to the region, even fueling a construction boom in Puntland (Kraska and Wilson 2009, 57) and forming a real-estate bubble in Nairobi as *badaadinta badah* shift their assets out of Somalia (Odula 2010). Piracy has also become a highly capitalized industry as local and regional entrepreneurs invest in pirate organizations, helping to outfit them with increasingly sophisticated weapons, global positioning systems, and satellite phones needed to conduct operations at greater distances (Dagne 2009, 105).

Today, the *badaadinta badah* have developed an intricate economy that includes distributing ransom money throughout the community. Boyah, a longtime *badaadinta badah* in the region, explains that "half [of the ransom] goes to the hijackers, a third to the investors who fronted cash for the ships and weapons, and 20 percent to everyone else, from the guards to the translators (occasionally high school students on a summer break). Some money is also given as charity to the local poor" (Bahadur 2009). In this context, the cause of defending the waters has become highly profitable. For example, in Haradheere a twenty-four-hour stock market draws investors and redistributes ransom money to those who materially support acts of piracy (Ahmed 2009). As another example, "a 22-year-old divorcée," Sahra Ibrahim, invested the rocket-propelled grenade launcher she received as alimony in a pirate "company" and, with the successful ransoming for a Spanish tuna fishing vessel, received seventy-five thousand dollars in return (ibid.).

While the United States government, the United Nations, and other foreign countries describe piracy as the result of statelessness, these claims ignore the arguments made by the *badaadinta badah themselves,* who defend their activities as attempts to protect themselves from the latest postcolonial form of economic dispossession, namely overfishing and toxic dumping. However, both Somalia's stateless as well as regional poverty should be recognized as symptoms of the region's asymmetrical integration into the world economy. Therefore, rather than simply reducing piracy to banditry made possible by the vacuum left by an absent state, piracy might instead be understood as a creative (and profitable) attempt to develop a vibrant economic sphere within places marginalized from the world economy for more than a century. While American and international policies to combat piracy in the Gulf of Aden that do not address the long-standing maldistribution of wealth—including efforts to reinforce the TFG and now FGS as a centralized Somali state—might reduce piracy as a particular form of political violence, in the end they fail to address the structural violence of which piracy is one symptom.

In the concluding section I examine how piracy in the Gulf of Aden creates the possibility to critique peacebuilding's emphasis on state building. Instead of reproducing the ideological claim that violence is caused by statelessness, I argue that academics, journalists, and policy researchers should refocus our attention to address how massive economic inequalities have produced the conditions in which piracy—and other forms of political violence—become increasingly viable.

## Piracy and Peacebuilding

So far foreign countries have responded to piracy in the Gulf of Aden by dispatching naval forces to the region under the auspices of the United Nations. In 2008 the UN Security Council issued numerous resolutions calling for an international and coordinated attack on piracy.[16] Since then many countries have deployed ships and airplanes to the area to reinforce "the sovereignty, territorial integrity, political independence and unity of Somalia," as embodied in the Transitional Federal Government and successor Federal Government of Somalia (UN 2008). Many analysts, however, argue that policing the Gulf of Aden is only a temporary solution to the problem and greater emphasis must be placed on state building (see, for example, UN 2009). However, taking the above narrative seriously, piracy—like Somalia's failed state—must be treated not as a local crisis to be solved through state building, but rather an effect of vastly unequal relations of capitalist circulation.

It is important to note, however, that while there exists a robust discourse calling for greater state building in Somalia, the United Nations and foreign countries have expressed little interest in actually participating in a concerted effort to build strong Somali state institutions. In fact,

16. In 2008, the UN issued a historic four resolutions targeting piracy in the Gulf of Aden, including Resolution 1816, making it possible for ships to pursue pirates within Somalia's territorial water, and Resolution 1838, encouraging nations to deploy naval vessels and aircraft to the area (Kraska and Wilson 2009, 56). These resolutions justified the use of military force to fight piracy as an enforcement of international law. For example, Resolution 1816 reaffirmed the UN's commitment to the fight against piracy in the Gulf of Aden, arguing that piracy threatens the "delivery of humanitarian aid to Somalia," violates "international navigation and the safety of commercial maritime routes," and disrupts activities, such as fishing, that are "in conformity with international law" (UN 2008).

the position of foreign countries toward Somalia looks much like Duff-ield's analysis of how "global liberal governance" walls off those spatial locations controlled by "non-liberal political complexes" (i.e., warlords, rebels, mafia groups, etc.) and therefore threaten capitalist circulation and liberal governance. These areas are then intervened on to prevent the spread of violence to areas that fully embrace economic and political liberalism (Duffield 2001). The current responses to piracy—namely, policing the ocean and supporting the FGS—are prime examples of this approach. Despite the many calls for robust state building, the actual policy toward Somalia is one of containment. Therefore when academics, journalists, and policy researchers blame piracy as simply the result of an absent centralized state in Somalia they effectively mask the fact that the institutions of global governance, as in preceding centuries, actually have little interest in building the Somali state in any meaningful way.

That being said, while pirates in the Gulf of Aden provide an example of a bottom-up group finding ways to survive (and even prosper) at the margins of a highly unequal capitalist world-system, their project is one of private profit and does not rework these historical and structural inequalities. Nevertheless, academics, journalists, and policy researchers should not hastily dismiss their actions as simply a *problem to be solved* through the intervention of foreign powers. The history of foreign intervention in Somalia reveals that such approaches are often based not on the interest and well-being of the Somali people, but rather on securing the transportation of capital through the Gulf of Aden as cheaply and efficiently as possible.

In conclusion, it is important to remember that the form Somalia's future ultimately takes is for Somalis and members of the diaspora to decide. Nevertheless, academics, journalists, and policy researchers can contribute to this discussion by critically reframing what it means to build peace. This involves not simply assuming that peace takes the form of disinterested, philanthropic states committing themselves to building a strong centralized Somali government (where one, by design, never existed). Rather, external actors should participate in the larger project of imagining and identifying emancipations capable of disrupting the existing political economy of violence. This involves taking seriously Somalia's forced integration into the world capitalist economy and using piracy as an opportunity to make visible the structural conditions that produce political violence. By critically examining the politics of our own knowledge production, we might use our intellectual labor to develop narratives that avoid reproducing the reified claim that violence stems primarily from statelessness, and therefore can be prevented by state building.

Reframing piracy as a symptom of structural inequality (rather than a logistical problem to be solved) opens up the possibility of addressing the structural—rather than particular—causes of violence. As knowledge producers, treating piracy as a symptom of structural inequality not only avoids reproducing the ideological claim that political violence results from statelessness but also demands that we ask the further question: How can a world be created that challenges the highly asymmetrical and exclusionary distribution, and circulation, of capital? Rather than reproducing the ideologically dangerous and historically inaccurate claim that Western states are the heroic builders of states (and therefore peace) in the previously colonized world, we can instead turn our academic labor toward creating an intellectual argument for the redistribution of wealth at a planetary scale. We can write for (and work with) social movements engaged in the project of addressing the structural inequalities that define contemporary capitalism. Only by taking seriously the structural and material causes of violence is it possible to use the "weapon of criticism" to "grasp the root of the matter" (Marx 1997). In doing so, it becomes apparent that without also tackling the massive structural asymmetries defining capitalist production and circulation the term "peacebuilding" has no meaning.

# 6

# Poisoned Patronage

*Appropriating Aid and Pulling Down*
*"Big Men" in Northern Sierra Leone*

## Catherine Bolten

Political power in democratic countries may be vested in the state itself, but in Sierra Leone, politics is personal. In a country with a political history built on patronage networks, only "big people," those who can harness the economic means to surround themselves with loyal clients willing to support them in any endeavor, can expect to maintain power or hold office for even a single term. In the aftermath of an eleven-year civil war, universal suffrage, democratically elected councils, and a sudden influx of aid money as a reliable resource have altered the power base of big men. A big man's ability to gain and maintain power depends on his willingness and ability to harness these institutions to support his socioeconomic networks.

In this chapter I use the case of the deposition of a town council chairman in the wake of an embezzlement scandal to examine how the project of the liberal peace to promote liberal democracy within the context of patronage networks poisons the political process and stymies postwar development. Through a discussion of the emergence of the "half-baked youths" as a political constituency, the infusion of development aid as the only source of revenue for a beleaguered and impoverished town council in the wake of the war, and the manipulation of social leveling as an instrument of political power wrangling, this chapter illustrates how the patronage system moved into an essentially unworkable conflict with democracy in the decade after the war. Here, democratic processes are harnessed in the service of traditional systems of power and inequality. Given the emphasis on channeling aid and development money through democratic structures in international development policy, this case provides a warning against assumptions that a country's embrace of democracy as part the postwar development process ensures that democracy will function as intended.[1]

Popular mobilization is linked with political contexts and networks in current research on social movements and collective action. While the case I examine here is not a social movement per se, the processes of localized collective action, and the way public mobilization is channeled, are conditioned by larger national and global structures. Youths feel that their actions have the power to influence government to improve their opportunities, whether or not those actions are either sustained or aimed at political transformation. The constraints on social welfare and employment opportunities that stem from Sierra Leone's marginal and yet dependent position in the global economic system feed the disaffection among youths. These youths have been mobilized by politicians/big men seeking access to public coffers as a means of generating individual benefits for their own supporters, while still remaining marginal to those networks. Moreover, the concentration of financial resources at the global level structures international aid flows in ways that contribute to the "unfreedoms" of Sierra Leoneans, perpetuating competition and conflict that undermine efforts at postwar peacebuilding (see Sen 1999).

The phenomenon of the "half-baked," and the power that an alienated, dispossessed section of youths have in influencing the deposition of a chairman, draws on two interrelated themes of social mobilization. The first, that all forms of social mobilization, whether positive or negative, resonate with and have their origins within the social norms or parent culture to which they pose a challenge, is widely documented

---

1. Though relevant, this is not the space for a discussion over whether donor organizations and countries should continue providing aid to African countries. For the purposes of this argument, suffice to say this is one of the reasons aid may end.

in dissimulative forms of action across Africa and elsewhere (see Branch 2006; Edelman 2001; Mooney 1998; Useem 1998; West 1998). The "half-baked youths," by being mobilized to challenge the authority of the chairman, hoped that they could prove themselves worthy of being incorporated into existing forms of power, specifically the new political patronage networks. Therefore, their action was motivated and molded by their social norms with the goal of achieving gains within those norms, rather than working on a broad form of cultural transformation. In essence, they were working to empower themselves within existing systems of inequality, rather than emancipating themselves from the system altogether. By being successful in their short-term goal of ousting a chairman but failing to gain incorporation, they reinforced the very inequalities that keep them on the lowest rung on the patronage ladder. Youths in this example are, in essence, brawn for hire.

The fact that youths mobilized for this challenge on the urging of the chairman's political challengers leads to a second, contested theme of social mobilization: whether or not their "non-routine" action of a sit-down strike, which brought them few gains and thus appears to resonate with breakdown theory (see Useem 1998), can be analyzed as the actions of the dispossessed and marginalized. Because the youths were merely the instruments of this action, rather than its architects, assigning theories of action to the actors themselves obscures our ability to accurately classify the diverse goals of this social movement. The youths themselves gained little aside from a momentary ability to express their anger and collective power; as Useem states, "while not irrational, [it is] also not politics by other means" (1998, 235). Big men, on the other hand, gained a power vacuum over which they could fight for access to the very same aid resources designed to create the development that would enhance the prospects of youths. This social mobilization was therefore not populist, except in the fact that power brokers harnessed popular anger to accomplish their own goals.

I propose a combined ideological and practical approach to the postwar political economy in order to address these dissimulative battles for resources. The "unfreedoms" experienced by postcolonial countries in the contemporary world economy—underresourced health infrastructure, lack of credit, poor education—hinder their ability to generate accountable and responsive democratic policies. Therefore, a better understanding of the links between economic well-being and political freedom is needed, as is an emphasis on basic welfare that will strengthen the possibility of democratic process. In the scramble to rebuild in the aftermath of war, electoral benchmarks are prioritized without knowledge of the social and economic contexts that are fundamental to achieving the goals for which elections have become a proxy marker. Moreover, these economic contexts are constrained in important ways by the very same donors who fund rebuilding. And in Sierra Leone, this situation generates an untenable paradox with traditional political-economic forms such as the big man. Big men are given access to external resources that they can use to enhance their own positions with less direct accountability to their clients. This serves to increase, rather than ameliorate, the dispossession suffered at the local level by largely marginalized women and youths. Aid also increases the willingness of big men to challenge one another through the destructive and easily harnessed rage of dispossessed youths. Restructured aid policies that are sensitive to structural inequalities, especially with respect to cultural expectations regarding power and opportunity, would not empower individuals within a poisoned patronage/democratic system, thereby reinforcing its inequalities. Instead, it would emancipate both marginalized individuals and the democratic process itself from the current polarizing, stratifying, and violence-prone relationship between economic and political power in postwar Sierra Leone.

### Personalized Politics and Big People

The intensely personal nature of politics in Sierra Leone—in essence the legacy of the patronage system—is best illustrated by the 2002 presidential election, during which incumbent President Ahmed Tejan Kabbah covered the country on the campaign trail. During one stay in the town of Makeni, the capital of the northern region, Kabbah visited the regional army headquarters. In a story that is now local legend, Kabbah advised the assembled soldiers to consider carefully when they voted for president, as the military's votes were tallied by battalion. Just by looking at the results as they were returned from the barracks, Kabbah would know who among his soldiers was loyal to the president. During the Makeni district and town council inauguration in May 2004, Kabbah was notorious for refusing to applaud when a member of the opposition party was sworn into office, and applauding wildly when a member of his own party took the stage. Neither he nor any other politician in Sierra Leone attempts to conceal the fact that party affiliation is a mark of loyalty to a particular politico-social network.[2] As a function of this loyalty, a political big man must serve as a distributor of resources for his clients, who owe him labor and support in return. Big men only retain their positions as long as they can maintain both resource bases and reputations as fair redistributors who, although they retain their own hefty share, are reasonable with the trickle down. Those who do not are deserted or pulled down by their supporters.

In the wake of a war that decimated seed stock, scattered familial labor pools, and left fields in a desultory state, the traditional avenues of becoming "big" were largely closed. Political office, as one of the few occupations with access to outside resources, had become the de facto avenue for would-be big men, even as they were forced to be accountable to both personal and wider political networks. Aid was one of the few fungible resources at their disposal in the decade after the war, and it continues to be true that everyone associated with a politician had a fair claim to a piece of the pie. Though council members are beholden to donors and their constituencies as producers of public good in the form of development, individuals who display overt political support for councilors in the form of votes are signaling clientelistic intent, or loyalty to that politician, and they expect benefits in return. Finally, members of the big man's personal social network—family, friends, and associates—also have a fair claim on resources. However, when politicians vested their

2. In his analysis of Kabbah's reelection in 2002, Kandeh states candidly that Kabbah was reelected because, as far as the people could see, he had held to his promise to end the war. In spite of the overt ethnic tribalism and known corruption of members of his party, loyalty to a promise fulfilled was the driving reason for supporting him (Kandeh 2003, 189).

ability to be big solely in their positions in a democratically elected polity with resources provided by aid organizations, the results had the potential to be personally disastrous. No matter the source of income, politicians who fail on any level—be it charges of corruption or the failure to support their client base—will fall victim to social leveling, and other big men will jockey to take their place. The combination of finite aid resources with patronage within a fragile democracy created a poisoned system: instead of promoting the postwar development meant to stabilize a fragile postwar economy, aid money supported a system of patronage by which would-be big men kept themselves in power. Rather than mobilizing to argue for the fair distribution of resources for the public good, youths instead mobilized to become part of big men's personal networks so that they too could share in the aid wealth by pulling down their would-be patron's rivals.

### Social Leveling and Resource Distribution: Making Aid "Fit"

Social leveling is a common practice among people who live in uncertain or marginal environments, where the survival and persistence of the group depends on the willingness of individuals to level disparities in household production and income (see Sugiyama 1987, 31; Fortier 2001, 199). In forms such as sharing of resources, ritual gift-giving, and forced redistribution, communities such as the Bemba in Zambia could maintain working communities in the face of perpetual food shortage. In Sierra Leone, intertribal warfare, prolonged but localized drought, and kin networks expanded through marriage and slavery were accompanied by the redistribution of seed, labor, and favors through far-reaching channels. Would-be big individuals became redistributors in order to cement their status and increase their resource base through labor. This had the added effect of maintaining at least minimal levels of nutrition and social functioning even in times of upheaval and desperate need. Through the relative sedentarization of populations that accompanied colonialization, social leveling morphed into a more localized and public process.

*Pul yu doŋ sindrom* is the name given to social leveling in Makeni. To "pull down" is to socially and financially topple someone who hoards personal successes. One is prone to being pulled down by people who feel they comprise the membership of that person's network, have themselves contributed in good faith, and are therefore entitled to share in the successes of every individual with whom they are linked. The pulling down can take many forms, from the spoiling of resources that someone secrets away instead of sharing them, to public shaming of an individual who is clearly greedy and has done his or her network wrong. *Pul yu doŋ sindrom* has the dynamic effect of destroying unworkable networks and creating the space for new patrons to rise. This is resonant with the "wealth in people" models, where big people's wealth is in their clients as much as their physical resources (see Leach 1994, 60). Ideally, it maintains accountability and equitable distribution of resources. In reality, it rarely works this effectively, especially when resources are not produced within the community, but are infused from outside. Pulling down one of these new big men will not ensure equitable distribution of resources; it will merely create a vacant spot for a new big man to gain control over their distribution.

Townspeople bemoan the fact that because of endemic poverty, jealousy and suspicion of greediness are emerging as the most potent emotions moving people to action. It is the phenomenon to which people consistently point when they talk about why Makeni is incapable of sustaining community development. "The problem," said one man, "is that whenever someone gets a little bit of anything, there is someone standing right behind him who wants some of it too, and their jealousy makes them do bad things."[3] With respect to the events described below, the chairman of the town council was toppled because his flagrant disregard of patronage meant he had no allies; *he was not sharing enough to protect his status because he treated aid as a public good.* The chairman was authoritarian in his control of the treasury and was unwilling to share the council's wealth with everyone in the community, even his fellow councilors. They had

3. Other examples are Smith (1994, 173) in Papua New Guinea; Ashforth (1998, 231) in South Africa, where people use witchcraft to limit the good fortune of their neighbors; and Sanders (2003, 164) in rural Tanzania, where witchcraft is part of a social economy of "nightmare egalitarianism." In Guinea-Bissau wealth is kept hidden to avoid jealousy and accusations of witchcraft that would result in leveling (Gable 1997, 213).

elected him, placing him in his position as big man, a position from which they expected he would grant access to council resources.

Institutions are resistant to change, but the resources that support them are the source of constant contention. With political patronage and social leveling placed in the context of a resource, namely, postwar development aid that was not intended to be shared by people except through the production of public good, making it useful for building patronage networks threatened the social stability of a fragile nation in which inequitable access to resources defined the government of the president/ dictator Siaka Stevens during the prewar "shadow state" (Reno 1995). Big men are under intense pressure to make public aid provide for individual good as well, particularly in the form of jobs, contracts, and cash distributions. Those who could not or would not force aid to perform both functions—thus being accountable to both donors and voters—were toppled on the pretense of being greedy, and other would-be big men took their place. Each big man must build and sustain his own networks of supporters, and being responsive to democracy means including citizens who feel that voting entitles one to access to a sociopolitical network that is both public and personal.

## The Town Council:
## The Democratic Experiment Returns to Makeni

The year 2004 marked the first time in thirty years that town council seats lost their status as prizes for party loyalty and were instead put to democratic vote. Because of their links with patronage, townspeople had learned to distrust the motives of councilors, who, in the words of one journalist, would "stay on the council until the money was gone. Once there was nothing left to 'eat' they would lose interest" (Bunting-Davis 1981). Councilors could and did treat the council as their own personal bank and as instruments for building their personal status. They had no one to be accountable to except the president, Siaka Stevens, and he did not care what happened to council funds as long as councilors extended the reach of his power through the districts. Naked embezzlement bled the town dry, with little money invested in public works or infrastructure.

Under intense international pressure to democratize the country following the war, Tejan Kabbah reinstated elections for town and district
council seats. Makeni, in the north, is in the traditional stronghold of Stevens's own party, the All People's Congress, or APC. Kabbah himself is
from the southeast, the stronghold of the Sierra Leone People's Party, the
SLPP. Well before his return to the presidency, Kabbah had a bad reputa-
tion in Makeni. In 1996, as the war raged in the south and east, Kabbah
announced to an assembled crowd how much he disliked the place and its
people. He stated bluntly that the residents should apologize to the rest of
the nation for the war, as several commanders from the rebel Revolutionary United Front (RUF) hailed from the north, which was derided in the
media as the "hail theory of war" (Anonymous 1996). The RUF invaded
and occupied Makeni from 1998 to 2001, and, instead of sending troops
to liberate the town, my interlocutors quoted Kabbah's announcement
in a radio broadcast to the nation that Makeni was "a place of collaborators." He stated that the town had forfeited its place in the nation, and
as such he was calling in a helicopter gunship to bomb it "down to the
last chicken and ant."[4] In the following months, repeated bombings of
Makeni resulted in a mass exodus from the town, leaving only the RUF,
the old and infirm, and a few sturdy holdouts (Bolten 2008).

Kabbah's destruction of the town was matched by his initial refusal
to funnel development money to Makeni in the aftermath of the war. The
town council reflected popular anger at his snub. According to one of my
interlocutors, "The residents here reacted very violently to Tejan Kabbah
refusing to develop the town. By electing an all-APC council, they are
saying they don't care to work together with the government, they still
blame Kabbah for abandoning them, they don't care that Kabbah takes
credit for ending the war, they will still do things their own way." Residents elected only those people who had remained in the town during

4. The practice in anthropology is to maintain complete confidentiality for all interlocutors except public figures. For this reason, the quotes that appear unattributed in
this work were made by people in Makeni during confidential interviews that took place
between May 2004 and April 2006.

the occupation; people whom they felt they could personally trust to love the town and not abandon it to pursue better opportunities. Even as they represented vastly different perspectives, all campaigned under the banner of the APC, which meant they were firmly locally oriented and were taking a personal stand against Kabbah and the SLPP.

Every elected councilor had played an important role in the town during the occupation; none had run away only to return once the town was deemed safe by the United Nations. The town council chairman, Musa Mansaray, was a former employee of a respected international humanitarian organization, and was responsible for bringing the first food relief to the town before it was demilitarized. Another member held political meetings in contradiction to RUF rules during the occupation. One councilor sheltered and trained women who had become homeless; another worked as the liaison between RUF command and the market women, demanding on their behalf greater access to food and medicine. All councilors were elected by large margins, and on their shoulders rested the hopes and expectations of the community. The new councilors had already proven their worth as unselfish patrons in times of crisis, and were loved and respected because they extended compassionate patronage to the very margins of society. Again, politics was personal, and the APC town council of Makeni represented the feelings of the town for the nation: in spite of Kabbah's huge margin of victory when he was reelected, no one in the town was going to reward him or his party for ostensibly ending the war. It was only those people who stood for office inside the town that could possibly represent truly caring patrons of Makeni's people.

As the council got down to business, problems emerged, and all were directly traceable to Kabbah's vindictiveness over being snubbed. His ministers refused Makeni its allotment of town council funds and equipment on the premise that the town was receiving enough assistance from abroad. All three town councils were supposed to receive new garbage trucks, and Makeni's truck was delivered to Koidu, the unofficial capital of the diamond mining area. The bishop of the Catholic mission appealed to his diocese in Italy to fund a substitute, which was delivered weeks later. In spite of the bishop's good intentions, this only proved Kabbah's point that the town council did not need government assistance to survive, and so could be left to its own devices. News emerged shortly afterward that the councilors would not receive salaries. On the heels of this announcement, the chairman revived a tax on traders—including young people with informal, mobile petty trade boxes—in order to raise revenue.

Taxes have a long and sordid history in Makeni (see Bolten 2008, 70–90), from their initiation under the colonial government, to their abuse by paramount chiefs in the 1950s, to prewar town and district councils taxing populations into destitution while the money was "lost" inside a flagrantly abusive council. Townspeople do not trust taxation, and openly admitted to dodging the council's revenue collectors whenever they saw them. The young people in particular—most notably the "box" traders with their tendency to close up shop and run when the taxman is near— openly refused to pay taxes to a council that had not proven itself worthy of trust; in essence one that proves itself through public development. In spite of the chairman's pleas, the council limped along in a crippled state until he convinced a large donor organization to fund all of the town's development projects. Mansaray conceived of this infusion as a way of restoring the trust that people had in his ability to run the council as an honest democratic institution. When it came to light that these funds were not being used in a transparent manner, it was the young people who coalesced as a movement to eject councilors for the benefit of those most wronged by the scandal: themselves. The disappearance of aid, with no visible benefit for anyone, meant that the council was not providing its largest voting bloc with the development benefits for which they assumed that councilors' proven loyalty to Makeni would result in. The betrayal, like politics itself, was taken personally.

### The "Half-Baked Youths" Emerge as a Coalition

Before analyzing how a self-proclaimed civil society movement toppled the chairman in the wake of an embezzlement scandal, I must first explore its origins. The coalition called itself the Makeni Union of Youth Groups, though its numerous critics in town called it the "half-baked youth union." Calling a young man "half-baked" is the ultimate insult; it implies he is the product of a social network that is paltry, poor, and backward. One who is "half-baked" lacks the training that would result in full socialization as an adult enmeshed in networks of mutual obligation with adults; and a "half-baked" person also thinks his (typically) three to four years of formal schooling entitles him to white-collar employment. It is a comment reserved for young men, many of whom were originally school migrants from villages and who, though they have completed only a little bit of schooling, reject manual labor on farms; these youths were called "dead-end kids" by colonial administrators in the 1950s (Fanthorpe, personal communication, October 2006).[5] They insist instead on staying in the towns and looking for salaried jobs, and while they are unemployed spend their time drinking *poyo* (palm wine), smoking marijuana, and talking politics in the town's ghettos.[6]

When Sierra Leoneans speak of youths, they are primarily talking about young men. Socially and culturally, a girl achieves adulthood by getting married and becoming a mother, no matter her personal economic prospects. Male adulthood, on the other hand, is a performance of a youth's ability to achieve certain goals. A *man* is marked by the fact that he earns enough income to get married (including the bride price he must pay to his future in-laws) and support a family. While rejecting agriculture as a backward occupation of the illiterate, most young men turn to education and the prospect of waged work to achieve manhood. They flock to the urban areas, dutifully pursue education in order to enhance their prospects, and spend their time waiting for success to find them (see

5. Conversation with Dr. Richard Fanthorpe at the Upper Guinea Coast conference held at the Max Planck Institute, Halle, Germany, in October 2006. Dr. Fanthorpe is an independent consultant who has worked for the United Nations and is a visiting fellow in the Department of Anthropology at the University of Sussex.

6. This phenomenon is present around the world. Peel noted that in Yoruba society, the youth who were not successful academically "were not prepared to live in rural society or work on farms" and instead moved to the urban areas looking for white-collar jobs (Peel 1978, 157). Papua New Guinean villagers talk about *rubis* youth, particularly semieducated migrants, who do not help their villages, but instead drift from town to town, working some but mostly living off friends and kin (M. F. Smith 1994, 227). The attribution does not exist for girls, for whom the transition to adulthood is marked more gradually, with initiation and marriage, and is less dependent on their work status (see Cole 2005, 894).

Jeffrey 2010 for similarities in India). Of the fifty youths I interviewed in Makeni in 2010, forty-two were unemployed and "sitting down waiting" for a "sponsor" to either employ them or pay for them to further their education. They were waiting for big men to incorporate them into the system of patronage.

Youths become urban migrants as a result of the efforts of their social networks to educate them, and stay partially because of their unwillingness to accept rural poverty—and close proximity to a network that expects benefits from their investments—as preferable to urban poverty. This situation echoes Southall's discussion of the paradox of "modernity" in places where it has brought few benefits to either country or city life (Southhall 1988, 4): "The question of whether rural-urban migrants are better off in town is not a question of whether modern life has brought improvements in traditional life—which it should and could but in the vast majority of cases has not—but whether modern urban life, even at its lowest, offers more to migrants than can the modern oppressed, exploited, impoverished countryside." Migrants hope that urbanization means progress, not least by offering the chance to engage with cash-centered networks of the exchange economy as waged laborers. For many of these youths, the disappointment they suffer when they fail leads to time spent conversing angrily with others in the same situation about how the government of Sierra Leone—bastion of the nation's ultimate big men—has failed them.

In 2006 most adults perceived these youths to be criminally idle and unproductive. They were concerned that the youths thought too much of their schooling, and the resulting half-witted intellectual and social arrogance was dangerous. Even more dangerous was their strength in numbers. Sierra Leone is demographically one of the "youngest" nations on earth, with over 40 percent of the population below the age of fifteen, and over 70 percent below the age of thirty-five (IMF 2005). A "youth" is anyone under the age of thirty-five who has not yet succeeded in effecting a transition to adulthood; essentially, he lacks a job that would allow him to support a family (Shepler 2004, 11; see Utas 2005, 141, for similarities in Liberia). This category of liminality is predicated on the state of unemployment, so the youths were and continue to be, for all intents and purposes, a single-issue coalition: they want jobs, they want the social and financial security that jobs would provide, and therefore they want patrons who will provide them with these jobs. Their power in numbers and their demands have become one of the primary movers for the political *pul yu doŋ sindrom*. In their own words, youths feel they have "attached themselves to progress." They believe their educations and their votes entitle them to positions in the networks of powerful members of a modern society. They demand recognition as urbane actors, and that politicians, as "modern big men" (see Goheen 1992; reprint Young 2003, 102), fulfill their "obligations" to their like-minded supporters.

Why do young people who fail to complete an education also fail to return to their extant networks in rural areas? The disdain that most youths have for farming is not a new phenomenon, but it was not always so obviously tied to demands for jobs and respect as educated people. At first, the youths just wanted to participate in the offerings of the developed world, and many intended to use their training to promote community development. In addition, as Michael Jackson discovered in his fieldwork in northern Sierra Leone in the 1960s, children pursued education because it freed them from subsistence agriculture, where they worked "like slaves" (Jackson 2004, 149). Fanthorpe (personal communication, October 2006) and Peters (2004, 26–28; 2006, 40) found that in the years before the civil war, young people in rural areas were effectively slaves to chiefs and other big people. They were subjected to forced labor, could not marry for lack of money, and lived under the thumb of the powerful. This mutated form of patronage, which found its ultimate expression in "the shadow state," was one of the many reasons the RUF cited in its manifesto for its existence, and why young recruits volunteered as rebels in the early years of the war (Peters 2004 and 2006).

For young people in a newly independent nation, education presented itself as the enlightened exit from agriculture for children who wanted greater opportunities. Forty years later, opportunities to help one's country by pursuing white-collar occupations were not present for semieducated youths, who achieved only the first aim of leaving their villages and extricating themselves from the control of powerful village elders. The implication of this categorization is that when farming was removed as a viable option for supposedly education-enlightened youths, waged jobs became one of the few possible routes to adulthood. The irony of this development is that the youths were actively choosing the same subject position they eschewed in village life: the need to find a patron, a powerful big man who could provide these jobs.

These youths possessed a modicum of control over the direction of their lives and a willingness to engage with a larger political world on their own terms. The sense of danger that accompanied their activities and demands put extra pressure on the instrument of patronage to provide for them, and meant that the threat of violence, especially intergenerational violence, was omnipresent. These youths—poor, unemployed, without prospects— were "a node of energetic discontent" in the public arena when they chose to be visible (Bastian 2003, 77). Scott (1990, 19) refers to their activities as "infrapolitics," which Fatton describes as "a social space [beyond the visible spectrum] where subordinates develop their own discourse" (Fatton 1995, 68; see also Hoffman 2003, 297). By retreating into the town's ghettos and conversing in a place invisible to the rest of society, youths keep their politics below the radar, and emerge as and when they please. From the first of Freetown's *pote,* gathering places where youths smoked, drank, and talked, came the bulk of the city's street violence. The *rarray boys,* alienated youths who frequented these precursors to the ghettos, were known for their antisocial tendencies, including murder, even when they emerged for ostensibly political reasons (Abdullah 2005, 176–77). This situation has been replicated in many places in Africa, such as Congo-Brazzaville, where in the 1990s the private militias of politicians were comprised almost entirely of unemployed graduates and dropouts with ambitions of mass political mobilization (Bazenguissa-Ganga 1999; and Young 2003, 91).

The ghettos themselves are spaces that define and situate the invisible and dangerous conversations and activities that occur there. One of Makeni's main ghettos was at the time of this event located just off the town's main business thoroughfare. Its big man is a Rastafarian who called himself "Opa" or "Father." He arrived in town with the RUF in 1998, and "established my business" in the dark back alleys out of view of most people. The legitimate face of his business—that which made the ghetto acceptable to people during the occupation—was a public restroom complete with washing facilities that he built and maintained. People paid a few hundred leones to use the facilities, and therefore "they do not bother us much," he said, offering me some *poyo* and directing me to a space where about a dozen young men were lounging, drinking, and passing around a cigarette. Though Opa was not young, he defined the interface that is the ghetto: it is an integral part of public space, one that provides a service, even as people decry the activities of its clients as morally suspicious. It is in this marginal space that unemployed young people gather to talk politics, and it is here that the Union of Youth Groups was spawned.

The primary goal of the youths within a rubric of the progress of urbanization is nested in an essential paradox. They want to have full control over their work as educated people and show their disdain for the extant sociopolitical order by concealing their activities in the ghettos, but admit to needing "a hand under them"—in essence a patron—in order to begin their careers. Any return to agriculture, unless it is accompanied by a massive mechanical input of tractors, grain mills, and other forms of technology that would link agriculture with progress and education, is eschewed as undignified and unbecoming for educated people. And so the youths sat in the ghettos, idly chatting, deriding the politicians who promised them jobs and failed to deliver. In 2005, their conversations turned increasingly to the failings of the town council, and most specifically chairman Musa Mansaray. Youths were, in their own words, "responding to grumbling" within the council that he was taking too high-handed an approach with the rest of the council and the town, using his educated status to run both as his personal kingdom. This is not how a true leader should run a council. If he expected to stay in power, he needed to understand that voters were technically his "clients" to whom he owed respect and resources.

### Mansaray Fails to Make Patronage and Democracy Compatible

What follows is an account of how Musa Mansaray was toppled from the town council chairmanship. There are two interlinked reasons for this downfall. First, he was being too authoritarian in his ruling style, overseeing all aid projects himself and not giving other councilors enough, be that responsibility, oversight, or shares in the aid pot. Second, he was unwilling to accept responsibility for the private big man activities of his embezzling treasurer, who was all too happy to solidify his own patronage networks with aid funds. Mansaray's unwillingness to make aid and loans a network resource as well as a public good led to both his treasurer embezzling funds for himself and the rest of the council calling for his resignation instead of supporting him against accusations of misdeeds. When the news broke, youths who assumed that jobs would flow readily from the donor's investment organized a sit-down strike in Makeni in order to force Mansaray out. In essence, Mansaray was pulled down because he failed to make aid an accessible resource for everyone in the forms in which they desired it, namely, client rewards.

As most states in Africa are less than a century old, political leadership on a large scale is a relatively new phenomenon and fraught with discontinuities with older styles of leadership. Some political scientists see authoritarianism as an almost necessary component of political rule in Africa because the state is not structurally tied to society, making it impossible for a leader to exercise systematic power (see Hyden 1983; and Young 2003, 26). In Mozambique, Alexander (1997; and Young 2003, 189) found that people wanted leaders who were "educated but not too educated, wealthy but not too rich, local but not too local," so that they could deal with people fairly and compassionately, though also intelligently and dispassionately. Similar qualities were sought among Kumasi's female traders when leaders were needed to represent them politically, which was often in confrontation with a distant and uncaring state (Clark 1994, 276). It is a fine line to tread, and is indicative of the poor fit between historical forms of leadership that occurred on smaller, more easily circumscribed local scales, and the current need to elect leaders on the scale of towns, districts, and states. For whom do they serve as leaders, and to whom are they responsible? What form does this responsibility actually take?

Traditional patronage becomes poisoned and poisonous when it is forced to fit with externally imposed forms of governance, even as these forms—specifically democracy—are actively pursued by people as the governance panacea, indeed perhaps the highest form of human governance. Democracy's only resonance with patronage and social leveling is the requirement for accountability, even as each system defines to whom one must be accountable differently. Mansaray chose democracy, to his ultimate detriment.

In March 2006, news broke in the Freetown newspapers that Le85 million from the town council's development budget, which had been provided by a donor, could not be accounted for.[7] Culverts that could have been built for Le5 million were recorded as costing Le20 million, contracts were awarded to contractors without being put out to bid, and contracts were paid for in cash instead of checks requiring multiple signatures (Anonymous 2006a; Anonymous 2006b). The APC and SLPP parties and Mansaray himself each set up their own investigating committees. According to Mansaray, none of them found him "personally wanting." The money had gone missing, and though he was the chairman of the council while this occurred, none of the money had gone into his own pockets nor had he authorized its distribution. It seemed his treasurer was intent on securing his own status as a big man with his own personal networks of allies, clients, and contractors.

Why was this scandal blamed on Mansaray? According to rumor in the town, council members had to dodge the complaints of their own clients by diverting blame onto him. Even though they were not getting full salaries from the government, he was unwilling to loosen his control over the budget. Though no one stated directly that other councilors wanted to pay themselves, it was implied that they fought for places on committees that had larger budgets. Other reasons—more acceptably aired than pure patronage—were stated publicly. People grumbled that Mansaray was trying to sabotage the council because he was Mende, a tribe from the south (see Fanthorpe 2005, 44). He has a Mende father, though the senior Mansaray lived in Makeni from 1930 until his death in the 1990s. In addition, as one of his first acts as chairman, Mansaray had fired local council workers who had been drawing salaries for years without doing any work and failed to pay them redundancy (see Bolten 2008, 101). Clearly he did not care about the welfare of the people.

---

7. Sierra Leone's national currency is the leone, abbreviated Le. In 2006, the exchange rate was approximately Le3000 to 1 US dollar.

Mansaray steadfastly refused to step down, despite general demands for his resignation. He claimed that he was not personally responsible, and there were other members of the council, such as the procurement officer and the treasurer, to whom the fingers could point directly. Both were forced out of the council with little ceremony, but Mansaray remained (Anonymous 2006c). The rumors that he was disliked because he refused to allow needy council members to dip into council funds to fill their own needs seems contradictory to this accusation of corruption, namely, that he allowed other members of the council to dip into council funds full stop.[8] Nevertheless, it resonated with a general disapprobation of politicians in Sierra Leone who, as Shaw discovered in her conversations with diviners, are castigated for "consum[ing] the foreign aid intended for the poorest people of Sierra Leone, arresting the flow of benefits which 'big persons' are expected to channel to their community" (Shaw 1996, 39). Money was expected to flow through the council to the community, from the biggest person, Mansaray, through other council members, to the townspeople. What was unacceptable was that the money stopped flowing at a high level within the council (see Bayart 1993, 233; Jackson 2006, 107).

Mansaray's refusal to resign was greeted with outrage because, as the largest big man on the council, he was responsible for everything that occurred. Former supporters, including Ibrahim Kargbo (the then editor of *The New Citizen* and, after the 2007 elections, the Minister of Information), called publicly for his removal. Ernest Koroma, who became president of Sierra Leone in 2007, was at the time the national leader of the APC, Mansaray's own political party, and threatened to expel him from the party if he did not resign. Still he refused, citing the fact that no accusations of corruption could be traced back to him, that he was, in the words of one of my interlocutors, "an honest man surrounded by thieves." Mansaray's own

8. The use of the word "corruption" is limited in this article because I feel strongly that it has become fetishized among academics and policy wonks when describing politics in Africa (see Hasty 2005, 271), to the detriment of real understanding of the mechanism and function of political patronage. Therefore I limit it here to its use in actual fact by people describing the pulling down of the chairman. "Corruption" in Sierra Leone can mean, quite basically, "someone who does not share enough."

perception of his position as a political big man in a democracy, namely, one who is responsible to fellow council members and voters only with respect to his production of public good, though technically "honest," was incongruent with councilors' perceptions of their own needs as his clients.

At this point, the Makeni Union of Youth Groups, composed of youths who had urged residents to vote for him two years earlier, called for a sit-down strike to protest. For one day the market was closed, no motorcycle taxis operated, and traders stayed home (Anonymous 2006d). Mansaray received numerous death threats that day, and so announced that he was stepping down (and moved his family out of Makeni), though he emphasized that he did not resign because he was guilty, but rather in the interest of maintaining peace in the township (Anonymous 2006e; Anonymous 2006f; Gbenda 2006). The success of the strike was not simply due to the political will or persuasive powers of the youths; rather this was the last brick removed from the dam, releasing a political tide that was already in motion. As Scott states, "Events that weaken the power of dominant groups are analogous to the weakening of a dam wall; thereby permitting more of the hidden transcript to leak through and increasing the possibility of a complete rupture" (Scott 1990, 219), even though, as the journalist Theophilus Gbenda noted, it was accomplished through "undemocratic means" (Gbenda 2006), thus undermining the legitimacy of the exercise.

According to several people, the turn on Mansaray had nothing to do with his honesty or capacity to run the council; rather, the youths' anger at their continued inability to succeed economically led them to believe outrageous rumors about his personal involvement in the embezzlement. The critics of the "half-baked youths" stated that the curse of having a town replete with the "half-baked" was that in the absence of reliable information or the education to think intelligently about information, the majority of people heard what they wanted to hear. Other councilors, angry at Mansaray's refusal to create a patronage network from his position, refused to protect him from popular wrath and encouraged the youths with rumors. Enraged at their inability to succeed in spite of the promise of a council flush with donor funds and making big development promises, the half-baked youths consumed the rumors of undemocratic dealings and pulled him down on these grounds. This was not a democratic state dealing with internal corruption, this was a patronage network rocked by one politician's will to operate in a democracy rather than use democracy to fund patronage. The intractability of the relationship between democracy and patronage was so apparent that even former Vice President Solomon Berewa admitted to embezzling funds from the national treasury. He explained his actions in a church meeting in Makeni by stating that he knew he would not be able to maintain his position forever. Therefore, he had to squeeze as much personal benefit out of the vice president's office as possible before he was deposed.

The actions of the "half-baked" resonates with researchers who pronounce "civil society" movements, especially in Africa, to not be "civil" at all (see Edelman 2001, 302). Ikelegbe states that many civil society movements in Nigeria have become "so parochial, divisive, divergent and disarticulative that they actually undermine democracy," often on platforms of ethnic militancy and violent confrontation with the state (Ikelegbe 2001, 1). Fatton (1995, 73) noted that the "big men" who lead movements in Nigeria seek to ally with or join the state, not to reform it, and Alexander (1997; and Young 2003, 182) found the same was true for civil society leaders in postindependence Mozambique. In Burundi, citizens do not trust the neutrality of civil society organizations, which are usually politically aligned and thus politically manipulative (Ngosi 2006, 236). In Makeni, this particular movement was inarticulate and poorly informed, but through anger and force of numbers it cowed the educated residents into silence and succeeded in challenging the populace to confront the council, even though it came to light that it was other would-be big men, those who did not attempt to be accountable within a democracy, who silently orchestrated Mansaray's downfall and ultimately benefited. The marriage of democracy and patronage, it seems, was more poisoned even than it appeared.

### Wither Big Men? Or, Are There Honest Politicians in Sierra Leone?

The paramount chief of the district was pleased that the new civil society movement was so vibrant that it succeeded in bringing down a corrupt politician. From his perspective, any civil society movement that is able to force political change is forcing the state to become more responsive to its people, thereby increasing its legitimacy (see Barkan, McNulty, and Ayeni 1991, 459–60). And the new council was better because it was shaped directly by the people and did not overstep its bounds. The chief liked the fact that the new council chairman was not trying to wrest power away from traditional authorities by framing himself as the authoritarian "leader" of Makeni, as he perceived Mansaray had done (see Fanthorpe 2005, 47). This council was finally falling in line with the reasons the United Nations had initially argued for the reinstatement of town and district councils after the war, namely, that they would "aid in the restoration of the beneficial role of the paramount chiefs and other native authorities" (Owusu 1997, 139). Owusu states outright that the United Nations was complicit in allowing patronage and democracy to continue as parallel and interlinking institutions. This begs the question: did the United Nations and donor organizations ever speak about their expectations for governance and use of aid? Or did donor organizations automatically assume that all democratic instruments run according to Western expectations?

The paramount chief was asked by the new chairman to appoint an advisor to the council among the older politicians so that it would not go astray in the future. The paramount chief chose his cousin, whom I will call "Abraham," for this position. I first met Abraham in 2003 when he was serving as the chief's representative in the latter's absence from town. When I arrived back in Makeni in 2004 after a year's absence, Abraham was not speaking to his cousin because he felt that the chief, loyal to one party, had deliberately sabotaged his own campaign with the other party to become a member of the new council. When, on my neighbor's advice, I sought them out in the wake of the council scandal in 2006, I found them lunching together in the chief's house. The chief had extended the olive branch in the form of a political appointment to his estranged cousin, and it had been accepted. Indeed, the paramount chief was a savvy enough politician to understand the branches of his own network that he needed to keep intact.

Abraham called Mansaray "a crook of the highest degree," and a man he had never trusted. He made this pronouncement even though two years earlier, at the inauguration, Abraham confided to me that Mansaray, as a highly educated man, was the best choice to run the council, and had supported him during his first two years. When the embezzlement scandal erupted, Abraham launched his own investigation and decided that Mansaray was personally responsible for LE80 million of the missing money. He asked Mansaray to repay the missing money and the latter refused; as a representative of the APC, he also suffered Mansaray's refusal to leave the party. Abraham then discussed how under the APC party constitution, the party can call for a politician's resignation in cases of corruption. However, because Mansaray argued that he was not corrupt, he could not be brought down under that clause. Failing to convince Mansaray to resign, Abraham planted the "grumbling" among the Makeni Union of Youth Groups and encouraged them to stage a strike. In the end he gained a position of power on the council that he was originally, and he felt unjustly, denied. He supported the new town council chairman, around whose financial activities in the council rumors were already swirling. "The other councilors do not like him," said my neighbor, "and they will pull him down too." Perhaps the grumbling around the new town council chairman had to do with his personal networks extending to the paramount chief, widely perceived as a powerful rival of democratic authority and interested in dismantling the council full stop. From where, then, would aid money flow?

One cannot know the truth of what happened with the missing money, who was to blame, and in whose pockets it ended up. Everyone in the town took a side on this issue; many did so simply to air grudges, or to express their dislike of someone who was too powerful and who did not share the benefits with his constituents, either in the form of jobs, contracts, or kickbacks. As Chabal and Daloz state, politicians only succeed in Africa if they are both wealthy and generous enough to keep their positions (Chabal and Daloz 1999, 34–35). Those who do not appear to be credible patrons do not last long in office, even if they are openly trying to clean up political offices and initiate development. By failing to maintain any balance in this regard, Musa Mansaray, "corrupt" or not, was not conforming to expectations that he would run the council to the direct benefit of the greatest number of clients, including both other council members and the wider community, and extending to the youths. The youths in this case, though acting in the public space, were what Diouf calls "stakes"; that is, the "civil society" movement sought to capture the youths and use them to proclaim success in the endeavor of pulling down the chairman (Diouf 2005, 229). The youths do not have any positive power in this situation, as they do not have jobs that would allow them to build their own networks. They hoped that by exposing themselves as active participants, they would prove worthy as potential clients to would-be patrons. They organized the strike, the death threats, and the potential for violence not as an act of righteous indignation in defense of democracy, but rather to reveal themselves to other politicians in the town as worth having in their own networks. They wanted patronage incorporation, with or without democracy.

Is civil society an effective alternative to corrupt states? I agree with Fatton that this is not possible, though our reasons are different. He states, "crippled by material limitations and class impairments it [civil society] constitutes at best a very uncertain substitute to what had previously been the corrupt and class-based patronage of a more profligate state" (Fatton 1995, 72). I argue instead that civil society movements like the "half-baked youths" in Sierra Leone actually comprise a search for belonging to patronage networks using the instruments and language of a democratic state. In short, the youths were not interested in overhauling a "corrupt" town council, they merely wanted someone in charge who might consider them. The angry, unemployed, uneducated youths did have the power as a voting and acting bloc to topple a man who clearly was not interested in being a personal patron, but they could do nothing above that except hope that someone more congenial to their needs would replace him. The linking of patronage with democracy in the absence of sufficient resources has created an impossible mutant: aid must be both personal and public, leaders both honest and good patrons, and their clients are also their constituents. Civil society movements do not coalesce around democracy, because democracy itself has no power aside from choosing the person who will distribute resources. Democracy here is merely elections: an instrument, an event around which the setting up and pulling down of big men occurs.

It is here that we return to the question of what makes a big man in present-day Sierra Leone, and what effect the persistence of patronage networks as a main organizing social principle will have on the future of democracy and development in the nation. Can big men run democratic governments that are largely aid-driven? As Fatton states, democracy is impossible without the empowerment of subordinate classes (1995, 89; also Monga 1995, 375), but in the case of places with strong patronage histories, what form should the empowerment of the subordinate classes take? President Siaka Stevens ran Sierra Leone for over twenty years as his personal patronage network, rewarding loyalty and punishing dissent, and using the country's resources as his own personal power base, William Reno's "shadow state" (1995). After successfully turning the country into a one-party state on the pretense that the traditional Sierra Leonean value of "unity" should be emphasized over a divisive imported system of multiparty democracy, his cronyism pushed the country to the brink of a war that exploded under his weak successor, Joseph Momoh. The perpetrators of war were largely those marginalized individuals who had been left or pushed out of the system.

In the aftermath, the call for democracy as a tonic for a country ailing under bloated patronage politics meant the reinstitution of elected town councils. However, within two years, two of three councils in the provinces were crippled by embezzlement scandals involving aid money, and democracy was left to prove itself as a viable system once again. It is clear from the political history of Sierra Leone that patronage masquerading as democracy cannot bring a country out of poverty, but would shedding democracy and returning to "honest" patronage provide for the incorporation of the most marginal, those most prone to airing grievances through force and violence? Would a democracy continually thwarted by patrimonialism be seen as viable by the donor countries that currently prop up the government?

### Usurping the Big Man: Harnessing *Metis* in Social Welfare

The way out of this conundrum may be deeply unpopular with champions of the combined electoral democracy and aid as a postwar cure-all package. According to Moyo, democracy is only a stable and enduring political form in countries that already possess economic stability (Moyo

2009, 42). She suggests a "benevolent dictator" model for African countries; someone who can push through economic reform before democratic elections are instituted. Though I would not go that far, in Sierra Leone and other countries with big men patronage systems and fragile postwar democracies, I suggest that one must start with a different perspective on who has the ability to create development, what constitutes this development, and what structures must initially be in place to promote it. I argue that an effective approach would synthesize Amartya Sen's argument that development can only occur when certain "unfreedoms"—physical and social constraints to self-developing activities—are removed by donors emphasizing social welfare in postwar contexts (Richmond 2008, 289). In addition, donors must support localized development directly through funding creative, cooperative economic systems born of practical experience, what James Scott (1998, 6) refers to as *metis*. In a peacebuilding context, it is critical to emphasize that working economies create the foundation for democratic government apparatuses that can support public works, and not the other way around.

The first task is taking the onus for economic development off of elected officials in fledgling democratic structures. As this chapter has shown, even honest politicians are subject to the strong arm of patronage, and asking them to use donor money to support essential functions often means that the critical foundations of development are left languishing. Those structures that comprise "unfreedoms" in postwar contexts—the decrepit hospitals, sewage-choked streets, and nonexistent agricultural infrastructure—must be considered basic tenets of social welfare for which the donor interested in a "liberal peace" is responsible, and must therefore be funded and supervised directly by donors for many years following a war. If people—no matter their poverty level—can go about their lives knowing that they can see a doctor and obtain medicine, that they will not succumb to infectious diseases regularly, and that food is affordable, they now have the freedom to pursue their individual economic strategies. In my own work in Makeni, people often cited the inability to see a doctor when ill or injured as the primary reason agriculture was languishing. Donor intervention with hospitals and roads supports agriculture indirectly, without involving a town council whose members have interested constituents/clients among the agricultural community. As Richmond observes, welfare-enabled local development proves to the international community that the "culture of corruption" so often observed in Africa in particular (see D. J. Smith 2007) is not a result of some intrinsic cultural flaw, but rather is the result of poverty (Richmond 2008, 290).

Having provided the community with the *freedom* to pursue economic development, donors may then harness *metis* to *support* economic activity by investing in locally created, small-scale, and clearly worthy people-driven projects (see also Easterly 2006). Makeni's inhabitants have their own ideas of what would make their lives better, and this never includes more money for governance structures. There are alternatives to the patronage system, and these include traditional rotating credit organizations, community-based cooperative agriculture, and cooperative artisanal workshops. By acknowledging the value of extant economic systems that oppose the patronage ethos, donors can prove that these alternatives are not only possible, but are also productive long-term strategies.

The emphasis on supporting *metis* does not mean instituting microfinance programs. Bateman (2008) provides ample evidence that emphasizing individual entrepreneurship as the silver bullet for postwar development actually undermines the ability of communities to create sustainable economies. Rather, donors would encourage those cooperative ventures—particularly emphasizing the collective activities of women and youths—that provide evidence of the potential for long-term development: the community agriculture organization needing seeds, tools, and support for several years until it achieves sustainable harvest; the association of motorcycle taxi drivers needing tools and training in mechanics so it can continue to provide cheap and reliable transportation for traders and farmers; the female traders needing capital to start a wholesale business. These sustainable, self-organized ventures should become targets for development money not just because they are viable alternatives to patronage, but also because they contribute to the welfare of the township, and thus enable development for all.

The impetus for this approach should be clear. First, deemphasizing the economic role of politicians—whose domain would be active engagement with legal, political, and constitutional reform, budgeting projects with money from their own national government, and limited engagement with external monetary inputs—would release individuals from the social pressure of trying to be patrons as they are politicians. In the words of Pugh, Cooper, and Turner, "donors must not give a corrupt state any chance to reassert itself" (2008b, 2). Those who intend to use political position as a conduit for becoming economically "big" would be discouraged, and perhaps a new brand of politician would emerge. Second, by giving everyone who can organize around a project—be it a business, a service, artisanal work, or food production—a chance to apply for money directly from donors, the drive to find and pressure would-be political big men to be economic patrons disappears. Groups of women, youths, farmers, businessmen, or anyone who has a viable proposal they can pitch to a local representative can have access to donor money.

This approach would also allow fairer competition in the business workplace. Contractors, keen to hire workers to build a road (and on which they could collect a small toll for loan repayment and maintenance), could also apply for loans. Businesses that formerly had to bid and bribe their way into work using their patronage networks could compete honestly to contribute to development. There is a greater likelihood of achieving gender justice as women's organizations have independent access to funds and are liberated from dependence on men to support them and their children (see Pankhurst 2008, 40). Combined with donor support of schools, education could become a viable development tool, and thus ease the socially troubling phenomenon of the "half-baked." Most important, those individuals, especially youths, whose political and economic toolkit is currently limited to social leveling or civil violence, would be given the opportunity to organize themselves productively. Once the economic foundation is in place, governments, and therefore democracy itself, would not be as susceptible to patronage politics. People who can stand on their own two feet do not need patrons, and those would-be clients who currently pressure likely patrons with their demands would disappear. With "unfreedoms" removed and sustainable dreams supported, everyone has the chance to improve their own lives, and the reasons to be a patron, let alone to pull one down, will, with time, disappear.

# Part Three

# Peacebuilding from Below

*Opportunities and Challenges*

# 7

# Peacebuilding as a Transformative and Deliberative Process

## James Bohman

An important and developing feature of contemporary democracy is free and open deliberation, on the basis of which it becomes possible to institutionalize processes of constant change and renewal. While deliberation has many other functions within a political system, one of its important functions is to establish and maintain social peace in cases of conflict. Applying this idea at the transnational level is fraught with difficulties. Even in democracies, violence leads to the suspension of the political process, often at the cost of handing over much of self rule to executive power, with the consequence that democracies can become dominators not only of others but also of their own citizens. Often this process is made possible by negotiations involving various elites or leaders closed from public view. Having excluded the public in order to make the process more open and impartial, such deliberations lack important sources of legitimacy and may even exacerbate festering conflicts.

Needless to say, it may be very difficult to initiate such processes after long-term conflict. This deficit of legitimacy, the overcoming of which is necessary for peace, can only be overcome by popular, deliberative, and multi-track peacebuilding. Peacebuilding must not only be deliberative; it must also involve the publics of each party in any conflict, lest it lack legitimacy. In cases of conflict, this sort of deliberative process cannot simply involve a small group of elites, nor even a small group of citizens, such as elected representatives or "minipublics," the term for a select group of citizens who make recommendations or decisions on behalf of others. Such political mechanisms of representation require already settled institutions if they are to deal successfully with societal grievances. Rather, postconflict peacebuilding requires difficult, crosscutting, macrodeliberative processes. This important kind of deliberation has not often been discussed by deliberative democrats. My argument aims to show that modern peacebuilding is a macro-deliberative process in three main steps. First, it is clear that the use of deliberative bodies enhances democratic legitimacy in a variety of ways, but in particular in cases of democratic reform. Indeed, peacebuilding as a form of democratic renewal must be legitimate along three dimensions: the process must become formally, deliberatively, and popularly legitimate across communities. But even this kind of legitimacy may be insufficient for the macro-deliberation necessary in many cases of peacebuilding. When confined to states, such processes are undermined by the structural features that lead to contests of sovereignty, in which one party succeeds at the cost of another, even if they occupy the same political space. This leads to my second main argument. As crosscutting, this political space in which peacebuilding occurs is transnational, and works when something analogous to "international society" emerges. The English School of International Relations used the term "international society" to describe a kind of normative order that is not based on an overarching authority. But "transnational society" may be the more apt term, precisely because such a normative order emerges as involving a variety of societies, groups, and individuals rather than sovereign states (Bohman 2007).

The third dimension of successful peacebuilding concerns the role of civil society. While transnational spaces necessarily include publics and civil society as constitutive of them, peacebuilding requires organizations that act as purveyors of publicity and intermediaries that cut across the parties and mediate the creation of new societal bonds through processes of deliberation. These types of intermediaries have included the Women's International League for Peace and Freedom founded after WWI and the World Social Forum, which seek to establish not only publicity but also the conditions of collective agency needed for peacebuilding. In order for peacemaking to become a deliberative process, intermediaries like these are necessary, as can be illustrated in various successful processes of peacebuilding, such as those that occurred in Northern Ireland. Given the need for society-wide or macro-deliberation, a more complex conception of transnational political legitimacy is required if we are to understand why such processes of peacemaking succeed, sometimes even in the face of deeply entrenched conflicts. The World Social Forum offers us a transnational understanding of peacebuilding based on processes of translation and mutual understanding that make it possible to promote more comprehensive and inclusive alternatives.

### Democratically Legitimate Reform

In order to explore a conception of transnational political legitimacy related to peacemaking, it is helpful to turn to other transnational cases of politically legitimate reform. Various polities distribute the capacity to reform themselves differently. In the existing structure of the European Union, for example, power to initiate reform is shared by the member states primarily through the Council of the European Union. Rather than democratic appeals to the will of the people, the Council relies in the first instance on institutional problem-solving capacity or effectiveness, which Fritz Scharpf has dubbed "outcome legitimacy" (1999). Outcome legitimacy is quite typical for traditional diplomacy and negotiations, since the point of such processes is to reach some outcome that is the basis of a modus vivendi. The case for peacebuilding as a deliberative process is precisely that it aims at the transformation of conflict rather than a modus vivendi. As deliberative, peacebuilding demands an overlapping consensus that provides the basis for a democratic settlement that is more than the end of hostility.

With the aim of transformation in mind, other forms of legitimacy become more salient. The *formal legitimacy* of any process of reform, including peacemaking, is found in the institutional authority to initiate it, through specified authority as in the case of the Truth and Reconciliation Commission in South Africa. Formal legitimacy is often required in order that peacebuilding be institutionalized. *Popular legitimacy* emerges to the extent that "the People" have genuine opportunities to shape or assent to such reform, minimally the popular ratification of proposed changes or amendments, and that these opportunities are common knowledge among citizens. In cases of conflict, popular legitimacy may not easily be attained without altering the distribution of power among social groups. Finally, democratic reform has *deliberative legitimacy*, to the extent that citizens (or their representatives) offer reasons to one another in a process of mutual justification. Deliberation promotes legitimacy when it is taken not just to be addressed to those who are doing the actual deliberation, but to all citizens insofar as it makes manifest the democratic features of the process. Of course, lingering hostility makes it likely that some citizens may not be willing to deliberate with their former enemies, at least not immediately.

An alternative might be to use some sort of random selection procedure of citizen representatives, such as the one used in the highly successful Citizens' Assembly in British Columbia. At the same time, this and other similar bodies are usually oriented to a very specific task, in this case a change in electoral systems. Macro-deliberative bodies are self-organizing and have very different goals, often generating them on their own. In any case they do not seek merely to settle particularly contentious issues, but rather to create the conditions that make it possible that they will be dealt with in a mutually acceptable way. Thus, macro-deliberation has broader goals than can be captured by some issue or even a set of issues, since its task is to create the conditions for deliberation rather than deliberation itself. Of course, such a process is itself deliberative, but not in a problem-solving sense. Rather, deliberation here begins the exchange of points of view and grievances, without which there can be no overlapping consensus that is transnational. In order to have macro-deliberation sufficient for peacebuilding, various deliberative forums and other institutions must emerge that publicly engage all sides, such as in some truth and reconciliation commissions.

As a constructed public (or, more precisely, a minipublic (Fung 2003, 338–67)), the Citizens' Assembly used its delegated popular authority by deliberating as citizen-representatives on behalf of the people, whose political will could best be formed under the more ideal conditions that were fulfilled in the assembly's deliberation (especially considering the complexities of various voting systems). The force of such a claim must be tested when the powers of the assembly are transferred back to the public as a whole. In order to secure popular as well as deliberative legitimacy, the assembly's proposal had to be voted on by *all* citizens. But macro-deliberation does not generate popular legitimacy as much as generate the conditions for reestablishing such legitimacy. Such groups or movements seek to create a basic minimum of democracy. The democratic minimum is based in the achievement of an important democratic power that belongs to all citizens, the capacity to change the existing legal order itself (including rights, duties, and boundaries), and in so doing reorder it so as to achieve the necessary conditions for securing nondomination. Macro-deliberation used in peacebuilding seeks to move civil society socially from domination to the nondomination needed for political legitimacy, security, and trust.

In order to bring about such secure nondomination, two forms of status are required for democratization that results from peacebuilding as a process. The first such status is the "communicative freedom" of members of publics, a form of freedom that may take on a constructive role by which members grant one another rights and duties in their roles as participants in the public sphere. Communicative freedom depends on this public status, which under the right institutional circumstances can become "communicative power," or decisional status shared with others. By acquiring such communicative freedom beyond the control of even a disaggregated authority, membership in a public uses the creative and constructive powers of communication and public opinion to reshape the operations of authority. For this reason publics have a special role in processes of democratization, so long as participants see themselves as addressing others and being addressed by them in turn. This communicative status allows each to exercise a two-way democratic power. Such communicative status allows not just that each member can address all other members, but that they also are addressed by others who have this same power. For this reason, communicative freedom can be transformed into communicative power, a decisional status the basis of which is the capacity not merely to contest what the powerful decide but also to share in that power with others to the extent that the procedure or context is democratic. However, the internal deliberative legitimacy achieved procedurally among participants does not automatically extend to those who have not participated in it. It is clear then that the procedures used to increase the deliberative legitimacy of democratic reform may fail to attain the proper threshold of popular legitimacy and are furthermore subject to the same sort of veto by others who may be outside the deliberative process.

By putting all these aspects of legitimacy together, a much more complex and demanding picture of democratic reform emerges. Even if institutions are in place that structure decision-making processes, they may not be sufficient to permit the democratic threshold to be met. In situations of conflict, the formal institutions may fail to create the conditions by which public deliberation can be the means to make decisions that are widely seen as legitimate. In some cases, conflict may undermine the efficacy of the formal structure to make fair decisions. Missing in this account thus far is some measure of the legitimacy of the system as a whole, and in the case of conflict the fault may not lie so much in the design of formal institutions. Instead, peace is required for the democratic process, and this is based not just on institutional structure, but also on the existence of something like a transnational society, in which various kinds of norms of interaction and communicative statuses are developed and exercised across social and political differences. I call this "transnational society" because the kind of peace that it produces does not require strong forms of solidarity or shared civil identity in order to promote deliberation and communicative action among its members. Constructivists have argued that various norms and forms of communication have evolved over time to regulate various kinds of interaction. Thomas Risse and Kathryn Sikkink have shown that there is indeed a high degree of communicative action and persuasion in international politics even without shared, authoritative institutions[1] (Risse and Sikkink 1999, 7–8). When peace is absent, even within a state, it is precisely these presuppositions of society that fail to hold and need to be re-created not only for democracy to prevail, but also

---

1. They discuss the ways in which human rights norms transform domestic regimes.

for peace to be established on an equitable basis. This may be true, as in the case of Northern Ireland, even without the formal political system (here the Westminster system) being in some way inherently unjust.

For this reason we may say that even within a state with a relatively successful form of democracy, peacebuilding is a task for which such settled democratic institutions are often not particularly well designed. While minipublics may work to establish trust under such a settlement, peacebuilding will likely not be so effective if it is confined to micro-level institutions. Such institutions may often be important at various stages in the process (particularly later), but macro-deliberation has a different and more demanding structure, since deliberators may not yet stand in settled social relations with one another, much less shared democratic citizenship. Nonetheless, deliberative peacebuilding requires that participants take the step of granting one another the same communicative freedom and communicative power if it is to be successful. The post-conflict situation is not yet a polity so much as a developing transnational society. Democracy is as much a consequence of peace as its cause, making macro-level deliberation more effective as a means to attain the self-reinforcing benefits of democratic deliberation. When democratic institutions fail to address such problems and conflicts, they may even work against peacebuilding in the way that they divide up powers and influence according to old antagonisms. By cutting across such cleavages, transnationalizing macro-deliberation is better suited to creating new norms and practices that reconstruct the social and political bases for mutual peace. Of course, one such basis may be mutual separation, but this is often asymmetrical in the distribution of the benefits and burdens, and may thus only exacerbate the problem. Even this solution, should it be mutually acceptable, will require macro-deliberation if it is to build peace rather than more conflict.

## Inclusion and Dialogue in Transnational Society

In the previous section, I have argued that there are limits to the formal institutional legitimacy of democracy in postconflict situations; in the absence of a layer of transnational society, it is difficult to give democracy the credit for social peace. In cases in which such social peace has already broken down, macro-deliberation and social interaction across the conflicting parties may serve to create shared norms and forms of communicative action that develop over time. It is in this terrain of transnational society that a dialogue about peace and justice is often located, even in the absence of effective institutions that cut across cleavages, such as those found in religious pluralism as an important and increasingly common cause of social conflict. As the case of religion shows, we should not give credit to constitutions as uniquely able to solve conflicts, since most liberal democratic constitutions generally presuppose religious conflict is already solved. Jürgen Habermas seems to think that religious pluralism requires a postsecular order that makes demanding claims on its participants, so that religious groups must already be subject to those normative requirements that are necessary for any such pluralistic endeavor, including the acceptance of human rights, religious freedom for all, and some form of the separation of church and state (Habermas 2008, 111).[2]

A postsecular order on this view simply presupposes social peace is consistent with broad religious pluralism. If religions were the source of the conflict, a dialogue on national peace and justice could succeed only as transreligious and deliberative peacebuilding. In many cases, transnational society could simply entrench rather than transform the opposition into one between secular Western elites on the one hand and religiously motivated opposition to a secular order. As an alternative, John Rawls and Allen Buchanan offer a more restricted set of requirements for participation in democratic society, excluding only those who do not respect a basic list of human rights. But religious contributions to deliberation cannot be left out because they are not shared, particularly when they are precisely what are at issue, nor should we in these cases regard macro-deliberation as simply confined to the informal public sphere, nor can demands for inclusion and the accessibility of reasons be decided prior to deliberation without argumentation losing its point (Cooke 2007, 228–29).

---

2. See also Jürgen Habermas, *Europe: The Faltering Project* (Cambridge: Polity Press, 2009), 59.

For these reasons, it is a mistake to think of peacebuilding as merely a byproduct of interaction between constitutional institutions and the informal public sphere. Such legal mechanisms and public spheres function properly only if they are not fragmented, as it is in cases of societal conflict. These problems of inclusion look different if macro-deliberation takes place at the level of transnational society, where there is an absence of settled formal institutions whose authority seems to suggest exercising strong constraints on deliberation about conflicts. Indeed, the state structure often produces contests over which the majority will effectively occupy the position of the sovereign and make its conception of social order authoritative. But rather than specific substantive commitments, we might argue with Habermas that what is required is a shared awareness of reflexive modernity on all sides, even if this modernization is now no longer always conjoined with secularization. How might the idea of transnational society help us consider macro-deliberation about religious conflict and the idea of a postsecular political order?

When thought of in the strategic terms of standard realism, the absence of any overarching political authority means that international society is in anarchy; but if it is organized as a society, even if initially a society of states, it is governed by some shared norms, discourses, and practices that have developed over time to regulate interactions and various domains of action. By civilizing conflict and by regulating through norms, international society puts a high premium on reaching understanding and shared deliberation. For example, as many international regimes give a greater role to participation and transparency, decisions must be oriented to the whole public (Payne and Samhat 2004, 6). According to John Dryzek, this situation marks a shift away from predetermined norms to engaging in discourse (such as in discussions of sustainability), which now become "the means to coordinate and structure actions and interactions"(2009).[3] Absent a sovereign, such deliberation does not necessarily issue in an authoritative decision. Even so, deliberative processes

---

3. Also John Dryzek, *Deliberative Global Politics* (Cambridge: Polity Press, 2008).

have often shaped the norms of international society, such as when the international community agreed to abolish the slave trade. In these cases, communicative status in the global public sphere over time became shared decisional status, even if these processes are rather slow when compared to legislation.

In this respect, peacebuilding refers to one sort of transnational deliberative process that aims at creating conditions and norms of trust and equity among long-time enemies, such as the Protestants and Catholics in Northern Ireland. While peace processes are often thought of as negotiations by both participants and observers alike, they also demand deliberation and have a highly deliberative goal: the transformation of the beliefs and preferences that sustain situations of conflict. Typically initiated among relatively small groups, peace processes that create the official agreements are kept from public view and carried on by agreements among the elites of the conflicting parties. While such forms of secrecy are useful for deliberation when conflicts are deep, such cases are normatively limited. Indeed, it cannot be assumed that the deliberative legitimacy attained internally to the deliberating group will transfer easily to the members of the larger public sphere who have not deliberated and remain in conflict. Rather, what begins as small group deliberation across the conflict must become multi-track, macro-level deliberation in a variety of forums and forms of communication from everyday talk to formal parliamentary debates, and from informal to empowered public spaces, all of which aim in the first instance at producing mutually recognized statuses with varying degrees of decisional authority. Such a macro-public space might house a variety of civil society groups, designed citizen forums, or transnational activist groups, and more; but to enable its transformative goal at least some of them must think of themselves as "purveyors of publicity" and "intermediaries" for macro- or society-wide deliberation if there are to be successful public capacities to build peace. Peacebuilding of this deliberative sort creates a transnational society, however narrow or wide, with an eye to converting the communicative freedom of publics into the communicative power of peaceful and stable institutions.

The attempt to create peace by transnationalizing solutions to the deep local conflicts has long characterized Northern Ireland. As Daniel

Wehrenfennig argues, what was distinctive about the Northern Ireland case was that "a continuous, multilevel dialogue process has been a key factor in the successful peace process" and its aftermath (2008, 356–75). By contrast, the Israel/Palestine peace process has achieved no such stable dialogue process or transnational framework. Peace networks created in the Northern Ireland case aimed at such a multilevel dialogue and formed peace networks with strong links across local, regional, national and global level actors. What is distinctive in this case is the way in which a multireligious networked public began to shift toward a more shared, transnational perspective. This was particularly evident in the joining together of Protestant and Catholic women's groups to make common cause against violence. As these new forms of political cooperation and new types of campaigning and arguments developed over time, they also provided the context for the emergence of shared values and aims. The extensiveness of these ties at various levels of society in Northern Ireland was crucial in pushing the formal negotiators toward a resolution to long-term and seemingly intractable zero-sum impasses.

As this example shows, the fundamental condition for creating a transnational society is communicative freedom; without which there is no possibility for initiating transnational interaction across borders. Communicative freedom is not primarily exercised within states alone, but is a common form of nonstate membership, the membership in a public or civil society that is a matter of mutual recognition tied to communicative and social status. Having such a space is the first step for the beginning of democratic control over such membership and the discourses within it. Communicative freedom is tied to a particular, reciprocally recognized informal communicative status that is the necessary condition for having a public sphere at all. Participants create a space for communicative freedom to the extent that they regard themselves as a public and interact with one another accordingly. It establishes what could be called a "two-way power," the normative power to both address claims to others and to be so addressed by them. In the first instance, a public sphere institutionalizes a particular kind of social relationship between persons and makes it possible to achieve a similar relation between the public and political authority. By acquiring such communicative freedom beyond the control of even a disaggregated authority, membership in a public uses the creative and constructive powers of communication and public opinion to reshape the operations of their authority. When it transforms the situation of conflict, communicative freedom becomes communicative power, that is, the power to make decisions that change the structure of the conflict. This possibility requires that transnational forms of social organization emerge within the public sphere, the purpose of which is not to use the public sphere as a means to political ends, but rather to realize the necessary conditions of publicity that make it possible for conflicting parties to grant each other a shared communicative status. This process is not spontaneous, but requires that some group or groups act as intermediaries within the public sphere as necessary purveyors of publicity where it does not exist. Intermediaries are especially necessary in situations of deep conflict. But these intermediaries emerge not from the outside, but rather, as the Northern Ireland case shows, from members of the conflicting groups who have come to regard transnational society as the open space for deliberative engagement with the aim of peacebuilding.

## Purveyors of Publicity

In the current system of global governance, states play a diplomatic role in conflicts, and leave it to nongovernmental organizations (NGOs) to act as surrogate publics, often attempting to expand the scope of those who can influence decision-making and to act to ensure some accountability. This role in the public sphere is played, as for example, when environmental groups monitor compliance to pollution and whaling regimes and represent environmental interests in discussions and negotiations of the regime's rules and policies. This kind of intermediation and representation connected to formal regimes is an important function of transnational society, but it is not the means by which communicative action could be employed to overcome differences that block deliberation. By contrast, some civil society organizations move from being facilitators to actors who help transform weak into strong publics with decisional as well as communicative status. In this regard the Women's International League for Peace and Freedom (WILPF) founded after the First World War illustrates how communicative status can be transformed into decisional status at the international level. The World Social Forum plays a similar intermediary role, although in very different circumstances.

The WILPF had a long history of advocacy around issues of peace and the opposition to war. Using Nancy Fraser's distinction between weak (influential) and strong (decisional) public, Molly Cochran has shown that the League formed itself into a "strong" international public over time and began to shape decisions made by nation-state and League of Nations officials through three mechanisms of normative leverage. First, they saw themselves as purveyors of "publicness" in the sense that they established a transnational public sphere and communicative status for women within it (Cochran 2008, 3–4). The transnational public sphere, they argued, was in danger of disappearing during and after the First World War, and they sought to revitalize it, primarily for the sake of new emerging publics. Second, they saw themselves as establishing a forum in which the distinct perspective of women could enrich discussions of international issues of war and peace. In this way, they regarded the public sphere that they established as significantly enriching the quality of discussions of such issues that were epistemically deficient because past discussions and negotiations had lacked an important perspective, the perspective grounded in the experience of women. Third, as a plural public sphere, the League could claim to represent women, at least in the sense that it provided a forum in which their communicative status could be realized and transmitted. Thus, it was not just an interstate actor, but also a self-conscious international public, that realized the conditions for communicative freedom and the epistemic advantages of its plurality of perspectives for solving problems in the international sphere.

The WILPF saw their task as twofold: they sought not only to form public opinion, but also to shape the decision of extant international institutions, the League of Nations in particular. It was a self-consciously formed public that sought to legitimate its influence on these decisions as representatives of women and humanity in general. This communicative freedom was effectively transformed in a campaign to influence the League of Nations to do something about the many stateless women and children who continued to be held in Turkey after World War I. In this case, the WILPF served as an intermediary that sought to build a transnational public that could interact with and shape the League of Nations as a formal organization with a postwar agenda, where the public for whom the organization was formed shifted from states and other formal actors to the public of humanity at large. The WILPF did not just influence specific decisions but also interacted with the League of Nations so as to reshape and direct this institution away from its initial statist orientation and toward emerging strong international publics that were at the time concerned with creating the conditions for peace through publicity.

The WILPF offers an example of an exemplary intermediary that had a transformative effect on extant international institutions. Who are the purveyors of publicity today? Given how dispersed global governance institutions are, it is not surprising that this role is occupied by a wide variety of organizations and groups, many of which attempt to influence a particular domain or policy issue. Nonetheless, there are still examples of broader intermediaries with similar goals as the WILPF. The World Social Forum (WSF) emerged primarily out of protests over the consequences of the global financial system, but shifted from a defensive strategy of protests to creating a space for global deliberation and organizing around the broad issues of global justice.

As Jackie Smith and her collaborators point out, the annual meeting of the WSF, which acts as an intermediating forum for many different groups, is not an end in itself, but rather a part of an overall process in which there is an exchange of ideas, the mobilization of networks, and the global expansion of deliberative spaces where people can reflect on and try to realize alternatives to neoliberalism (Smith and Karides et al. 2007, 178).[4] These forums provide the basis for the creation of further forums and networks at the local, national, and regional levels. The WSF seeks to organize a self-consciously enduring public sphere that creates transnational social bonds in which learning can take place across various levels of time and place. As in any attempt to create a transnational society, innovative norms

---

4. Such movements aim at establishing "an effective, coherent and more democratic global polity," by building up transnational society and its norms (Smith 2008, 178).

and forms of communication are necessary in order to create democratic legitimacy for this dispersed task of deliberating about alternatives to the present order. Thus, as a communicative space and as an ongoing process, the organizers of the WSF see themselves as making public substantial injustices and creating the necessary conditions for interconnecting local and global dimensions of justice. Much like the WILPF, the WSF realizes conditions of communicative freedom and basic communicative status as participants in discussions of global justice in an imagined community, even while aiming to secure the epistemic benefits of diversity.

Given the potential for conflict among transnational groups that differ widely among themselves, the deliberative process in such a diverse group takes the form of peacebuilding. This case is interesting precisely because such a group does not necessarily agree on a single general principle or uniting theory. Instead, as Boaventura de Sousa Santos suggests, the alternative is the work of translation, a cognitive process that "allows for mutual intelligibility among the experiences of the world" (Santos 2005, 15–22). Such a process recognizes shared communicative status as the basis for mutual translation, while at the same time not requiring full communicative agreement even as it provides for understanding what unites and divides various groups that may still share common ends. What is important here is that the translation is mutual, that when various conceptions of human dignity are considered, the shortcomings of each will be apparent from the point of view of the other, as when various non-Western perspectives could challenge the idea of strict symmetries between rights and duties that rule out rights of future generations. Or, consider the ways in which proponents of human rights might reject a bias in favor of the religious and social status quo, and neglect the ways in which conflict could lead to a richer form of harmony (Santos 2005, 17–18). Thus, mutual translation of this kind opens up a space for dialogue and shared knowledge that makes it possible for people who deliberate to engage in practical action together. This sort of process can be generalized beyond the World Social Forum to many different cases of conflict in which it is important to establish a multiperspectival form of communication as the basis for a common future. The advantage of this kind of mutual intelligibility is that each side takes on the perspective of the other and in that way forms new experiences. At the same time, translation in this sense permits new and plural forms of social justice that show "the possibility of a better world imagined from the vantage point of the present" (ibid., 21–22).

As in the Northern Ireland case, networks also serve the cause of peace as purveyors of publicity and facilitators of communication. Certainly some such groups exert pressure on state actors, such as in the International Campaign to Ban Landmines. But more than pressuring state actors and their diplomacy, nonstate actors extend the conditions of social space through the creation of mutually recognized communicative status out of which norms and solidarity emerge in transnational society. The WSF does not attempt to achieve specific goals as one of many civil society organizations, but rather to create the communicative and social space in which new forms of interaction and specific goals and tactics might emerge. Besides the more general intermediaries such as WILPF and the WSF, networks such as the International Campaign to Ban Landmines also generate political legitimacy through peacebuilding, creating the transnational ties and relationships that make the lingering consequences of conflicts more apparent. Citizen dialogue and communicative diplomacy are not merely instrumental but are constitutive for building a common society and for generating social norms that provide the basis for a shared future. Given the nature of the dialogue, communication is directed not only at the conflicting parties, but also at establishing wider, transnational relations.

In both the WILPF and the WSF, the role of a transnational intermediary takes shape along with the social transformation directed at achieving a functioning and broad transnational society of individuals and publics. In the case of the Northern Ireland peace networks, for example, the same concern for establishing the conditions of publicity also helped to form a new transnational society within a divided state. All these networks were concerned with establishing an inclusive dialogue about social justice, including of course a dialogue across religious identities. The exercise of such communicative freedom requires the existence not only of a civil society as such, but also the emergence of a transnational society concerned with publicity and agreements by overlapping consensus. The creation of a common ground that makes a transnational society possible is an achievement, not something that can be specified in advance except in the general terms of realizing peaceful spaces for communicative freedom. These spaces in turn can also function to generalize decisional powers among a broad range of actors who are affected by various decisions over which they have not exercised influence or control.

## Conclusion

The approach to peacebuilding that I have taken here has two levels. The first is to see peacebuilding as the product of reconstructing political society so that it becomes more transnational, not only in the sense of having greater diversity, but also in distributing decisional powers. A necessary condition for constructing a transnational society is to create the ties of communicative status across the borders of communities. In Northern Ireland, these borders were religious, and the multi-track processes across the boundaries of conflict helped to produce the ties that supported the settlement. In many cases, the construction of a transnational society with its own norms and forms of interaction and communication is facilitated by various intermediaries, such as the peace networks in Northern Ireland that cut across religious difference. Second, on this same model, a global multilevel dialogue about peace and justice also seems possible, especially as transnational public spheres expand the scope of interaction, and this process also is aided by the emergence of new intermediaries such as the World Social Forum; however, there are also other formal institutions that will act as forums, such as various international courts in which debates about the scope and applications of international criminal, humanitarian, and human rights norms are worked out in deliberation.

Traditional diplomacy based on closed-door negotiations takes place without public awareness at the level of international society. Even when closed doors are in fact necessary in order that the glare of publicity and the hardening of positions can be addressed, a large deficit of democratic legitimacy often emerges as new transnational norms are too narrowly understood. In such cases, macro-level deliberation has not played a strong enough role in establishing a shared social space for deliberation.

What is needed is an extended, multi-track, and macro-level form of deliberation that will also transfer the deliberative form of shared legitimacy to contexts of deep conflict. It is certainly still the case that transnational agreements and implementation will be fragile. The aim here is not so much to create or spread some specific set of norms (such as international law), but to fashion peace by an overlapping consensus that would contextualize such norms of transnational society and be open to influence from publics.

If my discussion of the WILPF and the WSF is correct, then this kind of macro-deliberative process will require intermediaries and purveyors of publicity in most large-scale settings. Given that communicative capacities now can be widely distributed at very low cost, intermediaries can also organize a counterdiscourse and counterdeliberative processes. To put it in a phrase, intermediation creates legitimation through macro-deliberation among all the members of transnational society. Accordingly, peace can be built when people organize themselves and promote common aims from that perspective. What is now called "second-" or "multi-track" diplomacy aims at creating a form of transnational society on the basis of which a feasible peace can be recognized in ongoing deliberation.

# 8

# The World Social Forums as Transformative Peacebuilding

## Jackie Smith, Rebecca Burns, and Rachel Miller

Most analysts of peacebuilding view civil society actors as essential to any postwar peace. Paffenholz and Spurk summarize seven key functions of civil society identified in the literature, including protection, monitoring, advocacy for marginalized groups, socialization for a culture of peace, and fostering social cohesion (Paffenholz and Spurk 2006). Several observations can be made about these expectations of civil society in regard to postwar peacebuilding. First, these functions require fairly extensive capacity on the part of civil society. Even in societies that have not undergone wars, such capacity is likely to be weak or underdeveloped. Second, civil societies in postwar contexts face particularly difficult challenges in undertaking these tasks, given the devastation and social polarization that occurs in wartime. Third, with globalization, the abilities of civil society actors to monitor and hold authorities accountable and to engage in advocacy depend on their ability to target international actors as well as national officials. Fourth, many social movements are actively engaged in peacebuilding-related activities in nonwar contexts around the world, and lessons about postwar peacebuilding and the prevention of violent conflict might be found by paying more explicit attention to the role of social movements in peacebuilding.

While few social movements articulate their goals in this way, in practice, many are engaged in work that contributes unambiguously to peace by: addressing latent conflicts before they manifest themselves in violent ways; cultivating social cohesion; socializing people in democratic norms, values, and practices; and developing analyses of social problems and their solutions. We discuss the World Social Forums as an important example of contemporary transnational social movement mobilization that is engaged in such peacebuilding work on a global scale. In making this argument, we are expanding notions of peacebuilding beyond the national context to the world-system level. We also argue that much significant peacebuilding work takes place in contexts of latent conflict, rather than in the postwar settings more commonly addressed in the literature. Our analysis leads to the conclusion that more scholarly attention should be devoted to uncovering and theorizing the peacebuilding work being done by critical social movements.

Before we begin our analysis, however, we must clarify what we mean by "civil society." Volumes have been written on this concept, and we don't intend to review these debates here. With Kaldor, we define civil society as "the sphere of ideas, values, organisations, networks, and individuals located primarily outside the institutional complexes of family, market, and state" (Kaldor 2003, 4).[1] Civil society can contain elements that are "uncivil" (Anheier 2007), including groups that promote intolerance, violence, and exclusivity as well as those fostering social cohesion and cooperation. The aim of peacebuilding should be to encourage processes that foster the latter and discourage or preempt the former.

## Clarifying Concepts: Peace and Peacebuilding

Any consideration of peacebuilding should begin with the question, what is peace? In his review of the peacebuilding literature, Jon Barnett critiques existing scholarship in peace research for failing to adequately theorize the connections between development and peace (Barnett 2008). Consistent with Bolten's conclusions in chapter 6 of this volume, he argues

---

1. Kaldor's book focuses on *global* civil society, which she sees as extending "beyond the confines of national societies, polities, and economies" (2003, 4).

for a definition of peace as freedom and opportunity rather than merely the absence of violence:

> By moving away from a theory based on what peace is not, by articulating the complex and interdependent characteristics of peace as freedoms and opportunities, and by focusing as much on processes as outcomes, the theory of peace as freedom facilitates a more nuanced and multivariate assessment of peace based on its contingent nature. In this view, it is not the case that there is either peace or violence, because peace is not constructed in such dualistic terms. Rather, peace as freedom suggests that peace is more or less present based on the degree to which each important freedom and opportunity is present and the degree to which they are collectively present. (Barnett 2008, 86)

This definition of peace resonates with those advocating a broader and more holistic understanding of the social systems that contribute to peace, war, and violence (see, e.g., Philpott and Powers 2010). It also stresses that peacebuilding is a task required in many more situations than the postwar settings currently emphasized in the literature. It also offers a method for evaluating the forces and social processes that contribute to peace or its reduction, complicating the rather simplistic notions of "conflict cycles" that move from latent conflict to greater levels of escalation and sometimes overt violence to de-escalation and (it is hoped) postwar peacebuilding. Finally, it is consistent with the visions put forward by many social movements working to promote social change in diverse contexts.

Achieving peace as defined in terms of freedom and opportunity requires more concerted efforts to address the larger problem of structural violence. As the introduction and other contributions in this volume argue, the global social and political order is rooted in structural violence, that is, the "denial, through the distribution of resources and opportunity, of people's means of realizing basic needs and potential" (Uvin 2003, 110).[2] The global economy is organized around an economic

2. Webster and Perkins define this concept as follows: "Structural violence occurs when political and economic systems are organized in ways that oppress, exploit, and

model that requires the perpetual accumulation of capital. This accumulation of wealth—which is assumed to generate constant economic growth that will eventually "trickle down" to benefit all—depends on the extraction of surplus value (profits) from the products made by workers. In other words, it requires the exploitation of people and the environment, at least in the short term. In practice, there has been little evidence that wealth trickles down in the longer term; to the contrary, many analyses find that economic globalization has contributed to further concentration of wealth both within and between countries (Korzeniewicz and Moran 2009; Milanovic 2005; Weisbrot et al. 2002).

The global political order is likewise founded in basic inequality and is inherently linked to the world economic system. The interstate political order was consolidated in the West, and was imposed on the peoples of the global South through processes of imperialism and colonial occupation (Escobar 1988; Escobar 2004). Although colonialism was discredited and abandoned in the post–World War II era, it left a lasting legacy of exploitation by requiring newly "independent" states to both adopt models of statehood derived from Western experience and to become integrated into a global political and economic order that was controlled by Western powers (see, e.g., Pogge 2008; Farmer 2004).

If the conditions generating violence and peace are fundamentally linked to the world capitalist economy, then scholarship on peacebuilding must pay attention to the efforts of social movements that are resisting this global neoliberal order. Moreover, if the world economy is an underlying source of violent conflicts, then civil societies in countries experiencing war must have the capacity to affect global structures if they are to be effective at peacebuilding within particular national contexts. To the extent that social movements are developing transnational networks of increasing scale and capacity, they can better address the root causes of violence and war.

In addition to refining our conceptualization of peace, it is essential for us to interrogate our understandings of peacebuilding. As defined

---

dominate certain segments of a population while privileging others who hold power and wealth" (Webster and Perkins 2001, 330).

originally by Johan Galtung, peacebuilding is distinguished from peace-keeping and peacemaking mainly by its role in advancing "positive peace," or the elimination of structural violence. For Galtung, "peace-building achieves positive peace by creating structures and institutions of peace based on justice, equity and cooperation" (Galtung 1975, 282–304, cited in Paffenholz 2010b, 44–45).

In the early 1990s, Boutros Boutros-Ghali's *Agenda for Peace* and the end of the Cold War contributed to the expansion of international interven-tion in national conflicts. It also led to the use of the "peacebuilding" term to refer quite narrowly to interventions in postwar situations that tended to take on a managerial and problem-solving orientation. The emphasis has thus become more on postwar state building than on the reduction of structural violence as a means of preventing violence. The "liberal peace" advanced through international peacebuilding prioritizes economic lib-eralization, thus serving to "modernize and relegitimize a fundamental status quo respectful of a national and international market economy" (Paffenholz 2010, 55–56).

It is this conventional understanding of peacebuilding—and its role in maintaining the structural violence inherent in the global economy—that authors in this volume and other critical peace researchers are con-testing. An improved conceptualization of peacebuilding would focus on the larger set of processes that shape social relations, rather than on strictly postwar contexts or settings of high conflict escalation. Thus, Bur-ton (1990) offers the concept of "provention"—the promotion of condi-tions that create cooperative relationships that help satisfy basic human needs—as both a strategy for preventing overt violence and a remedy to structural violence. Similarly, as Fetherston observed, Lederach "sees pro-tracted social conflict as a *system* and focuses his elicitive approach on the *relationships within that system*" (cited in Fetherston 2000, 204, emphasis added). Peacebuilding thus entails work on transforming relationships that are manifest in specific places and histories.

But such approaches still lack a critical analysis of power, which must be "as much about understanding our own participation in [discourses of war and militarization] as it is about understanding how they are being played out in the context of a specific conflict" (Fetherston 2000,

207). In this respect, the field of peacebuilding has often struggled to develop tools that can extend peacebuilding work outside the range of conventional actors and that can be applied at supranational levels. For instance, not only do conventional approaches downplay the importance of actors outside national contexts in peacebuilding, but they also tend to marginalize relatively powerless, nonviolent groups within postwar societies while privileging the voices of potential spoilers, who tend to be armed militants. Methods are needed that bring into focus the continuity of structural and manifest violence across societies and allow us to undertake the renegotiation of relationships in the vast spatial geography of today's global economy.

Finally, we point to some of the major challenges identified in the literature for external interventions seeking to help build lasting peace. As we noted above, virtually all studies of postwar peacebuilding efforts highlight the important role played by civil-society actors in securing a durable peace. Paffenholz's important work on this topic concludes that there is general agreement in the peacebuilding literature on the following: First, the role of outsiders should be limited to supporting domestic actors. Second, civil-society peace initiatives are as important as official or unofficial diplomatic efforts to advancing durable peace. Third, the proliferation of new nongovernmental organizations in response to international funding has a negative effect on peacebuilding, since it crowds out local efforts and actors (Paffenholz 2010, 59).

These conclusions reinforce the argument in the introduction to this volume that the notion of civil society "empowerment," as applied in much scholarly and practitioner discourse, is problematic. The term suggests that civil society can be strengthened from the top down in a one-way process of dropping in resources. But considerable experience attests to the fact that civil societies consist of complex sets of relationships, and outside interventions must account for these complexities, as well as the effects of external actors' asymmetrical relationships with the societies in which they engage, when doing peace work. Santos's (2007a) notion of "social emancipation" offers some critical leverage into our thinking about the relationships of civil society and peacebuilding while reinforcing the notions of peace as freedom and opportunity discussed above.

Replacing conventional notions of civil society "empowerment" with the idea that peace work should involve social emancipation emphasizes the long-term task of strengthening civil societies' capacities to advance social cohesion, articulate latent conflicts over resources and other inequities, and to support crosscutting ties and a culture of democracy. This sort of work is hardest in postwar settings, and is impossible without attention to global factors that affect social mobilization.

Putting together the strands of thinking we outline above, we argue that neither peace, defined as freedoms and opportunities, nor peace-building, as the elimination of structural violence and transformation of social relations, can be achieved without a fundamental reordering of the world economic and political system. States and other actors with a vested interest in maintaining the status quo are not likely to be the main catalysts of this kind of reordering. Nevertheless, they are generally regarded as the core players in conventional peacebuilding strategies. Such strategies therefore preclude the greatest possibilities for structural transformation, particularly insofar as they reproduce those dominant discourses of power that constrain the space for broader civil society participation in peace processes.

Because the task of social emancipation requires a rethinking of relationships and the social orders reproducing them, the types of activities that constitute peacebuilding may be as much cognitive and symbolic as structural. The act of deconstructing the discursive processes that reproduce consent for everyday violence is an important aspect of what Fetherston refers to as "transformative peacebuilding." Fetherston points to antihegemonic social movements as key agents of this process, emphasizing their role in creating and exploiting spaces for critical reflection and dialogue about existing social relations:

> A *minimal requirement* [for transformative peacebuilding] appears to be opening critical space, where the very foundations of social meaning and practice are examined and where a diversity of critical social movements contest the "regime of truth" without reproducing it. A *maximal potential*, encompassing some minimal shared normative base (produced through communicative action) would *attempt* to reconstruct a consensual basis

for local hegemony, repairing and reforging distorted communication networks at localized "everyday" sites of social structures and action. (2000, 213, emphasis original)

This opening of critical space and creation of a new, shared normative base is, moreover, key to the process of social emancipation. Given this understanding, we argue that social movements are indispensable and indeed are central to any transformative peacebuilding process. As a reflection and articulation of contemporary social movements around the world, the World Social Forum (WSF) has been explicit in its aim of creating "open space" for social movements opposed to the existing neoliberal global order to meet, exchange ideas and experiences, and build networks and strategies for bringing about "another world [that] is possible." The very questioning of the inevitability of the neoliberal model of globalization through the WSF slogan "another world is possible" begins to open the sort of critical space Fetherston views as minimally essential to transformative peacebuilding. The fact that the WSF articulates a critical analysis of *global* structures that activists see as reproducing inequality, social exclusion, and violence reflects its critique of conventional, state-centric responses to violence that fail to address the world-systemic causes of violence in all parts of the world.

## The World Social Forum Process
## as Transformative Peacebuilding

The World Social Forum process is the most prominent example of contemporary antihegemonic movements, and it is unique among historic movements for its ability to bring together a highly diverse array of movements and organizations under a single—albeit broad—banner. Begun in 2001 as an effort to help focus and strengthen a growing "movement of movements" opposing the many harmful effects of economic globalization, the World Social Forums have expanded over time and place to mobilize many hundreds of thousands of people. It is conceived not as an organization or a movement, but rather as an ongoing process of convening, conversing, and "movement-building" in movement-created "open spaces" (Blau and Karides 2008; Karides et al. 2010; Teivainen 2002). Thus activists refer to it as the World Social Forum *process*. Attesting to the vibrancy and expanding nature of the WSF process is the proliferation of social forums at local, national, regional, and global levels that are linked both through the networks that participate in them as well as through shared identities and discourses (see, e.g., Smith et al. 2007; Santos 2006; Smith and Doerr 2011; della Porta et al. 2006).

We argue in this chapter that the WSF is a global project of *transformative peacebuilding*. Its transformative potential emerges from its focus on the structural violence of the world capitalist economy as an underlying cause of violence around the world, its creation of "open spaces" for critical dialogue and networking that in turn help aggregate civil society resistance to global neoliberalism while supporting viable alternatives to the existing world-system. Figure 8.1 illustrates this dynamic, and its relationship to conflict dynamics.

The World Social Forum process creates a multiplicity of "open spaces" for people to come together across many differences and in more equitable and inclusive ways to deliberate (see Bohman, chapter 7) about what sort of world is desirable. Activists in the WSF process have worked to sustain dialogue and learning across the time and distance that separates the various social forums. Thus, the WSFs help foster new relationships, advance dialogue, and socialize people in the norms and practices of democracy, thereby strengthening the foundations for peaceful societies. Drawing from many years of research on the WSF process, and from participant observation work at World Social Forums and at regional, local, and national (US) Social Forums (USSF), we identify ways that the practices being promoted through this process can contribute to effective and sustainable peacebuilding work. Smith attended the World Social Forums in 2001 and 2005 in Porto Alegre, Brazil; the European Social Forum in 2004; Boston, New York, and Midwest social forums in the United States; and both US Social Forums. She also served as a member of the USSF National Planning Committee for the 2nd USSF in Detroit and organized local social forum activity in her community. Miller and Burns attended the USSF in Detroit.

The open space of the WSFs contributes to social movement efforts to develop unified and coordinated strategies for resisting neoliberal

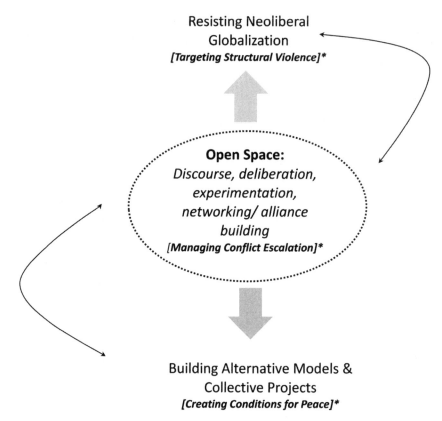

Resisting Neoliberal
Globalization
*[Targeting Structural Violence]*

Open Space:
*Discourse, deliberation,
experimentation,
networking/ alliance
building*
*[Managing Conflict Escalation]**

Building Alternative Models &
Collective Projects
*[Creating Conditions for Peace]**

*These practices reflect steps in the conventional "conflict cycle."
Figure 8.1: World Social Forum Dynamics

globalization and its many localized consequences. The WSF Charter of Principles explicitly opposes neoliberalism, and encourages movements to articulate their struggles around this shared understanding. In this sense, it confronts the structural violence of the world-system and therefore demands strategies to advance system-level change.

But mobilizing resistance to the existing order alone cannot bring peace. The strength of the WSFs and the spirit that motivates many to participate is the idea that "another world is possible." The open spaces of the forum provide opportunities for activists to share ideas about alternatives to globalized capitalism and to develop strategies and networks for making these alternatives viable. By providing alternatives to those generated by and reinforced through the existing patriarchal, militarized, and fundamentally conflictual global order, the WSFs offer a path toward global transformation. Below we explore the significance of the WSF's opposition to neoliberal globalization to peacebuilding. We then consider how the WSF notion of open space contributes to the work of advancing peace as freedom and opportunity. Our aim is to show how the practices of social movements can inform new thinking about transformative peacebuilding.

### Uniting Struggles against Global Neoliberalism.

Within the context of the global economy, efforts to advance peace—as freedoms and opportunities—require a fundamental transformation of the world economy. The countries of the global South, and the people who are marginalized in the global economy—including many workers, the unemployed, racial, gender, and other minority groups—lack many of the freedoms and opportunities enjoyed by those of the global North and those with greater access to power and wealth. By privileging the voices of the global South—including the marginalized "Souths" in the North—the World Social Forum process encompasses what Santos (2006) calls the "politics of emancipation," since it requires of those who seriously engage with it critical reflection on the operation of power in global, national, and local politics. The WSF process is perhaps most clear and unified on this point, even if debates remain over how to challenge existing power relations.

The World Social Forum aims to bring activists and organizations together with the explicit purpose of fostering dialogue and networking that builds global resistance to neoliberal globalization. Its significance in this regard is first that it provides a space for contact among activists that would otherwise not be available. The sort of contacts it fosters encourage new understandings of the common sources of the diverse problems activists confront in their local settings. Also, by uniting activists around explicit opposition to neoliberal globalization, the WSF process contributes to the articulation of new collective identities that transcend longstanding divides among nations and peoples, creating what della Porta calls "flexible identities and multiple belongings" (2005).

First, the WSF challenges neoliberalism by providing an arena for public testimony and the development of shared interpretations of global political and economic processes and their impacts. This allows activists to understand the effects of economic globalization for people around the world. Many are surprised to learn, for instance, that people in very different national contexts face similar problems. Others learn of the varied ways that neoliberal economic policies impact people in different settings, and they sometimes gain insights into how the policies of their own governments contribute to suffering elsewhere in the world. Hearing these stories helps activists forge shared understandings of their struggles to improve conditions in their own locales. It helps them see their local struggles as part of a much larger, global one that is being waged in many places. Testimony from activists around the world helps legitimate and validate their claims against the powerful forces that advance neoliberal globalization, aiding their work to challenge pervasive, dominant discourses. The knowledge that there are many activists in different parts of the world carrying out similar work can help motivate continued struggle in local settings, where many activists often feel alienated and overpowered.

Second, by providing spaces where activists can encounter one another across many differences, the WSFs foster the construction of collective identities that can form the basis of sustained coalitions. The critique of neoliberalism offered within the WSF helps activists see how globalized capitalism reinforces competition and division among people. It does so through multiple, overlapping hierarchies of patriarchy, racial inequality, and nationalism. Such an interpretation or framing of global capitalism and its effects helps groups transcend long-standing divisions among movements. But given that many activists work in "issue silos" in their routine, localized contexts, it is often difficult for them to see or to find ways to transcend the structures that reproduce deep social divisions.

As an arena for exchange, the WSF helps nurture "the politics of emancipation," by providing a platform from which groups and movements can identify the common forces that impact their lived experiences in different ways. This process of bearing witness and providing space for public testimony mirrors what scholars of truth commissions see as essential to the process of peacebuilding. As Priscilla Hayner notes of the truth commissions responding to mass human rights abuses, public testimony around the experience of such abuses often confirms generally held beliefs rather than revealing new facts. Thus, Hayner says, "the importance of truth commissions might be described more accurately as *acknowledging* the truth rather than finding the truth" (1994, 607). Having such an established public record can nevertheless be effective in condemning the crimes committed, identifying and rectifying the patterns of social behavior that led to the crimes, and granting moral recognition to the experiences of victims. In focusing on neoliberalism as the common target of resistance and providing a space for public testimony of its impacts, the World Social Forum advances a form of global truth telling that shares some of these functions of truth commissions.

If neoliberal globalization is an important cause of violence, then exposing it as a perpetrator of violence is important to altering the social relationships that generate violence. Paul Farmer discusses how the "erasure" of the history of colonialism, slavery, and other forms of institutionalized violence perpetuate structural violence:

> The concept of structural violence is intended to inform the study of the social machinery of oppression. Oppression is a result of many conditions, not the least of which reside in consciousness. We will therefore need to examine, as well, the roles played by the erasure of historical memory and other forms of desocialization as enabling conditions of structures that are both "sinful" and ostensibly "nobody's fault." . . . Erasing history is perhaps the most common explanatory sleight-of-hand relied upon by the architects of structural violence. Erasure or distortion of history is part of the process of desocialization necessary for the emergence of hegemonic accounts of what happened and why. (2004, 307–8)

Thus, by aggregating multiple realities as they are experienced, the World Social Forum process is able to bring to light alternative interpretations of historic and current events. Similar to conventional peacebuilding processes, it serves as a global truth commission that enables victims of structural violence to name their oppressor and seek redress. Any end to the violence depends on transforming the relationships between aggressor and victim, and thus the arena provided by the WSF should be seen as a vital space for peacebuilding work around the world. Below we provide examples of three campaigns operating within the WSFs that have used the space to advance shared understandings and to offer alternative collective identities and projects aimed at challenging the hegemony of global neoliberalism.

*Food Sovereignty*

Via Campesina has emerged as a preeminent network of activists advocating for greater local control of food production. Since the 1996 World Food Summit, Via Campesina has advocated for "food sovereignty," a notion that has gained greater prominence with the expansion of global justice activism and the World Social Forums. Food sovereignty has been a theme at multiple World Social Forums, where Via Campesina and its partner organizations have organized workshops to inform activists and recruit participation in a transnational network of groups and activists demanding greater access to secure sources of food.

This example illustrates how movements can advance new frameworks for popular understanding that can, over time, alter the dominant "discursive opportunity structure" (Ferree 2003, 209). The discursive opportunity structure affects the resonance a given set of ideas will have in the public sphere, thereby shaping the scope of politically acceptable demands, practices, and identities. Food sovereignty challenges the notion that food may be treated as a commodity and used as a means of making profits. Instead, it suggests that basic human rights depend on people's access to and control of the means of food production. Food sovereignty challenges the more conventional notion of "food security," which has been advanced in official intergovernmental negotiations. Whereas food security does not necessarily require a fundamental questioning of the dominant economic order, food sovereignty helps focus attention on the politics of food production.[3] It stresses the idea that food is a basic right, and it highlights the need for transforming policies regarding land distribution and access by linking them to notions of human rights and human needs. "Food sovereignty" thus challenges the globalized food industry by stressing the importance of locally produced and ecologically sustainable food sources that emancipate local populations from exploitative outside markets, energy-intensive global distribution networks, and expensive agricultural technologies and their industrial complexes.

The World Social Forum's structure as an ongoing, multilevel, and transnationally networked space for activist discourse and movement building has allowed food sovereignty activists to link otherwise dispersed struggles that range from small farmers defending their rights to land, local producers and consumer groups opposing corporate food production monopolies and the spread of biotechnology, and resistance to the spread of environmentally harmful agricultural practices such as confined animal feeding operations. Since social forum gatherings typically take place in urban areas, they encourage efforts to show connections between rural and urban interests, while illustrating the potential for alternative food markets. For instance, the 2010 US Social Forum in Detroit featured a "people's movement assembly" on food sovereignty that helped profile the ways activists in that postindustrial city are expanding people's access to healthy food while cultivating a broader critique of corporate food production that linked the interests of Detroit and other US activists with those of people around the world. This assembly on food sovereignty resulted in the formation of the US Food Sovereignty Alliance, which continues to foster networking with the United States and with international food sovereignty movements.

Activists from Detroit continued to deepen their analysis of the global sources of their local problems through the "Detroit to Dakar" initiative,

---

3. This effect is similar to that discussed in chapter 1 by Neil Cooper, who showed how conventional arms control discourses shift analyses and remedial efforts away from basic human needs.

which brought Detroit delegates to the WSF in Dakar, Senegal, in 2011. There, Detroit organizers learned of struggles in several African countries to resist land grabs by transnational corporations that were displacing them from their land and denying their ability to produce food. Language of food sovereignty and attention to land grabs has expanded in Detroit following these exchanges in the WSF process.

### Solidarity Economy Networks

While food sovereignty activists have sought to alter dominant discourses and assumptions about acceptable methods for determining people's access to food, other activists have worked to build local markets for a variety of products and services. The notion of solidarity economy begins with the recognition that capitalism's basis in competitive market dynamics is a basic obstacle to achieving peace and human well-being. Policies encouraging individuals to pursue narrow self-interests to achieve economic growth have not, activists point out, produced the intended "trickle down" effect capitalism's proponents have predicted. Instead, they encourage predatory and exploitative practices that weaken social cohesion and threaten long-term environmental health. Solidarity economy activists work to reorient economic practices in ways that nurture local, equitable, and ecologically sustainable markets.

The WSF's agenda of challenging neoliberalism has provided a "privileged space" for groups working to connect diverse movements advancing the solidarity economy (see Allard et al. 2008). Thus, it has helped support the strengthening of formal networks aimed at building and maintaining initiatives. For instance, the US Solidarity Economy Network (SEN) was launched at the first US Social Forum by solidarity economy activists who had been active at world forums and had maintained ties with some of the vibrant solidarity economy networks in Latin America and other countries of the global South. SEN sponsored a tent and cosponsored several workshops to help educate USSF participants in the ideas behind solidarity economy and to demonstrate its viability by presenting examples of and organizing tools for local solidarity economy initiatives. It later joined the USSF National Planning Committee and worked to build its national presence with the 2nd US Social Forum in 2010. This network thus engages in transformative peacebuilding by functioning as both a global truth-telling mechanism, showing the destructive tendencies of global capitalism, and a support system for alternatives to competitive market economies.

*Take Back the Land*

Take Back the Land is a US-based network that unites opposition to neoliberalism by advancing a platform of housing as a human right. Take Back the Land formed around an explicit recognition of a widespread housing crisis in the United States. It unites a variety of constituencies that have been impacted recently by practices of predatory lending and financial deregulation, as well as those who have historically been marginalized from access to land and housing. Local groups are able to articulate their agendas and goals autonomously, but spaces such as the US Social Forum provide the opportunity to build what activists refer to as a "translocal network." Differences of strategy and tactics and in ideas about the role of private property remain as creative tensions among activists in this network, but the principles of "housing as a human right" and "community control over land and housing" provide a shared set of goals and values around which groups and individuals of different backgrounds and ideological orientations can come together to address shared housing insecurities.

In this way, Take Back the Land network challenges the commodification of land that has been a central feature in the expansion of neoliberal capitalism and advances a critique that extends beyond the state of housing in the United States. Convened in 2009 by the US Human Rights Network's Land Housing and Action Group, Take Back the Land also bears strategic and symbolic connections to the Landless Workers Movement in Brazil. A 2009 "US Housing and Human Rights Tour" by organizers of the South African Western Cape Anti-Eviction Campaign also facilitated connections between the struggles of several Take Back the Land local action groups in the United States and poor communities in South Africa that have faced increasing marginalization as that state has embraced neoliberalism.

The 2010 US Social Forum subsequently provided an opportunity for US activists to deepen their analysis of the global nature of the housing crisis and demonstrate solidarity across borders. Members of the Chicago Anti-Eviction Campaign and other antipoverty and antiracist groups organized a soccer game in Detroit to raise awareness of official harassment and displacement of poor people and movements in advance of the 2010 World Cup in South Africa. They also staged a parallel "Poor Peoples' World Cup" organized by the Poor Peoples' Alliance and Western Cape Anti-Eviction Campaign (Western Cape Anti-Eviction 2010). The Take Back the Land and allied movements, including the Right to the City Alliance which has been part of the US Social Forums, are thus engaged in contesting one of the most fundamental conditions that structures social relations: the ownership of and access to land. Landlessness and homelessness are key elements of structural violence that perpetuates social exclusion and violent conflict across the globe, and Take Back the Land is using the WSF process to bear witness to the pervasiveness and systemic causes of homelessness. It thereby challenges the legitimacy of a global economic order that denies so many people this basic right of access to shelter.

## The World Social Forums, Open Space, and Conflict Transformation

The World Social Forum's open space ideal helps characterize it as a movement-defined space where social movements and civil society groups have largely unrestricted access, and where there is the explicit goal of fostering dialogue and collaboration across many social divides. The only groups formally restricted from participating are those espousing violence and those rejecting the Charter of Principles and its explicit opposition to global neoliberalism.[4] This contrasts the kinds of civil-society spaces emphasized in the peace studies literature, which tends to focus

---

4. In practice, there is relatively limited enforcement of this rule, which is articulated in the Charter of Principles, although explicitly violent groups are excluded and workshops that counter these principles are not accepted.

on the performance of discrete peacebuilding functions once violent conflict has ended. In such spaces, the groups invited or most able to participate are typically those already relatively privileged. Many groups,
moreover, remain dependent on external resources in order to participate.
As a space that is explicitly devoted to not just engaging but also supporting the leadership of groups that have been historically marginalized, the
WSF process addresses latent conflicts based in long-term social exclusion
and deprivation. Thus, activists have debated extensively the question of
whether and how to accept funding from foundations and other powerful
entities as well as how to generate resources to expand participation by
the very poor.

As Fetherston argued, a minimal requirement for transformative
peacebuilding is the creation of a critical space where movements can contest the existing "regime of truth" (2000, 213). The refrain of "another world
is possible" that is repeated at different forums is an important retort to
Margaret Thatcher's famous statement that "there is no alternative" to liberal capitalism. In this sense, the World Social Forum's commitment to
creating "open space" for dialogue, reflection, and strategizing forms the
basis of a platform for global scale conflict transformation. The open space
created by the WSF process is used by movements to experiment with
alternative discourses and symbols that can be used to legitimize challenges to "mis-framing" (Fraser 2005) and other discursive dynamics that
serve to reinforce existing power asymmetries.

The 2010 US Social Forum revealed important efforts to transform
movement discourses and thinking about the work of advancing social
justice. In the titles of workshops and in the language used in plenary sessions and official publications, USSF organizers reinforced language such
as "gender justice," "climate justice," and "disability justice" in order to
challenge conventional discourses and socialize activists in new ways of
thinking about their own demands and about the perspectives and concerns of groups that tend to be marginalized even in movement settings.

While gender and disability issues have traditionally been discussed
in terms of "gender rights," "disability rights," or "disability access,"
groups discussed how a "justice" framework highlights intersections
between struggles and moves beyond single-issue and state-centered

approaches to advocacy. And considering environmental issues in terms of justice helps overcome common misperceptions that poor people are not interested in healthy environments, or that there is a hierarchy of issues and needs separating environmental concerns from other matters of equity and social justice. Such efforts should be seen as responses to the experiences of marginalization, "discursive demobilization" (see chapter 2 of this volume by Cecelia Lynch), and subversion of activist agendas through securitization and other processes documented in earlier chapters. They serve as a crucial starting point for the advancement of dialogue across difference and the work of "translation" (Santos 2006).

Organizing the open spaces of the WSF process has not been easy, and has generated some of the most vibrant and contentious debates within the WSFs. In the process of organizing the 2004 European Social Forum, for example, divides developed between the "horizontals," who demanded a greater degree of self-organization, and those whom they dubbed "the verticals," including traditional left political parties, who adhered to top-down organizing (Juris 2008). This reflects the fact that in the process of bringing diverse groups together around the project of organizing social forums, activists confront the reality of power and its operation, even in the spaces of movements working to resist oppression, hierarchy, and inequality (Juris 2008; Patomäki and Teivainen 2004). Smith and Karides and their colleagues' discussion of the tensions between those arguing for the preservation of the WSF as "open space" as opposed to a platform for collective action reflects one of the core "creative tensions" driving the WSF's dynamism and innovation (Smith and Karides et al. 2007). The two US Social Forums that have taken place have sought both to uphold the principles of open space and to challenge historical patterns of exclusion through a deliberate process that relies on leadership by those most harmed by economic globalization—specifically poor people and people of color. Organizations on the USSF National Planning Committee have been selected for their ability to mobilize grassroots leadership in marginalized communities. This organizing strategy reflects an *intentionality* that challenges the conventional understandings of "open space" in the WSF process while also potentially helping advance the basic principles articulated in the WSF charter (Juris 2008; Smith and Doerr 2011).

The leadership and participation by indigenous peoples in the 2010 Social Forum exemplifies this practice of intentionality. In addition to a role in planning, indigenous peoples caucused each day prior to the start of USSF sessions to reinforce this shared identity within the larger space of the USSF and to identify and address conflicts, concerns, and challenges as they arose during the forum itself. Experimenting with this open-space caucus helped strengthen organizational capacity among indigenous activists and organizations dispersed across North America while also helping advance forms of engagement with the forum that better reflected the cultural traditions, norms, and knowledges of indigenous communities. This work has been ridden with conflict for many years, and prior engagements between indigenous leaders and the US and World Social Forum process have been far from smooth (Becker and Koda 2011). But as Becker and Koda show, indigenous leaders and organizations have remained engaged with the WSF process, and in the course of this work have helped inform nonindigenous activists' understandings of the violence that economic globalization and Western cultural imperialism have done to indigenous peoples around the world.

The indigenous people's water ceremony at the Detroit USSF, for instance, opened space for dialogue and understanding of the issues facing indigenous communities by inviting nonindigenous participants to observe and be present during the sacred ritual. The water ceremony makes explicit the connection between humans and the environment, raising awareness of the need to care for and protect precious water resources, as well as acknowledge broader environmental injustices. The water ceremony linked the broader concerns of indigenous peoples from the Detroit area of the co-optation and commercialization of spiritual practices, as well as of continuing marginalization from historic lands and resources. By bringing indigenous issues to the center platform of discussion, and by inviting nonindigenous peoples to observe and participate in this ritual, indigenous activists were able to utilize open spaces within the forum to cultivate mutual concern and respect and foster awareness of the connections between indigenous and nonindigenous activists' needs and concerns. By continuing to engage with the WSF, leaders in the Indigenous movement are helping advance a broad and fundamental critique of the global economic order as a principal source of violence and inequality.

This example demonstrates the important role that the WSF's articulation of "open space" can play in peacebuilding. The open space ideal articulated in the WSF Charter of Principles aims to avert conflicts over strategies and tactics that have traditionally divided movements. By remaining a space for dialogue and convergence, the WSF explicitly rejects any attempts to take action in the name of the WSF. While activists within the process have debated the utility of the concept, and while some have pushed for more attention to collective action, thus far the principle of open space has remained, largely because of the remaining challenge many activists see of incorporating the voices and perspectives of those most harmed by economic globalization. Advocating a particular course of action without greater assimilation of the perspectives of these marginalized communities is seen as reproducing the failures of earlier movements.

Yet participants in the WSF process are impatient for social change and are eager to find ways of advancing their struggles for justice. Thus, one sees in the WSFs a variety of efforts to rectify the tensions between open space and action, most notable among these being the Social Movement and (in the United States) People's Movement Assemblies (PMAs). These are assemblies typically held at the end of social forum gatherings where activist groups and networks put forward calls for specific collective actions and campaigns. They allow groups to find allies and collaborators in their work, and facilitate action that can strengthen alliances that unite people across sectoral, racial, cultural, and national divides.

The people's movement assembly of the antiwar movement at the 2010 USSF reflected the critical work of creating bridges between diverse groups and across power levels. Comprised of diverse groups with varying agendas, the PMA in Detroit addressed a critical gap in involvement from Palestinian groups by recognizing the importance of expressing antiwar demands as a broader set that includes US policies in the Israeli-Palestinian conflict. While much of the focus remained on the US-led wars in Iraq and Afghanistan, the PMA opened a space for a more dynamic and equitable conversation of the role of the United States in a more diverse set of situations and included a call for changes in US policies toward Israel.[5] Thus, through learned experiences of a more narrow focus within the antiwar movement, activists saw the need to expressly create a tie to more marginalized and typically separate Palestinian groups and include those issues within the antiwar forum.

As Smith and Doerr (2011) observe, and as the above discussion suggests, the forum process involves significant reflection on the processes and power relations present within social movements while simultaneously seeking to create processes and structures that foster more equitable practices. This resonates with what Lederach, Neufeldt, and Culbertson (2007) write on the role of reflexivity in learning from experiences and thus developing experienced-based theory to support the work of transformative peacebuilding. The forums are recognized spaces of contestation in which power dynamics exist and are consistently challenged (see Smith and Karides et al. 2007; Teivainen 2004). While much has already been written on the challenges facing the WSF and its regional forums in regard to power relations and dynamics, there remains among many leaders and participants a clear commitment to a reflexive engagement in working within the existing open-space framework to transform power relations. Santos thus characterizes the WSF as "a space on the move" (2008), suggesting a process able to transform political realities through the intentional renegotiation of relationships and the formation of new modes of thought and interaction. The functions of open-space notions advanced through the WSF process thus present important opportunities for peacebuilders to think further about the possibilities for conflict transformation that exist in the realm of consciousness, culture, and discourse.

With open space, the WSF explicitly confronts the dualistic thinking that is characteristic of Western cultural traditions. One aspect of this that we can see in this discussion of open space is the WSF's challenge to the notion that cultural work is separate from and less important than work

5. This work was continued through the participation of a joint US-Canada delegation to the World Social Forum Free Palestine in Porto Alegre, Brazil, in the fall of 2012 (see: http://www.ussocialforum.net/node/437).

focused on policy processes and institution building. Such an "underestimation of the political nature of the cultural" (Osterweil 2004, 497) also functions to preserve a results-oriented conceptualization of political work that tends to marginalize civil society actors, especially those groups least prepared to engage in the conventions of institutionalized politics—such as poor people, ethnic minorities, and indigenous peoples (Osterweil 2004). It thus narrows the scope of action to formal policies and political institutions that are exclusive and essentially designed to reproduce existing social hierarchies and inequalities. Transformative peacebuilding, in contrast, requires efforts to imagine institutions and policies grounded in differently ordered social relations, and therefore must privilege cultural work that can help articulate alternative values and models of social organization while fostering collective identities and commitments to support new institutions. The WSFs' public performances, plenary sessions, celebrations, and information-sharing bazaars are thus important examples of the sort of activities that contribute to transformative peacebuilding.

We saw in the articulation of alternative discourses in the USSF that open space also supports positive framings of conflict that provide opportunities both for social emancipation and deliberation across difference. This parallels what Lederach calls the "moral imagination" (2005), which consists of efforts to imagine conflict in new ways and to accept the possibility of positive developments to emerge through relational engagement.[6] Similarly, many activists in the WSF discuss "new movement subjectivities" and "political imaginations" that are emerging through the process. Frequent references to variations on the Zapatista slogan *"Somos todos Subcomandante Marcos"*[7] emphasize both activists' rejection of hierarchy and

6. Of course, given that the WSF process focuses on the *structural violence* and often latent conflicts resulting from the inequities of economic globalization, this rethinking of relationships may first require an escalation of conflict as marginalized groups come to advance new collective identities and claims for justice.

7. For instance, in the first USSF in 2001, the French farmer-activist José Bové was arrested for his role in "decontaminating" a Monsanto-owned field of genetically engineered soybeans, which were being grown in a province that banned GMOs. Stickers saying *"Somos todos José Bové"* were quickly distributed and participants chanted this upon

the movement's decentralized leadership, while also signaling awareness of interdependencies and the possibility of "becoming the Other" (Sullivan 2005, 371). Such processes of subjective transformation do not occur naturally or easily. They require time and repeated opportunities for groups to encounter one another and to discuss their differences. Activists urging more "horizontal" forms of organization stressed how such forms are "modes of producing identities" that contribute to the renegotiation of identities, while vertical organizations more typical of earlier movements assume the "representation of given identities" (De Angelis 2004, 593). The sequential organization of at least nominally linked social forums thus provides a context for exchange, reflection, and learning that can contribute to the transformation of social relations and structures around the principles of inclusiveness and participation.

The crucial contribution of open space to transformative peacebuilding, then, is that it facilitates alliance building by expanding what Santos calls "contact zones," in which actors and ideas are "render[ed] porous and hence permeable to other NGOs, practices, strategies, discourses, and knowledges" (Santos 2004, 342). Such a formulation recognizes the central position that language and identity can have in escalating or deescalating potential conflicts and echoes Lederach's description of the moral imagination as requiring "a paradoxical curiosity that embraces complexity without reliance on dualistic polarity" (2005, 5). Participants' willingness to devote the time, resources, and energy to participating in the WSFs' open spaces signal their desire for dialogue and a commitment to building and rethinking relations across multiple divides. A commitment to "language justice" and the presence of multilingual discussion at many social forum workshops is a good example of this, as it often requires a rethinking of conventional strategies based in political expediency and efficiency (Doerr 2008). Participatory working sessions, which exemplify the notion of "contact zones," similarly focus on transformational aspects of relationships and building alliances rather than conventional

hearing the news of Bové's imminent deportation. The slogan has also been chanted to support international migrants and other targeted groups.

results-oriented frameworks. In a session on community-based economies, participants bridged diverse backgrounds and locales to question
discourses encountered in their daily work and to create strategies for
working in their local context, while forging relationships across political,
social, cultural, and economic divides. The WSF process can facilitate the
construction of alliances and mutual respect without explicit agreement,
thus functioning as a dynamic form of conflict management that circum-
scribes conflict within negotiated boundaries of civility (Anheier 2007).
These boundaries remain fluid, however, and such a process is thereby
potentially able to avoid the over-institutionalization of conflict (Anheier
2007, 44) that entrenches unequal power relations between participants.

## Conclusion

While civil society has been seen as vital to the effective implementation
of postwar peacebuilding projects, there has been relatively little effort to
develop our theories about how particular civil society formations and
practices affect the prospects for achieving sustainable peace. Countering
the assumptions inherent in the "liberal peace" theory, we have argued
that critical social movements both within and outside of societies experiencing wars are essential to any serious effort to cultivate sustainable
peace, since they help address issues of structural violence that emanate
from the global economic order. They engage in what Fetherston has
called "transformative peacebuilding," addressing the larger structures
of violence and therefore improving prospects of generating lasting and
just peace processes. Not only do these social movements help focus
attention on the underlying sources of many violent conflicts around the
world, but contemporary transnational movements have also developed
models of action aimed at bridging multiple differences among people
from different class, race, ethnic, and national backgrounds. They also
have developed structures to facilitate collective action that articulates
and supports alternatives to dominant structures that are based in
inequality and exclusion.

However, the cultivation of new models of economic and social
engagement, the development of identities that crosscut dominant social

cleavages, and the strengthening of people's commitment to collective political projects are tasks that are extremely difficult, even for civil societies operating without the challenges of violent conflict. To expect civil-society groups to be able to take on these tasks in an effective way in the aftermath of wars is highly problematic, and most efforts to do so will likely fail in the short term. Moreover, they will be dependent on external funding, thereby limiting the potential for local leadership development and the visions of social emancipation and open space that have been articulated by analysts and activists in the World Social Forums.

The World Social Forum is an important example of the kind of social movement activity that contributes to peacebuilding, because it focuses explicit attention on the world economic system as the main source of the grievances many local communities and activist groups are working to change. Moreover, it is not designed as a conventional movement campaign, but rather as a *process* that aims to develop relationships among diverse activists working across geographic space as well as time. It is a reflexive process that seeks to learn from the diverse experiences of movements around the world and to constantly improve its own operations to better achieve ideals of ever-more inclusive participation and solidarity around shared principles if not actions. Over time, it has helped build trust among groups with little experience working together. By cultivating ongoing dialogue and exchange, it generates new collective identities that help activists see themselves in new ways, where belonging is not restricted as it is with conventional class and national divisions. It has fostered in its first ten years the commitment among activists to a nonviolent process oriented toward large-scale social change. The practices in the WSF thus constitute functions that peace researchers have deemed important civil-society contributions to peacebuilding.

Transformative peacebuilding requires the fundamental reordering of large-scale social and economic relations, and this is impossible without efforts of movements to develop new collective identities that can transcend historical cleavages and unite people in long-term collective struggles for justice. Peacebuilding scholarship and practice should support critical social movements and identify practices and forms that reinforce civil society projects for social emancipation. Scholars must expand their conceptual lens to consider the world-systemic context of peacebuilding and to appreciate the need for "peacebuilding" work outside the particular contexts of postwar societies and even states. Work to imagine new relationships outside of existing structures (including states) that serve to perpetuate inequality and violence is impossible in settings polarized by war and other forms of violence. The work required of civil society peacebuilders is best done in situations of more limited polarization and minimal overt violence, and this sort of work to prevent the escalation of conflicts into violence needs greater material and symbolic support.

The narrow focus on civil society in postconflict peacebuilding in the peace research literature promotes a reductionist view of civil society because it limits its role to a stage when civil society is weakest and its involvement in peacebuilding is instrumentalized and linked to the aims of foreign donors. Instead, the work of civil society peacebuilders to prevent the escalation of conflicts into violence needs greater material and symbolic support. It is this kind of work that can yield important lessons about the imagining of new relationships outside of structures perpetuating inequality and violence. Because of its explicit focus on the structures that reproduce hierarchy, inequality, and violence, the World Social Forum, then, is a crucial case for considering both how social movement actors are already involved in peacebuilding at the world-systemic level and how this understanding of peacebuilding can help build strong civil-society networks that can prevent the escalation of conflict into violence.

# Conclusion

## Ernesto Verdeja and Jackie Smith

The past several decades have seen major changes in approaches to peace-building. Scholars and practitioners have moved beyond the early efforts of conflict management, which sought to contain violence, to more sophisticated strategies of conflict "resolution" and "transformation" (Richmond 2010) with the aim of addressing the deeper causes of violence. Some of these recent approaches have shown a welcome awareness of civil society demands, but peacebuilding is still largely driven by international and transnational elites and institutions that show little concern for substantive transformations of power relations (Jabri 2007). In this volume we have offered a critical review of the literature on peacebuilding, and have argued that the field of peace research needs to do more to embrace critical and truly multidisciplinary approaches to the study of peace, conflict, and violence. Moreover, the material presented in this volume supports our contention that more international resources and attention need to be devoted to the work of peacebuilding *before conflicts escalate into wars*. In short, our notions of peacebuilding need to be expanded to emphasize a focus on the underlying sources and structures that reproduce violence. We have illustrated how research on economic globalization and global institutions as well as on social movements can address limitations in much of the existing work on peacebuilding. In doing so, we have developed analyses of particular conflicts that suggest some basic lessons or conclusions for the larger field.

The approach to globalization, peacebuilding, and social movements in this collection is motivated by three theoretical concerns. First, we have sought to rethink the background and proximate causes of violence, as well as its accelerators. We have drawn particular attention to general factors such as neoliberalism that create the conditions for recurring and structural violence. This analytical orientation is not meant to dismiss the importance of meso- and micro-level analyses (which are evident in the contributions of the volume), but rather seeks to highlight the complex interactions through which national and subnational dynamics of violence and peacebuilding emerge, develop, and are constrained by transnational processes and structures. Given that the mainstream of current scholarly and policy literature assumes that the policies of the dominant international actors are normatively benign (though perhaps occasionally problematic in practice), such a fundamental reexamination of the causes of violence is especially pressing.

Second, we have promoted a critical interrogation of the assumptions and presuppositions underlying the norms of peacebuilding. This includes rethinking the proper place of social movements, domestic and international state actors, and civil society, as well as bringing under further scrutiny the ahistorical, statist, and Western-centric perspectives that frame much of contemporary thinking about peace and its relation to economic development, democracy, and stability. A critical interrogation of this sort investigates not only the practical outcomes of particular policies—such as market liberalization and privatization—but also the ideological justifications on which they rest and the interests they serve, which often remain opaque.

Finally, we have promoted an alternative analytical framework that privileges the perspectives and claims of people on the ground. Rather than begin from the perspective of national or international elites, we start with the problem of exclusion and domination of already vulnerable groups (such as women, racial and ethnic minorities, the economically disenfranchised, and others) within communities. This approach offers greater sensitivity and responsiveness to local contexts and the people who experience and resist violence firsthand. By focusing on these local experiences, our framework calls for greater transparency and accountability on the part of international actors and institutions—including dominant states whose interests largely define and constrain the options of local actors. It also requires a fundamental questioning of the security paradigm adopted by mainstream peacebuilding, which essentially treats populations as "biopolitical" (Agamben 1998), that is, as something to be regulated, managed, secured, and protected: ultimately, as something passive to be controlled and kept in place. One thinks of the security approaches used in Afghanistan and Iraq as well the slums in Brazil, Central America, and elsewhere that continue to inform peacemaking efforts, with often savage results.

The alternative framework presented here seeks to clear a space for envisioning and promoting economic models that (a) reverse the logic of free market dogma, and (b) are based on the welfare and agency—emancipation—of the population, rather than aggregate economic growth criteria that may mask increased inequality in weakened states. Our analytical framework takes as its normative basis the desire for an economy designed to serve the needs of society, rather than requiring societies to be restructured to meet the needs of capital. As Karl Polanyi (1944) argued, the economy needs to be reembedded in society and made to serve its needs, rather than vice versa.

This volume has made three general arguments: first, neoliberalism fails to address the underlying causes of violence; second, neoliberalism is more accurately seen as a project for advancing wealth accumulation in the hands of the few, and as such is a driver of inequality and conflict; and third, peacebuilding needs to engage in creating and sustaining counter-hegemonic alliances of marginalized groups and to promote an alternative project of "social emancipation" (see, e.g., Fetherston 2000, 210). We summarize these arguments in the following pages, with special attention provided to the idea of social emancipation.

First, as Valentine Moghadam discusses in her chapter on Afghanistan and Iraq, globalized capitalism fails to address the systemic causes of violence, and in fact reproduces and even exacerbates, if not causes, structural violence. Moghadam's chapter argues for greater attention to how conflicts within particular countries and locales are embedded within a larger world-system. She shows, for instance, that the contemporary conflicts in Afghanistan and Iraq cannot be reduced to localized differences, but rather need to be reframed as part of a world-scale competition in which the leading world power is struggling to maintain its control of key resources and therefore its hegemony in the world-system. Given that the causes of the war are part of this larger systemic struggle, solutions will only be found by looking at global processes and dynamics of state formation, development, constraint, and collapse. Addressing the root causes of violence, then, requires the transformation of states and the interstate system itself, since these structures have developed and solidified largely in response to the needs of global capital.

Second, neoliberalism should be seen as a project for advancing wealth accumulation by those who control capital on a global scale (Harvey 2005). Actors favoring neoliberalism influence key decisions by states, and they have significantly shaped inter- and intrastate policies regarding peacebuilding. Thus, efforts to address persistent failures of conventional peacebuilding efforts must strengthen the power of groups advancing alternative projects that aim at addressing human needs rather than the accumulation of profits.

Third, any political project that addresses the structural violence of the world economic and political order will require peacebuilding that focuses on building and supporting a counterhegemonic coalition among less powerful groups. This involves more than simply "empowering" civil society. Indeed, the term "empowerment" has effectively been appropriated by neoliberal discourse and drained of much of its normative force and vitality. This is unsurprising given neoliberalism's hegemonic position in peacebuilding programs, but it has resulted in the premature closing of the discursive and operational space available for civil-society actors to address problems and meet public needs (see chapter 2 by Cecelia Lynch). We argue that peacebuilding should advance "social emancipation" (Santos 2007a) and in particular take up a preferential option for groups that are most marginalized by dominant forces in society. A perspective informed by social emancipation seeks greater agency for those who are denied full participation in the economy, society, and politics. It is not enough, for instance, for external peacebuilders to provide basic material goods to a traumatized society but limit popular access to political voice and material well-being through programs that institutionalize a weak and unresponsive state. Emphasizing agency requires different strategies for peacebuilding, including the structural analysis of power, in contrast to ostensibly less politicized forms of social empowerment favored by international peacebuilders.

Social emancipation involves both cognitive (epistemic) and operational (praxis) dimensions (Santos 2007b). We contend that both are required for more effective and transformative peacebuilding efforts. From a cognitive standpoint, social emancipation concerns a transformation in how we understand (and thus analyze) power. In other words, it involves efforts to "shift the basis on which everyday life and meaning are constituted and practised" (Fetherston 2000, 195).

This not only involves critically interrogating the manifestations of domination, exclusion, and violence, but also problematizatizing some of our basic analytical categories. For instance, as Neil Cooper notes in his contribution, the main discourses on international arms regulation have drawn complex distinctions between "legitimate" and "illegitimate" trade in weapon systems that benefit continued arms sales by major global powers, while leaving unexplored the analysis of the consequences of conventional arms trade. So-called pariah weapons are defined, banned, and where necessary tracked, all while a massive conventional arms trade continues to flourish. The epistemic transformation at the center of the social emancipation framework requires not only a careful examination of the regulations in place, but also the basic categories of legitimate and illegitimate weaponry and the functional consequences of current arms control agreements. Who benefits from these categorizations, and how?

Cecelia Lynch has shown how the "NGO-ization" of peacebuilding and its attendant "discursive demobilization" divides civil society programs into issue silos, which in turn undermines coalition building by fostering competition for funding. Given the sources of much funding, civil society efforts are channeled in ways that support elite projects, rather than enabling organic or grassroots responses to local needs. Moghadam employs a gendered lens on the sources of violence and peacebuilding. This approach not only draws attention to the ways conventional peacebuilding efforts have neglected and even exacerbated the suffering of women in armed conflicts, but it also identifies gender-based hierarchy (patriarchy) as a basic cause of the persistent structural violence that characterizes the world-system. She discusses the role of "hegemonic masculinities" as they are developed both by dominant powers and by groups seeking to contest hegemony within the existing interstate framework. Women are thus marginalized within counterhegemonic struggles. She calls essentially for a feminist counterhegemony that moves the terms of debate outside the presumed values and hierarchies of the existing patriarchal and hegemonic order.

These authors engage in an epistemic reorientation by calling into question the basic analytical (and normative) categories used in contemporary analyses of peace and violence. Without such a reorientation—without, in other words, an analysis of the fundamental constitutive categories that underpin our understandings of legitimate and illegitimate power—peacebuilding will continue to focus on the symptoms rather than the causes of political, social, and economic exclusion. More important, it will serve to reinforce existing power relations and dominant political projects, reducing the abilities of marginalized groups to address basic needs. If neoliberalism is a political project that contributes to social exclusion, transformative peacebuilding calls for the creation of space for an alternative project that enhances people's stakes in a shared set of social and political institutions.

Social emancipation also includes an operational dimension. This concerns the empirical effects of modern relations of power and the practical strategies for transforming them in ways consonant with human needs and welfare. Peacebuilding efforts must be attentive to how the interstate system's structuring of states and demands on them affect the space in which civil society operates.

Moghadam's call for feminist-informed counterhegemony offers an important idea for articulating new and more effective approaches to peacebuilding than those predominating today. She shows how feminist groups operating across national boundaries have been responding to the needs of women and building other bases of power and discourse. While these groups are still vulnerable and constrained by the discursive, policy, and resource structures that other chapters have shown to limit civil society impact, they offer autonomous spaces where women can envision alternatives to dominant structures and begin to lay the foundations for enacting these alternatives. In similar ways, other civil society groups support the envisioning and enacting of alternatives, creating structures that can reinforce effective peacebuilding; in other words, peacebuilding that redresses structural violence. But feminist groups are particularly important leaders in this regard, since they confront a basic exclusion in the capitalist world order and offer a framework that is sensitive to the ways the world-system divides and marginalizes people as it supports the private accumulation of profits. Given Moghadam's analysis, it is not surprising that feminist organizations are at the forefront of the peace-building work traced by Bohman and by Smith, Burns, and Miller in their chapters on deliberative democracy and the World Social Forums.

Dia Da Costa shows how neoliberalism's demands on states affect the ways groups within India articulate conflicts and mobilize adherents. Da Costa traces how the context of interparty competition led groups to embrace competitive frames that exacerbated social differences rather than assisted in uniting across differences and in support of community aims. Isaac Kamola analyzes how the interstate system causes the chronic "failures" of states like Somalia while also offering "solutions" in the form of international intervention ostensibly aimed at rectifying state collapse. However, because the causes of piracy in places like the Gulf of Aden are systemic rather than anomalous, such interventions serve mainly to reinforce existing power configurations rather than address the underly-ing factors that lead people to engage in and support piracy. Under these conditions, international efforts will remain ineffective as solutions to the violence in the region.

Similar to the analysis offered by Kamola, Catherine Bolten argues that the Western characterization of politics in Sierra Leone and other conflict-prone countries of Africa as a form of deviance—in this case, corruption—is actually a rational and (for some) effective response by local actors to the structural context of the highly unequal economic and political system, which is exacerbated by problematic interventionist strat-egies. Conventional "peacebuilding" efforts and aid thus fuel such "devi-ance" by taking advantage of local institutions' weaknesses to advance elite projects, thereby deepening the unequal relations already embed-ded in the system. Addressing the problems of maldistribution of goods and services in poor and war-torn countries like Sierra Leone requires attention not only to the problem of corruption, but also to the ways these countries are embedded in the world economy. Furthermore, international strategies must account for how local traditions and systems of relations operate in response to external intervention. For Bolten, effective peacebuilding requires careful and direct attention to how the interaction of global and national systems of relations reproduce, at local levels, the "unfreedoms" that restrict people's abilities to meet their basic needs. She calls for peacebuilding that enables or creates space for the emergence of "metis," or local knowledge, that has proved essential to human survival.

These contributors highlight the practical consequences of uneven power relations across a variety of cases, and show the numerous ways in which local-level actors struggle for emancipation or new positions of domination. Ultimately, what these chapters underscore is how peacebuilding must remain sensitive to the broad transnational structures and policies that create—and constrict—social conflicts.

### Peacebuilding: A Way Forward

In his work on social emancipation, Santos often advocates greater respect for a "plurality of knowledges," a kind of subaltern and democratic response to the dominance of "expert" rational and scientific knowledge that claims authority to reconstruct societies without regard to their particular histories, cultures, or wishes. For Santos, the struggle between expert and subaltern pluralist knowledge dates to the beginning of the European imperial projects of the fifteenth century and is still evident today.

In the context of contemporary peacebuilding, we see these struggles mirrored as external demands for radical social and governmental reengineering according to the formal needs of global capital and power, versus myriad forms of local and national opposition drawing on particular self-understandings of freedom and collective well-being. In this respect, the need for a plurality of knowledges at the heart of Santos's social emancipation is really a call for greater democracy. Emancipation is premised on the idea that societies contain a variety of values and beliefs, sometimes conflicting, and through open deliberation and critical self-reflection civil-society actors are able to form (and reform) public opinions that shape and influence political elite behavior and state action. The crucial element here is a vibrant public sphere, the domain where civil society groups operate. The public sphere is not a formal institution or organization, but rather a network where citizens can share information and contest differing views on issues of common interest, including appropriate responses to legacies of conflict and violence.

Our final chapters by James Bohman and Jackie Smith, Rebecca Burns, and Rachel Miller illustrate the importance of civil society and the public sphere for peace. They show actual civil society initiatives taking place today that are engaged in work that can and should be interpreted as "transformative peacebuilding." Bohman discusses how civil-society efforts to create spaces for democratic and egalitarian deliberation—however limited by the structural constraints in which civil society groups must function—serve as a crucial remedy to the failures of existing peacebuilding approaches.

Bohman and Smith, Burns, and Miller highlight an actual counterhegemonic project of civil society, the World Social Forum (WSF), as a potential focal point for efforts to generate the power civil society needs if it is to effectively challenge and transform the world economic and political system. As an autonomous space of civil society, the WSF is not constrained by the terms of debate and the solutions put forward through interstate institutions like the United Nations. Indeed, the state itself can be problematized as part of the cause of persistent violence (both structural and direct) rather than remain outside of critical scrutiny, and solutions to violence can be sought outside the existing structures of the state. While groups operating in these spaces may be more or less aware of their role in envisioning new sorts of institutional arrangements, they play a vital role in helping give voice to new ideas about how best to order social relations and eliminate the persistent inequity and exclusion that characterize the dominant world order and sustain cycles of violence. Indeed, the point is not to romanticize civil-society peacebuilding efforts, but rather to recognize that sustainable peace is achievable only when all who have a stake in the future are able to articulate their concerns and participate in the decisions that affect them.

In closing, we have sought with this volume to advance a critical discussion across scholarly fields about preventing violence and achieving a just peace. As the world witnesses unprecedented financial, social, and ecological crises, the search for alternatives to the predominant ways of ordering social relations as well as consciousness is increasingly urgent. We hope that this work can contribute to the search for more effective ways of both ending collective violence and building a world where such violence is truly an anomaly rather than inherent to the functioning of the system.

*Bibliography*

*Contributors*

*Index*

# Bibliography

Abdullah, Ibrahim. 2005. "'I Am a Rebel': Youth Culture and Violence in Sierra Leone." In Honwana and de Boeck, *Makers and Breakers*, 172–87.

Aborigines Protection Society to the President of the International Conference in Brussels. 1889. In F.0.881/5983, Part 1: Correspondence Respecting the Conference Relating to the Slave Trade Held at Brussels, December 16, no. 294, 223–24. London: National Archives.

Abrams, Philip. 1988. "Notes on the Difficulty of Studying the State." *Journal of Historical Sociology* 1, no. 1: 59–89.

Achuth. 2002. "We Cannot Tell What Will Happen Tomorrow." *Seagull Theatre Quarterly* 32–33: 104–9.

Ackerly, Brooke. 2000. *Political Theory and Feminist Social Criticism.* Cambridge: Cambridge University Press.

Afzal-Khan, Fawzia. 2001. "Exposed by Pakistani Street Theater: The Unholy Alliance of Postmodern Capitalism, Patriarchy, and Fundamentalism." *Social Text* 19: 67–91.

Agamben, Giorgio. *Homo Sacer: Sovereign Power and Bare Life.* Stanford: Stanford University Press, 1998.

Ahmad, Aijaz, 2002. "Communalism after Gujarat." *Seagull Theatre Quarterly* 32–33: 48–61.

Ahmed, Mohamed. 2009. "Somali Sea Gangs Lure Investors at Pirate Lair." *Reuters,* December 1.

Alexander, Jocelyn C. 1997. "The Local State in Post-War Mozambique." *Africa* 67, no. 1: 1–25. Reprinted in Young, *Readings in African Politics,* 182–92.

———. 2006. *The Civil Sphere.* Oxford: Oxford University Press.

Al-Jawaheri, Yasmin Husein. 2008. *Women in Iraq: The Gender Impact of International Sanctions.* Boulder, CO: Lynne Rienner.

247

Allard, Jenna, Carl Davidson, and Julie Matthaei. 2008. *Solidarity Economy: Building Alternatives for People and Planet.* U.S. Solidarity Economy Network. Chicago: ChangeMaker.

Althusser, Louis. 1970. *For Marx.* Translated by B. Brewster. New York: Vintage Books.

Anheier, Helmut. 2007. "Bringing Civility Back In—Reflections on Global Civil Society." *Development Dialogue* 49: 41–50.

Anonymous. 1996. "Why Should the North Apologize?" *The New Citizen,* November 28,3.

Anonymous. 2002. "This Heart Desires More, Guruji" [Yeh Dil Mangey More, Guruji]. *Nukkad* 5, nos. 14–15: 116–22.

Anonymous. 2006a. "Makeni Town Council Chairman Must Vacate—Ernest Bai Koroma." *The New Citizen,* February 1, 2.

Anonymous. 2006b. "Makeni Town Council Chairman a Disgrace." *The New Citizen,* February 2,4.

Anonymous. 2006c. "Commentary: Musa Mansaray Must Resign." *The New Citizen,* February 7, 3.

Anonymous. 2006d. "Civil Society Rises against Makeni Town Chairman." *The New Citizen,* February 13, 1.

Anonymous. 2006e. "Makeni Council Chairman Resigns." *The New Citizen,* February 14, 1.

Anonymous. 2006f. "I Resigned Because of Peace—Makeni Town Council Chairman." *Awoko,* February 16,1.

Appiah, Kwame Anthony. 2006. *Cosmopolitanism: Ethics in a World of Strangers.* New York: Norton.

Ashforth, Adam. 1998. "Witchcraft, Violence, and Democracy in the New South Africa." *Cahiers d'Etudes Africaines* 38 (150): 505–32.

Axworthy, Lloyd. 1998. "Towards a New Multilateralism." In *To Walk without Fear: The Global Movement to Ban Landmines,* edited by Maxwell A. Cameron, Robert J, Lawson, and Brian W. Tomlin, 448–59. Oxford: Oxford University Press.

Babb, Sarah. 2001. *Managing Mexico: Economists from Nationalism to Neoliberalism.* Princeton: Princeton University Press.

———. 2005. "The Social Consequences of Structural Adjustment: Recent Evidence and Current Debates." *Annual Review of Sociology* 31: 199–222.

Bahadur, Jay. 2009. "'I'm Not a Pirate, I'm the Saviour of the Sea.'" *The Times (of London),* April 16.

Baker, Aryn. 2009. "The Warlords of Afghanistan." *Time,* February 23, 40–41.

———. 2010. "Afghan Women and the Return of the Taliban." *Time,* August 9, 18–28.

Baker, Raymond W., Shereen T. Ismael, and Tareq Y. Ismael, eds. 2010. *Cultural Cleansing in Iraq: Why Museums Were Looted, Libraries Burned, and Academics Murdered.* London: Pluto Press.

Barber, Benjamin. 1995. *Jihad vs. McWorld.* New York: Random House.

Barkan, Joel D., Michael L. McNulty, and M. A. O. Ayeni. 1991. "Hometown Voluntary Associations, Local Development, and the Emergence of Civil Society in Western Nigeria." *The Journal of Modern African Studies* 29, no. 3: 457–80.

Barker, Juliet. 2005. *Agincourt: Henry V and the Battle That Made England.* London: Back Bay Books.

Barnett, Jon. 2008. "Peace and Development: Towards a New Synthesis." *Journal of Peace Research* 45: 75–89.

Barnett, Michael. 2009. "Evolution without Progress?: Humanitarianism in a World of Hurt." *International Organization* 63: 621–63.

Barnett, Michael, and Thomas G. Weiss, eds. 2008a. *Humanitarianism in Question: Politics, Power, Ethics.* Ithaca: Cornell University Press.

Barnett, Michael, and Thomas G. Weiss. 2008b. "Humanitarianism: A Brief History of the Present." In Barnett and Weiss, *Humanitarianism in Question,* 1–48.

Bastian, Misty L. 2003. "Diabolic Realities: Narratives of Conspiracy, Transparency, and 'Ritual Murder' in the Nigerian Popular Print and Electronic Media." In *Transparency and Conspiracy,* edited by Sanders and West, 65–91.

Basu, Amrita, and Srirupa Roy, eds. 2007. *Violence and Democracy in India.* Calcutta: Seagull Books.

Bateman, Milford. 2008. "Microfinance and Borderlands: Impacts of Local Neoliberalism." In Pugh, Cooper, and Turner, *Whose Peace?,* 245–65.

Bayart, Jean-François 1993. *The State in Africa: Politics of the Belly.* New York: Longman.

Bazenguissa-Ganga, R. 1999. "The Spread of Political Violence in Congo-Brazzaville." *African Affairs* 98, no. 390: 389–411. Reprinted in Young, *Readings in African Politics,* 89–96.

Beachey, R. W. 1962. "The Arms Trade in East Africa in the Late Nineteenth Century." *The Journal of African History* 3, no. 3: 451–67.

Becker, Marc, and Ashley N. Koda. 2011. "Indigenous Peoples and Social Forums." In Smith, *Handbook of the World Social Forums*, 105–24.

Beier, J. Marshall. 2011. "Dangerous Terrain: Re-reading the Landmines Ban through the Social Worlds of the RMA." *Contemporary Security Policy* 32, no. 1: 159–75.

Bell, Stewart. 2009. "Somali Militants Training Pirates: 'Relationship of Convenience': Canadian Report." *National Post*, December 3, http://www.biyoku lule.com/view_content.php?articleid=2378.

Bergman, Marcelo. 2009. "Rising Crime in Mexico and Buenos Aires: The Effect of Changes in Labor Markets and Community Breakdown." In *Criminality, Public Security, and the Challenge to Democracy in Latin America*, edited by Marcelo Bergman and Laurence Whitehead, 62–92. Notre Dame: University of Notre Dame Press.

Bernstein, Henry, Colin Leys, and Leo Panitch. 2009. "Reflections on Violence Today." In Panitch and Leys, *Violence Today*, 5–22.

Besteman, Catherine. 1996. "Violence Politics and the Politics of Violence: The Dissolution of the Somali Nation-State." *American Ethnologist* 23, no. 3: 579–96.

———. 1999. *Unraveling Somalia: Race, Violence, and the Legacy of Slavery*. Edited by C. K. Mahmood. Philadelphia: University of Pennsylvania Press.

Beyer, Cornelia. 2007. "Non-Governmental Organizations as Motors of Change." *Government and Opposition* 42: 513–35.

Bharucha, Rustom. 2006. "Muslims and Others: Anecdotes, Fragments, and Uncertainties of Evidence." *Inter-Asia Cultural Studies* 5: 472.

Blau, Judith, and Marina Karides, eds. 2008. *The World and US Social Forums: A Better World Is Possible and Necessary*. Leiden, The Netherlands: Brill.

Bohman, James. 2007. *Democracy across Borders: From Demos to Demoi*. Cambridge: MIT Press.

Bolten, Catherine. 2008. "'The Place Is So Backward': Durable Morality and Creative Development in Northern Sierra Leone." PhD diss., University of Michigan.

Bond, Patrick, ed. 2005. *Fanon's Warning: A Civil Society Reader on the New Partnership for Africa's Development*. 2nd ed. Trenton, NJ: Africa World Press.

Bono. 2009. "Rebranding Africa." *The New York Times*, July 10.

Boone, Jon. 2009a. "Kabul Passes No Sex, No Food Law." *The Guardian Weekly*, 21 August, 13.

———. 2009b. "Taliban Murders Women's Champion." *The Guardian Weekly*, 17 April, 11.

———. 2010. "Afghan Campaigners for Female MP Killed." *The Guardian Weekly*, 3 September, 4.

Borchgrave, Arnaud de. 2009. "Al Qaeda's Navy?: A Militant Lesson from the Past." *The Washington Times,* August 17, 19.

Borrie, John. 2009. *Unacceptable Harm: A History of How the Treaty to Ban Cluster Munitions Was Won.* Geneva: UNIDIR.

Borrie, John, and Vanessa Martin Randin, eds. 2006. *Disarmament as Humanitarian Action: From Perspective to Action.* Geneva: UNIDIR.

Boyce, James K. 2002. *Investing in Peace: Aid and Conditionality after Civil War.* Oxford: Oxford University Press.

Bradbury, Mark. 2008. *Becoming Somaliland.* Oxford: Progressio.

Branch, Daniel. 2006. "Loyalists, Mau Mau, and the Elections in Kenya: The First Triumph of the System, 1957–58." *Africa Today* 53, no. 2: 27–50.

Brecht, Bertolt. 1977. *Brecht on Theatre: The Development of an Aesthetic.* New York: Hill and Wang.

Breines, Ingeborg, Robert Connell, and Ingrid Eide, eds. 2000. *Male Roles, Masculinities, and Violence: A Culture of Peace Perspective.* Paris: UNESCO.

Brim, Sand. 2003. "Report from Baghda." *Off Our Backs,* March–April, 10–12.

British Plenipotentiaries to the Marquis of Salisbury, Brussels. 1890. In F.O. 881/6197, Part 2: Further Correspondent respecting the Conference relating to the Slave Trade Held at Brussels, February 25, 1890, 111. London: National Archives.

Broad, Robin, and John Cavanagh. 2006. "The Highjacking of the Development Debate: How Friedman and Sachs Got It Wrong." *World Policy Journal* 23, no. 2: 21–30.

Brunelle, Dorval. 2007. *From World Order to Global Disorder: States, Markets, and Dissent.* Vancouver: University of British Columbia Press.

Bunting-Davis, F. 1981. "An Experiment in Local Government That Spelt a Big Flop until . . . So, It Can Be Done!" *We Yone,* October 11.

Burawoy, Michael. 1998. "The Extended Case Method." *Sociological Theory* 16: 4–33.

Burchell, Graham, Colin Gordon, and Peter Miller. 1991. *The Foucault Effect: Studies in Governmentality.* Chicago: University of Chicago Press.

Bureau of Industry and Security, United States Department of Commerce. 2011. "Export Control Reform Initiative: Strategic Trade Authorization License Exception," June 16, http://www.bis.doc.gov/news/2011/bis_press06162011.htm.

Burns, Richard Dean. 1971. "Regulating Submarine Warfare, 1921–41: A Case Study in Arms Control and Limited War." *Military Affairs* 35, no. 2: 56–63.

———. 1993. *Encyclopedia of Arms Control and Disarmament.* New York: Scribner's.

———. 2009. *The Evolution of Arms Control: From Antiquity to the Nuclear Age.* Oxford: Praeger Security International.

Burton, John W. 1990. *Conflict Resolution and Prevention.* Vol. 1. Basingstoke: Macmillan.

Buzan, Barry, and Ole Waever. 2009. "Macrosecuritisation and Security Constellations: Reconsidering Scale in Securitisation Theory." *Review of International Studies* 35, no. 2: 53–276.

Calhoun, Craig. 2008. "The Imperative to Reduce Suffering: Charity, Progress, and Emergencies in the Field of Humanitarian Action." In Barnett and Weiss, *Humanitarianism in Question*, 73–97.

Carazzolo, Barbara, Aberto Chiara, and Luciano Scalettari. 1998. "'E la nave va.'" *Familia Cristiana* 13, http://www.stpauls.it/fc98/1398fc/fc38.htm.

Carbonnier, Gilles. 2002. "The Competing Agendas of Economic Reform and Peace Process: A Politico-Economic Model Applied to Guatemala." *World Development* 30, no. 8: 1323–39.

Carpenter, R. Charli. 2011. "Vetting the Advocacy Agenda: Network Centrality and the Paradox of Weapons Norms." *International Organization* 65, no. 1: 69–102.

Carr, Christopher D. 1990. "The Other Arms Control: The Management and Control of Conventional Arms Transfers." *United States Air Force Journal of Legal Studies* 23: 23–49.

Carroll, Anthony J., and B. Rajagopal. 1993. "The Case for the Independent Statehood of Somaliland." *American University Journal of International Law & Policy* 8: 653–81.

Chabal, Patrick, and Jean-Pascal Daloz. 1999. *Africa Works: Disorder as Political Instrument.* Oxford: James Currey.

Chalk, Peter. 2008. "The Maritime Dimension of International Security: Terrorism, Piracy, and Challenges for the United States." Santa Monica, CA: RAND.

———. 2009. "Maritime Piracy: Reasons, Dangers, and Solutions." Washington, DC: RAND.

Chalk, Peter, and Laurence Smallman. 2009. "Piracy Still Threatens the Freedom of the Seas." *Radio Free Europe and Radio Liberty,* April 3, http://www.rand.org/commentary/2009/04/03/RFERL_piracy.html).

Chandrasekaran, Rajiv. 2009a. "Obama's New Deal for Afghan Farmers." *The Guardian Weekly,* August 7, 45.

———. 2009b. "U.S. Pursues a New Way to Rebuild in Afghanistan." *The Washington Post,* June 19, A1.

Chase-Dunn, Christopher. 1998. *Global Formation: Structures of the World-Economy.* 2nd ed. Lanham, MD: Rowman & Littlefield.

Chase-Dunn, Christopher, et al. 2009. "The New Global Left: Movements and Regimes." IROWS Working Paper no. 50, University of California, Riverside. http://irows.ucr.edu/papers/irows50/irows50.htm.

Chatterjee, Ashish. 2002. "Brotherhood Is Not Enough." *Seagull Theatre Quarterly* 32–33: 126–33.

Chaturvedi, Vinayak. 2011. "From Peasant Pasts to Hindutva Futures: Some Reflections on History, Politics, and Methodology." *South Asia* 34, no. 3: 402–20.

Christensen, Janne Bjerre. 2011. *Drugs, Deviancy, and Democracy in Iran.* London: I. B. Tauris.

Chua, Amy. 2003. *World on Fire: How Exporting Free Market Democracy Breeds Ethnic Hatred and Global Instability.* New York: Anchor Books.

Clark, Gracia. 1994. *Onions Are My Husband: Survival and Accumulation by West African Market Women.* Chicago: University of Chicago Press.

Cochran, Molly. 2008. "The Normative Power of International Publics: The Case of the Women's International League for Peace and Freedom, 1919–1925." American Political Science Association 2008 Annual Meeting, Boston, MA.

Coker, Christopher. 2001. *Humane Warfare.* London: Routledge.

Cole, J. 2005. "The Jaombilo of Tamatave (Madagascar), 1992–2004: Reflections on Youth and Globalization." *The Journal of Social History* 38, no. 4: 891–914.

Collier, Paul. 2005. "Iraq: A Perspective from the Economic Analysis of Civil War." Department of Economics, Oxford University (June), http://users.ox.ac.uk/~econpco/research/conflict.htm.

Collier, Paul, Lisa Chauvet, and Haarvard Hegre. 2008. "The Security Challenge in Conflict-Prone Countries." Copenhagen: Copenhagen Consensus Center.

Collier, Paul, V. L. Elliott, Havard Hegre, Anke Hoeffler, Marta Reynal-Querol, and Nicholas Sambanis. 2003. *Breaking the Conflict Trap: Civil War and Development Policy.* Washington, DC: The World Bank and Oxford University Press.

Collier, Paul, and Anke Hoeffler. 2002. "Aid, Policy, and Peace: Reducing the Risks of Civil Conflict." *Defense and Peace Economics* 12, no. 6: 435–50.

———. 2004. "Greed and Grievance in Civil War." 2004. *Oxford Economic Papers* 56 no. 4: 563–95. http://econpapers.repec.org/article/oupoxecpp/default56.htm.

Collier, Paul, and Nicholas Sambanis. 2005. *Understanding Civil War: Evidence and Analysis.* Washington, DC: World Bank.

Confortini, Catia. 2010. "Reclaiming Agency for Social Change." In *Twenty Years of Feminist International Relations,* edited by Ann Tickner and Laura Sjoberg, 22–47. New York: Palgrave MacMillan.

Connell, Raewyn. 1998. "Masculinities and Globalization." *Men and Masculinities* 1, no. 1: 1–20.

Constable, Pamela. 2009. "Kabul's Cobblers Sweat It Out." *The Guardian Weekly,* April 24, 44.

Cooke, Maeve. 1997. *The Business of Death: Britain's Arms Trade at Home and Abroad.* London: I. B. Tauris.

———. 2006a. "What's the Point of Arms Transfer Controls?" *Contemporary Security Policy,* Special Issue: Future Directions on Small Arms, 27, no. 1: 85–99.

———. 2006b. "Chimeric Governance and the Extension of Resource Regulation." *Conflict, Security, and Development* 6, no. 3: 315–35.

———. 2007. "A Secular State for a Postsecular Society?: Postmetaphysical Political Theory and the Place of Religion." *Constellations* 14, no. 2: 224–38.

———. 2010. "Training Goldfish (in a Desert): Transforming Political Economies of Conflict Using Voluntarism, Regulation, and Supervision." In Richmond, *Palgrave Advances In Peacebuilding,* 307–26.

———. 2011. "Humanitarian Arms Control and Processes of Securitization: Moving Weapons along the Security Continuum." *Contemporary Security Policy,* Special Issue: Arms Control for the Twenty-first Century: Controlling the Means of Violence, 32, no. 1: 134–58.

Corbridge, Stuart, and John Harriss. 2000. *Reinventing India: Liberalization, Hindu Nationalism, and Popular Democracy.* Oxford: Oxford University Press.

Cordovez, Diego, and Selig Harrison. 1995. *Out of Afghanistan: The Inside Story of the Soviet Withdrawal.* NY: Oxford University Press.

Cortright, David. 2008. *Peace: A History of Movements and Ideas.* Cambridge: Cambridge University Press.

Cottrell, M. Patrick. 2009. "Legitimacy and Institutional Replacement: The Convention on Certain Conventional Weapons and the Emergence of the Mine Ban Treaty." *International Organization* 63: 217–48.

Cox, Robert. 1986. "Social Forces, States, and World Orders: Beyond International Relations Theory." In *Neorealism and Its Critics,* edited by R. O. Keohane, 204–54. New York: Columbia University Press.

———. 1995. "Critical Political Economy." In *International Political Economy: Understanding Global Disorder,* edited by B. Hettne, 31–45. London: Zed Books.

Croft, Stuart. 1996. *Strategies of Arms Control: A History and Typology.* Manchester: Manchester University Press.

Da Costa, Dia, and Philip McMichael. 2007. "The Poverty of the Global Order." *Globalizations* 4: 588–602.

Dagne, Ted. 2009. "Somalia: Prospects for a Lasting Peace." *Mediterranean Quarterly* 20, no. 2: 95–112.

Dagnino, Evelina. 2008. "Challenges to Participation, Citizenship, and Democracy: Perverse Confluence and Displacement of Meanings." In *Can NGOs Make a Difference: The Challenge of Development Alternatives,* edited by A. J. Bebbington, S. Hickey, and D. C. Mitlin, 55–70. New York: Zed Books.

Daly-Harris, Sam. 2009. *State of the Microcredit Campaign Report.* Washington, DC: Results Educational Fund.

Darby, John, ed. 2006. *Violence and Reconstruction.* Notre Dame: University of Notre Dame Press.

Das, Veena. 1990. *Mirrors of Violence: Communities, Riots, and Survivors in South Asia.* New Delhi: Oxford University Press.

De Angelis, Massimo. 2004. "Opposing Fetishism by Reclaiming Our Powers: The Social Forum Movement, Capitalist Markets, and the Politics of Alternatives." *International Social Science Journal* 56: 591–604.

Defense News. 2009. "Obama Orders Broad Review of Export Control Regs." *Defense News,* August 14, http://www.defensenews.com/.

della Porta, Donatella. 2005. "Multiple Belongings, Tolerant Identities, and the Construction of 'Another Politics': Between the European Social Forum and the Local Social Fora." In *Transnational Protest and Global Activism,* edited by D. della Porta and S. Tarrow, 175–202. Lanham, MD: Rowman & Littlefield.

della Porta, Donatella, Massimiliano Andretta, Lorenzo Mosca, and Herbert Reiter. 2006. *Globalization from Below: Transnational Activists and Protest Networks.* Minneapolis: University of Minnesota Press.

della Porta, Donatella, Abby Peterson, and Herbert Reiter, eds. 2007. *The Policing of Transnational Protest.* London: Ashgate.

Desai, Radhika. 2004. "Nation against Democracy: The Rise of Cultural Nationalism in Asia." In *Democracy and Civil Society in Asia,* edited by Fahimul Quadir and Jayant Lele, 81–110. New York: Palgrave Macmillan.

Deshpande, G. P. 2002. "'. . . We Still Don't Know the Enemy We Wish to Attack. . . .'" *Nukkad,* 43–46.

Deshpande, Sudhanva, ed. 2007. *Theatre of the Streets: The Jana Natya Manch Experience.* New Delhi: Janam.

De Waal, Alex. 2006. *Famine Crimes: Politics and the Disaster Relief Industry in Africa.* Bloomington: African Rights and The International African Institute, in association with James Currey and Indiana University Press.

Diouf, M. 2005. "Afterword." In Honwana and de Boeck, *Makers and Breakers,* 229–34.

Doerr, Nicole. 2008. "Deliberative Discussion, Language, and Efficiency in the World Social Forum Process." *Mobilization* 13: 395–410.

Doornbos, Martin. 2002. "Somalia: Alternative Scenarios for National Reconstruction." *African Affairs* 101, no. 402: 93–107.

Dryzek, John. 2009. "Soup, Society, or System: On Global Democratization." Presented at a conference on Democracy and the Deliberative Society, University of York, June 24–26.

Duffield, Mark. 2001. *Global Governance and the New Wars.* London: Zed Books.

Duvall, Raymond, and Latha Varadarajan. 2007. "Travelling in Paradox: Edward Said and Critical International Relations." *Millenium: Journal of International Studies* 36, no. 1: 83–99.

Easterly, William. 2006. *The White Man's Burden: Why the West's Efforts to Aid the Rest Have Done So Much Ill and So Little Good.* London: Penguin Books.

Edelman, M. 2001. "Social Movements: Changing Paradigms and Forms of Politics." *Annual Review of Anthropology* 30: 285–317.

Editor. 2009. "Not Just a Pirate Movie." *The Boston Globe,* April 14, http://www.boston.com/bostonglobe/editorial_opinion/editorials/articles/2009/04/14/not_just_a_pirate_movie/.

Edwards, Michael. 2008. *Just Another Emperor?: The Myths and Realities of Philanthrocapitalism.* New York: Demos. http://www.nonprofitquarterly.org/images/fbfiles/files/Just_Another_Emperor.pdf.

Eisenstein, Zillah. 2004. *Against Empire: Feminisms, Racism, and the West.* London: Zed Books.

Engelbrecht, H. C., and F. C. Hanighen. 1934. *Merchants of Death: A Study of the International Armaments Industry.* New York: Dodd, Mead.

Enloe, Cynthia. 1990. *Bananas, Beaches, and Bases: Making Feminist Sense of International Politics.* Berkeley and Los Angeles: University of California Press.

———. 2006. "Macho, Macho Military." *The Nation,* March 7, http://www.thenation.com/doc/20060320/enloe.

———. 2007. *Globalization and Militarism: Feminists Make the Link.* Lanham, MD: Rowman & Littlefield.

Eschle, Catherine. 2001. *Global Democracy, Social Movements, and Feminism.* Boulder, CO: Westview Press.

Escobar, Arturo. 1988. "Power and Visibility: Development and the Invention and Management of the Third World." *Cultural Anthropology* 3: 428–43.

———. 2004. "Development, Violence, and the New Imperial Order." *Development* 47: 15–21.

Escobar, Arturo, and Sonia E. Alvarez, eds. 1992. *The Making of Social Movements in Latin America: Identity, Strategy, and Democracy.* Boulder CO: Westview Press.

Fanthorpe, R. 2005. "On the Limits of Liberal Peace: Chiefs and Democratic Decentralization in Post-war Sierra Leone." *African Affairs* 105, no. 418: 27–47.

Farmer, Paul. 2004. "An Anthropology of Structural Violence." *Current Anthropology* 45: 305–25.

Fatton, R. 1995. "Africa in the Age of Democratization: The Civic Limitations of Civil Society." *African Studies Review* 3, no. 2: 67–99.

Fearon, James. 2008. "The Rise of Emergency Relief Aid." In Barnett and Weiss, *Humanitarianism in Question,* 49–72.

Fearon, John, and David Laitin. 2003. "Ethnicity, Insurgency, and Civil War." *American Political Science Review* 97, no. 1: 75–90.

Ferguson, James. 1994. *The Anti-Politics Machine: "Development," Depoliticization, and Bureaucratic Power in Lesotho.* Minneapolis: University of Minnesota Press.

———. 2006. *Global Shadows: Africa in the Neoliberal World Order.* Durham: Duke University Press.

Ferree, Myra Marx. 2003. "Resonance and Radicalism: Feminist Framing in the Abortion Debates of the United States and Germany." *American Journal of Sociology* 109: 304–44.

Fetherston, A. Betts. 2000. "Peacekeeping, Conflict Resolution, and Peacebuilding: A Reconsideration of Theoretical Frameworks." *International Peacekeeping* 7: 190–218.

Filkins, Dexter. 2009. "A School Bus for Shamsia." *New York Times Magazine,* August 23.

Fitzgerald, Valpy. 2000. "Paying for the War: Economic Policy in Poor Countries." In *The Economic and Social Consequences of Conflict,* edited by Frances Stewart and Valpy Fitzgerald, 45–68. Oxford: Oxford University Press.

Fletcher, Max E. 1958. "The Suez Canal and World Shipping, 1869–1914." *The Journal of Economic History* 18, no. 4: 556–73.

Fortier, J. 2001. "Sharing, Hoarding, and Theft: Exchange and Resistance in Forager-Farmer Relations." *Ethnology* 40, no. 3: 193–211.

Foucault, Michel. 1991. "Governmentality." In *The Foucault Effect: Studies in Governmentality,* edited by Graham Burchell, Colin Gordon, and Peter Miller, 87–104. Chicago: University of Chicago Press.

Fox, F. W. 1889. Letter from Mr. F. W. Fox to Lord Salisbury, October 17. In F.0. 881/5983, Part 2: Correspondence respecting the Conference relating to the Slave Trade Held at Brussels, no. 84, 45–46. London: National Archives.

Franceschet, Antonio. 2006. "Global Legalism and Human Security." In *A Decade of Human Security: Global Governance and New Multilateralisms*, edited by Sandra J. Maclean, David R. Black, and Timothy M. Shaw, 31–38. Aldershot: Ashgate.

Fraser, Nancy. 2005. "Reframing Justice in a Globalizing World." *New Left Review* 36: 69–88.

Fujii Takeshi, and Oshikawa Fumiko, eds. 2000. *Fussing Modernity: Appropriation of History and Political Mobilization in South Asia*. Osaka: The Japan Center for Area Studies, National Museum of Ethnology.

Fung, Archon. 2003. "Recipes for Public Spheres." *Journal of Political Philosophy* 11, no. 3: 338–67.

Gable, E. 1997. "A Secret Shared: Fieldwork and the Sinister in a West African Village." Cultural Anthropology 12, no. 2: 213–33.

Galtung, Johan. 1975. *Essays in Peace Research*. Vol. 1. Copenhagen: Christian Ejlers.

Gbenda, Theophilus. 2006. "Former Makeni Town Council Chairman under Death Threat." *Awareness Times*, April 3, 1.

Gettleman, Jeffrey. 2008. "Pirates Tell Their Side: They Want Only Money." *The New York Times*, October 1, A6.

Gibbs, David. 2009. *First Do No Harm: Humanitarian Intervention and the Destruction of Yugoslavia*. Nashville: Vanderbilt University Press.

Gibson, Clark C., Krister Andersson, Elinor Ostrom, and Sujai Shivakumar. 2005. *The Samaritan's Dilemma: The Political Economy of Development Aid*. Oxford: Oxford University Press.

Gilpin, Raymond. 2009. "Counting the Cost of Somali Piracy." In *United States Institute of Peace Working Papers*. Washington, DC: United States Institute of Peace.

Glasius, Marlies, and Mary Kaldor. 2002. "The State of Global Civil Society: Before and After September 11." In *Global Civil Society Yearbook*, edited by M. Glasius, M. Kaldor, and H. Anheier, 3–34. Oxford: Oxford University Press.

Goheen, M. 1992. "Chiefs, Sub-Chiefs, and Local Control." *Africa* 62, no. 3: 389–411. Reprinted in Young, *Readings in African Politics*, 97–106.

Goldman, Marshall I. 2008. "Moscow's New Swagger." *Chronicle of Higher Education*, September 1.

Goldring, Natalie. 2006. "Establishing Controls for SALW and Major Conventional Weapons." *Contemporary Security Policy*, Special Issue: Future Directions on Small Arms, 27, no. 1: 85–99.

Goose, Stephen D. 2008a. "Cluster Munitions: Ban Them." *Arms Control Today*, January–February, http://www.armscontrol.org.act/2008_01-02/goose.

————. 2008b. "Cluster Munitions in the Crosshairs: In Pursuit of a Prohibition." In Williams, Goose, and Wareham, *Banning Landmines*, 217–39.

Green, Owen. 2010. "Examining Arms Control Processes: Reframing for Priority Setting." Paper for the International Studies Association Conference, New Orleans, February 17–20.

Grillot, Suzette R., Craig S. Stapley, and Molly E. Hanna. 2006. "Assessing the Small Arms Movement: The Trials and Tribulations of a Transnational Network." *Contemporary Security Policy* 27, no. 1: 60–84.

Habermas, Jürgen. 1996. *Between Facts and Norms: Contributions to a Discourse Theory of Law and Democracy.* Cambridge: MIT Press.

————. 2008. *Between Naturalism and Religion.* Cambridge: Polity Press.

Hafez, Mohammed. 2003. *Why Muslims Rebel: Repression and Resistance in the Islamic World.* Boulder, CO: Lynne Rienner.

Hari, Jonathan. 2009. "You Are Being Lied to about the Pirates." *The Independent,* January 5, http://www.huffingtonpost.com/johann-hari/you-are-being-lied-to-abo_b_155147.html.

Harkavy, Robert E. 1974. *The Arms Trade and International Systems.* Cambridge, MA: Ballinger.

Harriman, Ed. 2005. "Where Has All the Money Gone?" *London Review of Books,* July 7.

Hartung, William. 2008. "The International Arms Trade." In *Security Studies: An Introduction,* edited by Paul D. Williams, 345–60. Abingdon: Routledge.

Harvey, David. 2003. *The New Imperialism.* Oxford: Oxford University Press.

Harvey, Paul and Jeremy Lind. 2005. *Dependency and Humanitarian Relief: A Critical Analysis.* London: Humanitarian Policy Group, The Overseas Development Institute. http://www.odi.org.uk/sites/odi.org.uk/files/odi-assets/publications-opinion-files/277.pdf.

————. 2005. "From Globalization to the New Imperialism." In *Critical Globalization Studies,* edited by Richard P. Appelbaum and William I. Robinson, 91–100. London: Routledge.

————. 2006. *Spaces of Global Capitalism: Towards a Theory of Uneven Geographical Development.* New York: Verso.

Hasty, J. 2005. "The Pleasure of Corruption: Desire and Discipline in Ghanaian Political Culture." *Cultural Anthropology* 20, no. 2: 271–301.

Hayes, Christopher. 2007. "Hip Heterodoxy." *The Nation,* June 11, http://www.thenation.com/doc/20070611/hayes/2.

Hayner, Priscilla B. 1994. "Fifteen Truth Commissions—1974 to 1994: A Comparative Study." *Human Rights Quarterly* 16: 597–655.

High Seas Task Force (HSTF). 2006. "Closing the Net: Stopping Illegal Fishing on the High Seas." London: IUU Fishing Coordination Unit.

Hobsbawm, E. J. 1959. *Primitive Rebels: Studies in Archaic Forms of Social Movement in the Nineteenth and Twentieth Centuries.* New York: W. W. Norton.

Hoffman, D. 2003. "Like Beasts in the Bush: Synonyms of Childhood and Youth in Sierra Leone." *Postcolonial Studies* 6, no. 3: 295–308.

Holton, Paul, Mark Bromley, Pieter D. Wezeman, and Siemon T Wezeman. 2010. Trends in International Arms Transfers, 2009. SIPRI Fact Sheet, March 2010. http://books.sipri.org/product_info?c_product_id=404.

Honwana, A., and F. de Boeck, eds. *Makers and Breakers: Children and Youth in Postcolonial Africa.* Oxford: James Currey.

House of Commons Foreign Affairs Committee. 2009. *Global Security: Non-Proliferation.* Fourth Report of Session 2008–2009, HC 222. London: The Stationery Office. http://www.publications.parliament.uk/pa/cm200809/cmselect/cmfaff/222/222.pdf.

House of Commons Foreign Affairs Committee. 2010. *Global Security: UK-US Relations.* Sixth Report of Session 2009–2010, HC 114. London: The Stationery Office.

Howden, Daniel. 2009. "Africa's Best-Kept Secret: As Somalia Gains Infamy as a Haven for Pirates, Its Smaller Peaceful Neighbour Is Pleading for International Recognition." *The Independent,* May 6, http://www.garoweonline.com/artman2/publish/Somalia_27/Somaliland_Africa_s_best-kept_secret_printer.shtml.

Human Security Center. 2005. *Human Security Report 2005: War and Peace in the Twenty-first Century.* New York: Oxford University Press.

Huntington, Samuel. 2003. "The Clash of Civilizations?" *Foreign Affairs* 72, no. 3: 22–49.

Hyden, G. 1983. "Conditions of Governance." In *No Shortcuts to Progress: African Development Management in Perspective,* edited by Goran Hyden, 36–45. Los Angeles: University of California Press. Reprinted in Young, *Readings in African Politics,* 23–27.

Hynek, Nikola. 2007. "Humanitarian Arms Control, Symbiotic Functionalism, and the Concept of Middlepowerhood." *Central European Journal of International and Security Studies* 1, no. 2: 132–55.

Ikelegbe, A. 2001. "The Perverse Manifestation of Civil Society: Evidence from Nigeria." *The Journal of Modern African Studies* 39, no. 1: 1–24.

International Commission on Intervention and State Sovereignty (ICISS). 2001. *The Responsibility to Protect.* Ottawa: International Development Research Centre.

International Monetary Fund. 2005. *Sierra Leone: Poverty Reduction Strategy Paper—Joint Staff Advisory Note.* June. Washington DC: IMF Publication Services.

Ishay, Micheline. 1995. *Internationalism and Its Betrayal.* Minneapolis: University of Minnesota Press.

Jabri, Vivienne. 2007. *War and the Transformation of Global Politics.* London: Palgrave.

Jackson, M. 2004. *In Sierra Leone.* Durham: Duke University Press.

Jackson, P. 2006. "Reshuffling an Old Deck of Cards?: The Politics of Local Government Reform in Sierra Leone." *African Affairs* 106, no. 422: 95–111.

Jaggar, Allison M. 2001. "Is Globalization Good for Women?" *Comparative Literature* 53: 298–314.

Jan, Ameen. 2001. "Somalia: Building Sovereignty or Restoring Peace?" In *Peacebuilding as Politics: Cultivating Peace in Fragile Societies,* edited by E. M. Cousens and C. Kumar, 53–88. Boulder, CO: Lynne Rienner.

Janam. 2002. *Weapons [Hatyarey]. Nukkad* 5, nos. 14–15: 55–60.

Janega, James, and Antonio Olivo. 2009. "Abandoned, Adrift, Enduring: Weary Iraqi Refugees Describe How Life in Chicago and America Has Left Them with Very Little Hope." *Chicago Tribune,* October 25, 1.

Jeffrey, C. 2010. *Timepass: Youth, Class, and the Politics of Waiting in India.* Stanford: Stanford University Press.

Joya, Malalai. 2009. *Raising My Voice.* NY: Simon & Shuster.

Juris, Jeffrey. 2008. "Spaces of Intentionality: Race, Class, and Horizontality at the United States Social Forum." *Mobilization* 13: 353–72.

Kaldor, Mary. 1999. *New and Old Wars: Organized Violence in a Global Era.* Cambridge: Polity Press.

———. 2003. *Global Civil Society: An Answer to War.* Cambridge: Polity Press.

Kaldor, Mary, and Robin Luckham. 2001. "Global Transformations and New Conflicts." *IDS Bulletin* 32, no. 2: 48–69.

Kaldor, Mary, and Marika Theros. 2008. "Secure Afghanistan." *OpenDemocracy,* November 12, http://www.opendemocracy.net/article/kaldor/secure-afghanistan.

Kamola, Isaac A. 2007. "The Global Coffee Economy and the Production of Genocide in Rwanda." *Third World Quarterly* 28, no. 3: 571–92.

Kandeh, J. 2003. "Sierra Leone's Post-conflict Elections of 2002." *The Journal of Modern African Studies* 41, no. 2: 189–213.

Kaplan, Robert B. 2009. "Anarchy on Land Means Piracy at Sea." *The New York Times,* April 12, http://www.nytimes.com/2009/04/12/opinion/12kaplan.html?_r=0.

Kaplan, Seth. 2008. "The Remarkable Story of Somaliland." *Journal of Democracy* 19, no. 3: 143–57.

Karat, Brinda. 2002. "Genocide in Gujarat." *Seagull Theatre Quarterly* 32–33: 90–95.

Karides, Marina, Walda Katz-Fishman, Rose M. Brewer, Jerome Scott, and Alice Lovelace, eds. 2010. *The United States Social Forum: Perspectives of a Movement.* Chicago: Changemaker.

Karp, Aaron. 1988. "The Trade in Major Conventional Weapons." In *SIPRI Yearbook of World Armaments and Disarmament.* Stockholm International Peace Research Institute. London: Oxford University Press.

———. 2006. "Escaping Reuterswärd's Shadow." *Contemporary Security Policy* 27, no. 1: 12–28.

Keck, Margaret, and Kathryn Sikkink. 1998. *Activists without Borders.* Ithaca: Cornell University Press.

Keen, David. 2000. "Incentives and Disincentives for Violence." In *Greed and Grievance,* edited by Mats Berdal and David Malone, 19–42. Boulder, CO: Lynne Rienner Publishers.

Khaleeli, Homa. 2011. "Afghan Women Fear for the Future." *The Guardian Weekly,* March 11, 30.

Kingfisher, Catherine, ed. 2003. *Western Welfare in Decline: Globalization and Women's Poverty.* Philadelphia: University of Pennsylvania Press.

Kirk, Sir John. 1891. Memorandum, August 15. In FO 403-169, Correspondence respecting the Ratification of the Brussels Act, 1891–1892. London: National Archives.

Klare, Michael. 2008. "Past Its Peak: On the Oil Crisis." *London Review of Books,* August 14, 38–39.

Klein, Joe. 2008. "Why Are We in Helmand?" *Time,* September 28, 26.

Klein, Naomi. 2007. *Shock Doctrine: The Rise of Disaster Capitalism.* NY: Henry Holt.

Klotz, Audie. 1995. *Norms in International Relations: The Struggle against Apartheid.* Ithaca: Cornell University Press.

Knight, Graham, and Jackie Smith. 2007. "The Global Compact and Its Critics: Activism, Power Relations, and Corporate Social Responsibility." In *Discipline and Punishment in Global Politics: Illusions of Control,* edited by J. Leatherman, 191–214. New York: Palgrave Macmillan.

Kolodjiej, Edward A. 1987. *Making and Marketing Arms: The French Experience and Its Implications for the International System.* Princeton: Princeton University Press.

Korzeniewicz, Roberto Patricio, and Timothy Patrick Moran. 2009. *Unveiling Inequality: A World-Historical Perspective.* New York: Russell Sage Foundation.

Kraska, James, and Brian Wilson. 2008/2009. "Fighting Pirates: The Pen and the Sword." *World Policy Journal* 25, no. 4: 41–52.

———. 2009. "Maritime Piracy in East Africa." *Journal of International Affairs* 62, no. 2: 55–68.

Krause, Keith. 1992. *Arms and the State: Patterns of Military Production and Trade.* Cambridge: Cambridge University Press.

———. 2011. "Leashing the Dogs of War: Arms Control from Sovereignty to Governmentality." *Contemporary Security Policy* 32, no. 1: 20–39.

Krause, Keith, and Andrew Latham. 1998. "Constructing Non-proliferation and Arms Control: The Norms of Western Practice." In *Contemporary Security Policy*, Special Issue: Culture and Security: Multilateralism, Arms Control, and Security Building, edited by Keith Krause, 19, no. 1: 23–54.

Krause, Keith, and Mary K. MacDonald. 1992. "Regulating Arms Sales through World war II." In Burns, *Encyclopedia of Arms Control and Disarmament*, 707–24.

Krepon, Michael. 1974. "Weapons Potentially Inhumane: The Case of Cluster Bombs." *Foreign Affairs* 52, no. 3: 595–611.

Laitin, David D., and Said S. Samatar. 1987. *Somalia: Nation in Search of a State.* Boulder, CO: Westview Press.

Langman, Lauren, and Daniel Morris. 2004. "Hegemony Lost: Understanding Contemporary Islam." In *Globalization, Hegemony, and Power: Antisystemic Movements and the Global System*, edited by Thomas Reifer, 181–206. Boulder, CO: Paradigm.

Laskar, Baharul Islam. 2000. "Child Labour in the Aligarh Lock Industry." *Economic and Political Weekly* 35: 510–13.

Lattimer, Mark. 2008. "Iraqi Women Count the Cost of Freedom They Have Lost." *The Guardian Weekly*, February 22, 4–5.

Leach, M. 1994. *Rainforest Relations: Gender and Resource Use among the Mende of Gola, Sierra Leone.* Washington DC: Smithsonian Institute Press.

Lederach, John Paul. 2005. *The Moral Imagination.* New York: Oxford University Press.

Lederach, John Paul, Reina Neufeldt, and Hal Culbertson. 2007. *Reflective Peacebuilding: A Planning, Monitoring, and Learning Toolkit.* Notre Dame: Joan B. Kroc Institute for International Peace Studies, University of Notre Dame Press.

Leesen, Peter T. 2007. "Better Off Stateless: Somalia Before and After Government Collapse." *Journal of Comparative Economics* 35, no. 4: 689–710.

Lewis, I. M. 2002. *A Modern History of the Somali: Revised, Updated, and Expanded.* Oxford: James Currey.

———. 2008. *Understanding Somalia and Somaliland.* New York: Columbia University Press.

Li, Tania. 2009. "Reflections on Indonesian Violence: Two Tales and Three Silences." In Panitch and Leys, *Violence Today,* 163–80.

Little, Peter D. 1992. "Traders, Brokers, and Market 'Crisis' in Southern Somalia." *Africa: Journal of the International African Institute* 62, no. 1: 94–124.

Lobo, Lancy. 2002. "Adivasis, Hindutva, and Post-Godhra Riots in Gujarat." *Economic and Political Weekly* 37: 4844–49.

Luft, Gal, and Anne Korin. 2004. "Terrorism Goes to Sea." *Foreign Affairs* 83, no. 6: 61–71.

Luxner, Larry. 2004. "Suez Canal Is Raking in the Revenues." *The Middle East* 349: 46–47.

Lynch, Cecelia M. 1998. "Social Movements and the Problem of 'Globalization.'" *Alternatives* 23, no. 2: 149–93.

———. 1999. "The Promise and Problems of Internationalism." *Global Governance* 5: 83–101.

———. 2000. "Acting On Belief: Christian Perspectives On Suffering And Violence." *Ethics & International Affairs* 14: 83–97.

———. 2009. "Liberalism and the Contradictions of Global Civil Society." In *The Ethics of Global Governance,* edited by Antonio Franceschet, 35–50. Boulder, CO: Lynne Rienner.

———. 2011a. "Religious Humanitarianism and the Global Politics of Secularism." In *Rethinking Secularism,* edited by Mark Juergensmeyer, Jonathan Van-Antwerpen, and Craig Calhoun, 204–24. New York: Oxford.

———. 2011b. "Local And Global Influences on Islamic Ngos In Kenya." *Journal Of Peacebuilding And Development* 6, 1: 1–14.

Macalister, Terry. 2011. "BP 'Has Gained Stranglehold over Iraq' after Oilfield Deal Is Written." *The Guardian Weekly,* August 5, 10. http://www.guardian.co.uk/business/2011/jul/31/bp-stranglehold-iraq-oilfield-contract.

Macdonald, Laura. 1997. *Supporting Civil Society: The Political Role of Non-Governmental Organizations in Central America.* New York: St. Martin's Press.

Macwan, Joseph. 2002. "This 'Unique' Land." In *Seminar,* Special Issue, "Society under Siege: A Symposium on the Breakdown of Civil Society in Gujarat," 513. http://www.india-seminar.com/2002/513/513%20joseph%20macwan.htm.

Malkki, Liisa. 2009. "A Tale of Two Affects: Humanitarianism and Professionalism in Red Cross Aid Work." Paper prepared for the conference "Critical Investigations into Humanitarianism in Africa," University of California Irvine, January.

Mamdani, Mahmood. 2004. *Good Muslim, Bad Muslim: America, the Cold War, and the Roots of Terror.* New York: Pantheon Books.

Mani, Rama. 2002. *Beyond Retribution: Seeking Justice in the Shadows of War.* London: Polity Press.

Manson, Janet M. 1992. "Regulating Submarine Warfare." In *Encyclopedia of Arms Control and Disarmament,* edited by Richard D. Burns, 737–47. New York: Scribner's.

Marchand, Marianne, and Anne Sisson Runyan, eds. 2000. *Gender and Global Restructuring: Sightings, Sites, and Resistances.* London: Routledge.

Markoff, John, and Veronica Montecinos. 1993. "The Ubiquitous Rise of Economists." *Journal of Public Policy* 13: 37–68.

Marquis of Salisbury to Lord Vivian. 1890. In F.O. 881/6197, Part 2: Further Correspondence respecting the Conference relating to the Slave Trade Held at Brussels, April 23, 1890, no. 225, 226–27. Kew: United Kingdom National Archives.

Marshall, Katherine, and Lucy Keough. 2005. *Finding Global Balance: Common Ground between the Worlds of Development and Faith.* Washington, DC: The World Bank.

Marx, Karl. 1997. *Critique of Hegel's "Philosophy of Right."* Cambridge: Cambridge University Press.

Mason, T. David, and James D. Meernik, eds. 2006. *Conflict Prevention and Peacebuilding in Post-war Societies: Sustaining the Peace.* New York: Routledge.

Mathew, Richard A., and Kenneth R Rutherford. 2003. "The Evolutionary Dynamics of the Movement to Ban Landmines." *Alternatives* 28: 29–30.

Mathur, Shubh. 2008. *The Everyday Life of Hindu Nationalism: An Ethnographic Account.* Delhi: Three Essays Collective.

McDonald, Mark. 2009. "Record Number of Somali Pirate Attacks in 2009." *The New York Times,* December 29, http://www.nytimes.com/2009/12/30/world/africa/30piracy.html.

McMichael, Philip. 1990. "Incorporating Comparison within a World-Historical Perspective: An Alternative Comparative Method." *American Sociological Review* 55: 385–97.

———. 2006. *Development and Social Change: A Global Perspective.* 4th ed. Thousand Oaks, CA: Pine Forge.

McNeill, William H. 1982. *The Pursuit of Power: Technology, Armed Force, and Society since AD 1,000.* Chicago: The University of Chicago Press.

Menkhaus, Ken. 2006/2007. "Governance without Government in Somalia: Spoilers, State Building, and the Politics of Coping." *International Security* 31, no. 3: 74–106.

Meznaric, Sylvia. 1994. "Gender as an Ethno-Marker: Rape, War, and Identity Politics in the Former Yugoslavia." In *Identity Politics and Women: Cultural Reassertions and Feminisms in International Perspective,* edited by Valentine M. Moghadam, 76–97. Boulder, CO: Westview Press.

Mgbeoji, Ikechi. 2003. *Collective Insecurity: The Liberian Crisis, Unilateralism, and Global Order.* Vancouver: University of British Columbia Press.

Milanovic, Branko. 2005. *Worlds Apart: Measuring International and Global Inequality.* Princeton: Princeton University Press.

Milazzo, Linda. 2005. "Code Pink: The Twenty-first Century Mothers of Invention." *Development* 48, no. 2: 100–104.

Moghadam, Valentine M. 2002. "Patriarchy, the Taliban, and the Politics of Public Space in Afghanistan." *Women's Studies International Forum* 25, no. 1: 19–31.

———. 2003. *Modernizing Women: Gender and Social Change in the Middle East.* Boulder, CO: Lynne Rienner.

———. 2005, 2013. *Globalizing Women: Transnational Feminist Networks.* Baltimore: Johns Hopkins University Press.

———. 2007. "Peace-building and Reconstruction with Women: Reflections on Afghanistan, Iraq, and Palestine." In *From Patriarchy to Empowerment: Women's Participation, Movements, and Rights in the Middle East, North Africa, and South Asia,* edited by Valentine Moghadam, 327–52. Syracuse: Syracuse University Press.

———. 2010. "Confronting 'Empire': The New Imperialism, Islamism, and Feminism." In *Political Power and Social Theory: A Research Annual,* vol. 20, edited by Diane E. Davis and Julian Go, 201–28. UK: Emerald Group.

———. 2011. "Women, Gender, and Economic Crisis Revisited." *Perspectives on Global Development and Technology* [PGDT] 10: 30–40.

———. 2012. *Globalization and Social Movements: Islamism, Feminism, and the Global Justice Movement.* 2nd ed. Lanham, MD: Rowman & Littlefield.

Mojumdar, Anohita. 2009. "Code Pink Rethinks Its Call for Afghanistan Pullout." *Christian Science Monitor,* October 6, www.csmonitor.com/2009/po6s10-wosc.html.

Monga, C. 1995. "Civil Society and Democratisation in Francophone Africa." *The Journal of Modern African Studies* 33, no. 3: 359–79.

Montecinos, Veronica. 2001. "Feminists and Technocrats in the Democratization of Latin America: A Prolegomenon." *International Journal of Politics, Culture, and Society* 15: 175–99.

Montgomery, David. 2008. "Pillage People: Until Their Legacy Becomes a Punch Line, Somali Pirates Sail Scary Cultural Seas." *The Washington Post*, December 6, C1.

Mooney, K. 1998. "'Ducktails, Flick-Knives, and Pugnacity': Subcultural and Hegemonic Masculinities in South Africa, 1948–1960." *The Journal of Southern African Studies* 24, no. 4: 753–74.

Moore, Pete. 2009. "Making Big Money on Iraq." *Middle East Report* 252 (Fall), http://www.merip.org/mer/mer252/making-big-money-iraq.

Morgan, Crystal. 2011. "Tabula Rasa?: Conceptions of Microfinance in Juba, Sudan." Unpublished PhD thesis, University of California, Irvine.

Moyo, Dambisa. 2009. *Dead Aid: Why Aid Is Not Working and How There Is a Better Way for Africa*. New York: Macmillan.

Munck, Ronaldo. 2002. *Globalization and Labour: The New Great Transformation*. London: Zed Books.

Murphy, Crystal. 2011. "Microfinance on the Ground in Post-conflict Juba, South Sudan." Washington, DC: Wilson Center, Comparative Urban Studies Project. http://www.wilsoncenter.org/publication/microfinance-the-ground-post -conflict-juba-south-sudan.

Mutimer, David. 2006. "A Serious Threat to Peace, Reconciliation, Safety, Security: An Effective Reading of the United Nations Programme of Action." *Contemporary Security Policy* 27, no. 1: 29–44.

National Security Council. 2008. "Countering Piracy off the Horn of Africa: Partnership and Action Plan." Washington, DC: National Security Council.

Near East Arms Coordinating Committee, Minutes. 1954. In Records Pertaining to the Near East Arms Coordinating Committee, Box 2, 66D428, NEACC-M-38, November 14. Washington, DC: United States National Archives.

Neumann, Iver B., and Ole Jacob Sending. 2010. *Governing the Global Polity*. Ann Arbor: University of Michigan Press.

Ngosi, A. 2006. "The Voice of Civil Society in the Rebuilding of Burundi." In *Postconflict Reconstruction in Africa*, edited by A. Sikainga and O. Alidou, 224–36. Trenton, NJ: Africa World Press.

Nigam, Aditya. 2005. *The Insurrection of Little Selves: The Crisis of Secular-Nationalism in India.* New Delhi: Oxford University Press.

Obieta, Joseph A. 1970. *The International Status of the Suez Canal.* The Hague: Martinus Nijhoff.

O'Brien, Robert. 2004. *The International Monetary Fund, The World Bank, and Labour in Developing Countries.* Hamilton, Ontario: McMaster University.

Odula, Tom. 2010. "Pirate Ransom Money May Explain Kenya Property Boom." *Associated Press,* January 1, http://www.huffingtonpost.com/2010/01/02/pirate-ransom-money-kenya_n_409219.html.

Office of the Foreign Trade Adviser, Department of State, to Mr. Millspaugh. 1922. 511.3b1/102. April 7. College Park, MD: United States National Archives.

Ohanyan, A. 2008. *NGOs, IGOs, and the Network Mechanisms of Post-conflict Global Governance in Microfinance.* New York: Palgrave-MacMillan.

Onuf, Nicholas. 2004. "Humanitarian Intervention: The Early Years." *Florida Journal of International Law* 16, no. 4: 753–56.

Osterweil, Michal. 2004. "A Cultural-Political Approach to Reinventing the Political." *International Social Science Journal* 56: 495–506.

Owen, Taylor. 2008. "The Critique That Doesn't Bite: A Response to David Chandler's 'Human Security: The Dog That Didn't Bark.'" *Security Dialogue* 39, no. 4: 445–53.

Owusu, M. 1997. "Domesticating Democracy: Culture, Civil Society, and Constitutionalism in Africa." *Comparative Studies in Society and History* 39, no. 1: 120–52.

OXFAM/ACBAR. 2008. Report on Aid Effectiveness in Afghanistan. http://www.oxfam.org/en/news/2008/pr080325_donors_failing_afghanistan.

Oxfam America. 2006. *Annual Report.* Boston, MA.

Paffenholz, Thania, ed. 2010a. *Civil Society and Peacebuilding: A Critical Assessment.* Boulder, CO: Lynne Rienner.

———. 2010b. "Civil Society and Peacebuilding." In Paffenholz, *Civil Society and Peacebuilding,* 43–64.

Paffenholz, Thania, and Christoph Spurk. 2006. "Civil Society, Civic Engagement, and Peacebuilding." Washington, DC: World Bank.

———. 2010. "A Comprehensive Analytical Framework." In Paffenholz, *Civil Society and Peacebuilding,* 65–76.

Panich, Leo, and Colin Leys, eds. 2008. *Violence Today: Actually Existing Barbarism.* UK: The Merlin Press.

Pankhurst, Donna. 2008. "The Gendered Impact of Peace." in Pugh, Cooper, and Turner, *Whose Peace?*, 30–45.

Paris, Roland. 2002. "International Peacebuilding and the 'Mission Civilisatrice.'" *Review of International Studies* 28: 637–56.

———. 2004. *At War's End: Building Peace after Civil Conflict.* Cambridge: Cambridge University Press.

Paris, Roland, and Timothy D. Sisk, eds. 2009. *The Dilemas of Peacebuilding: Confronting the Contradictions of Postwar Peacebuilding.* New York: Routledge.

Patomäki, Heikki, and Teivo Teivainen. 2004. "The World Social Forum: An Open Space or a Movement of Movements?" *Theory, Culture & Society* 21: 145–54.

Payne, Rodger, and Nayef H. Samhat. 2004. *Democratizing Global Politics.* Albany: State University of New York Press.

Payne-Gallwey, Ralph. 2007. *The Crossbow: Its Military and Sporting History, Construction, and Use.* Ludlow: Merlin Unwin Books.

Peel, J. D. Y. 1978. "Ọlaju: A Yoruba Concept of Development." *The Journal of Development Studies* 14: 135–65.

Perkins Richard, and Eric Neumayer. 2010. "The Organized Hypocrisy of Ethical Foreign Policy: Human Rights, Democracy, and Western Arms Sales." *Geoforum* 41: 247–56.

Perrin, Noel. 1979. *Giving Up the Gun: Japan's Reversion to the Sword, 1543–1879.* Boston: G. K. Hall.

Peters, Krijn. 2004. *Re-examining Voluntarism: Youth Combatants in Sierra Leone.* Institute for Security Studies Monograph 100. Pretoria, South Africa.

———. 2006. *Footpaths to Reintegration: Armed Conflict, Youth, and the Rural Crisis in Sierra Leone.* PhD thesis, Wagenigen University.

Peterson, Scott. 2001. *Me Against My Brother: At War in Somalia, Sudan, and Rwanda.* London: Routledge.

Peterson, V. Spike. 2003. *A Critical Rewriting of Global Political Economy: Integrating Productive, Reproductive, and Virtual Economies.* New York: Routledge.

Peterson, V. Spike, and Ann Sisson Runyan. 2010. *Global Gender Issues in the New Millennium.* 3rd ed. Boulder, CO: Westview Press.

Philpott, Daniel, and Gerard Powers, eds. 2010. *Transforming Conflict in a Violent World.* New York: Oxford University Press.

Pincus, Walter. 2009. "U.S.: Up to 56,000 More Contractors Likely for Afghanistan." *The Washington Post,* December 16, http://www.corpwatch.org/article .php?id=15492.

Piquet, Caroline. 2004. "The Suez Company's Concession in Egypt, 1854–1956: Modern Infrastructure and Local Development." *Enterprise and Society* 5, no. 1: 107–27.

Poaletta, Michael. 1997. "Somali Waste Imports." Washington, DC: The Environment Database, American University.

Pogge, Thomas. 2008. *World Poverty and Human Rights: Cosmopolitan Responsibilities and Reforms.* 2nd ed. Cambridge, UK: Polity Press.

Polanyi, Karl. 1944. *The Great Transformation.* Boston: Beacon Press.

Pollock, Sheldon, Homi K. Bhabha, Carol A. Breckenridge, and Dipesh Chakrabarty. 2002. "Cosmopolitanisms." In *Cosmopolitanism,* edited by Breckenridge, Pollock, Bhabha, and Chakrabarty, 1–14. Durham: Duke University Press.

Price, Richard. 1997. *The Chemical Weapons Taboo.* Ithaca: Cornell University Press.

Prokosch, Eric. 1995. *The Technology of Killing: A Military and Political History of Antipersonnel Weapons.* London: Zed Books.

Pugh, Michael, and Neil Cooper. 2004. *War Economics in a Regional Context: Challenges of Transformation.* Boulder, CO: Lynne Rienner.

Pugh, Michael, Neil Cooper, and Mandy Turner, eds. 2008a. *Whose Peace?: Critical Perspectives on the Political Economy of Peacebuilding.* New York: Palgrave Macmillan.

Pugh, Michael, Neil Cooper, and Mandy Turner. 2008b. "Introduction." In Pugh, Cooper, and Turner, *Whose Peace?,* 1–10.

———. 2008c. "Conclusion: The Political Economy of Peacebuilding—Whose Peace? Where Next?" In Pugh, Cooper, and Turner, *Whose Peace?,* 390–97.

Raffaele, Paul. 2007. "The Pirate Hunters." *Smithsonian,* 38–44, http://www.smithsonianmag.com/people-places/pirate_main.html.

Rajagopal, Arvind. 2001. *Politics after Television: Religious Nationalism and the Reshaping of the Indian Public.* New York: Cambridge University Press.

Rajagopal, Balakrishnan. 2003. *International Law from Below: Development, Social Movements, and Third World Resistance.* New York: Cambridge University Press.

———. 2006. "Counter-Hegemonic International Law: Rethinking Human Rights and Development as a Third World Strategy." *Third World Quarterly* 27: 767–83.

Rashid, Ahmed. 2000. *Taliban: Militant Islam, Oil, and Fundamentalism in Central Asia.* New Haven: Yale University Press.

Redfield, Peter. 2008. "Sacrifice, Triage, And Global Humanitarianism." In Barnett and Weiss, *Humanitarianism In Question,* 196–214.

Rees, John. 2006. *Imperialism and Resistance.* London: Routledge.

Reno, W. 1995. *Corruption and State Politics in Sierra Leone.* Cambridge: Cambridge University Press.

Report by European NGOs. 2004. *Taking Control: The Case for a More Effective European Union Code of Conduct on Arms Exports.* London: Saferworld.

Richmond, Oliver P. 2008. "Welfare and the Civil Peace: Poverty with Rights?" In Pugh, Cooper, and Turner, *Whose Peace?*, 287–301.

———. 2010. "A Genealogy of Peace and Conflict Theory." In Richmond, *Palgrave Advances in Peacebuilding*, 14–40.

Richmond, Oliver P., ed. 2010. *Palgrave Advances in Peacebuilding: Critical Developments and Approaches.* London: Palgrave.

Risse, Thomas, and Katherine Sikkink. 1999. "The Socialization of Human Rights Norm." In *The Power of Human Rights*, edited by Thomas Risse, Stephen C. Ropp, and Kathryn Sikkink, 1–38. Cambridge: Cambridge University Press.

Rivage-Seul, Marguerite K. 1987. "Peace Education: Moral Imagination and the Pedagogy of the Oppressed." *Harvard Education Review* 57: 153–69.

Roberts, Cynthia. 1983. "Soviet Arms–Transfer Policy and the Decision to Upgrade Syrian Air Defenses." *Survival* 25, no. 4: 154–64.

Roberts, David. 2008. *Human Insecurity: Global Structures of Violence.* London: Zed Books.

Robinson, William. 2004. *A Theory of Global Capitalism.* Baltimore: Johns Hopkins University Press.

Rogers, Paul. 2010. *Losing Control: Global Security in the Twenty-first Century.* 3rd ed. London: Pluto Press.

Rose, Nikolas, Pat O'Malley, and Mariana Valverde. 2006. "Governmentality." *Annual Review of Law and Social Science* 2: 83–104.

Rought-Brooks, Hannah, Salwa Duaibis, and Soraida Hussein. 2010. "Palestinian Women Caught in the Crossfire between Occupation and Patriarchy." *Feminist Formations* 22, no. 3: 124–45.

Roy, Ananya. 2010. *Poverty Capital: Microfinance and the Making of Development.* London: Routledge.

Rubin, Barnett. 1995. *The Fragmentation of Afghanistan: State Formation and Collapse in the International System.* New Haven: Yale University Press.

Rudra, Nita. 2002. "Globalization and the Decline of the Welfare State in Less-Developed Countries." *International Organization* 56: 411–45.

Saferworld. 2003. *Independent Audit of the 2001 UK Government Annual Report on Strategic Export Controls.* London: Saferworld.

Saiwal, Rajinder, 2002. "A Very Difficult Battle." *Seagull Theatre Quarterly* 32–33: 112–16.

Samatar, Abdi Ismail. 1987. "Merchant Capital, International Livestock Trade, and Pastoral Development in Somalia." *Canadian Journal of African Studies* 21, no. 3: 355–74.

———. 1992. "Destruction of State and Society in Somalia: Beyond the Tribal Convention." *The Journal of Modern African Studies* 30, no. 4: 625–41.

Samatar, Abdi, Lance Salisbury, and Johathan Bascom. 1988. "The Political Economy of Livestock Marketing in Northern Somalia." *African Economic History* 17: 81–97.

Samatar, Abdi, and A. I. Samatar. 1987. "The Material Roots of the Suspended African State: Arguments from Somalia." *The Journal of Modern African Studies* 25, no. 4: 669–90.

Sanders, T. 2003. "Invisible Hands and Visible Goods: Revealed and Concealed Economies in Millenial Tanzania." In Sanders and West, *Transparency and Conspiracy*, 148–74.

Sanders, T., and H. West, eds. 2003. *Transparency and Conspiracy: Ethnographies of Suspicion in the New World Order.* Durham: Duke University Press.

Santos, Boaventura de Sousa. 2004. "The World Social Forum: Toward a Counter-Hegemonic Globalization." In *Challenging Empires,* edited by J. Sen, A. Anand, A. Escobar, and P. Waterman. Choike.org, http://www.choike.org/2009/eng/informes/1557.html.

———. 2005. "The Future of the World Social Forum: The Work of Translation." *Development* 48: 15–22.

———. 2006. *The Rise of The Global Left: The World Social Forums and Beyond.* London: Zed Books.

———. 2007a. "Reinventing Social Emancipation: Toward New Manifestos." In *Democratizing Democracy: Beyond the Liberal Democractic Canon,* edited by Boaventura de Sousa Santos, xvii–xxxiii. London: Verso Books.

———. 2007b. "Human Rights as an Emancipatory Script?: Cultural and Political Conditions." In *Another Knowledge is Possible,* edited by Boaventura de Sousa Santos, 3–40. New York: Verso Books.

———. 2008. "Interview: WSF Is as Much a Cultural Struggle as a Political One." Inter Press Services, http://www.ipsnews.net/news.asp?idnews=40866.

Sarkar, Sumit. 2002. "Hindutva and History." In Sarkar, *Beyond Nationalist Frames: Postmodernism, Hindu Fundamentalism, History,* 244–62. New Delhi: Permanent Black.

———. 2008. "Nationalism and Poverty: Discourses of Culture and Development in Twentieth-Century India." *Third World Quarterly* 29, no. 3: 429–45.

Scahill, Jeremy. 2008. *Blackwater: The Rise of the World's Most Powerful Mercenary Army.* NY: Nation Books.

Scharpf, Fritz. 1999. *Governing in Europe: Effective or Legitimate?* Oxford: Oxford University Press.

Scott, James C. 1990. *Domination and the Arts of Resistance: Hidden Transcripts.* New Haven: Yale University Press.

———. 1998. *Seeing Like a State: How Certain Schemes to Improve the Human Condition Have Failed.* New Haven: Yale University Press.

Sen, Amartya. 1999. *Development as Freedom.* New York: Anchor Books.

———. 2006. *Identity and Violence: The Illusion of Destiny.* New York: Norton.

Sending, Ole, and Iver B. Neumann. 2006. "Governance to Governmentality: Analyzing NGOs, States, and Power." *International Studies Quarterly* 50, no. 3: 651–72.

Shani, Ornit. 2005. "The Rise of Hindu Nationalism: The Case Study of Ahmedabad in the 1980s." *Modern Asian Studies* 39, no. 4: 861–96.

Shaw, R. 1996. "The Politician and the Diviner: Divination and the Consumption of Power in Sierra Leone." *The Journal of Religion in Africa* 26, no. 1: 20–55.

Shepler, S. 2004. "The Social and Cultural Context of Child Soldiering in Sierra Leone." Paper for the PRIO Sponsored Workshop on Techniques of Violence in Civil War. August 20–21. Oslo, Norway.

Silver, Beverly J. 2003. *Forces of Labor: Workers' Movements and Globalization Since 1870.* New York: Cambridge University Press.

SIPRI–Stockholm International Peace Research Institute. 2009. *SIPRI Yearbook 2009: Armaments, Disarmament, and International Security.* Oxford: Oxford University Press.

———. 2010. *SIPRI Yearbook 2010: Armaments, Disarmament, and International Security.* Oxford: Oxford University Press.

Sklair, Leslie. 1997. "Social Movements for Global Capitalism: The Transnational Capitalist Class in Action." *Review of International Political Economy* 4: 514–38.

Smart, Barry. 2005. "Empowering the Powerful, Enriching the Rich: On Neoliberalism, Economic Globalization, and Social Criticism." In *Confronting Globalization: Humanity, Justice, and the Renewal of Politics,* edited by Patrick Hayden and Chamsy el-Ojeili, 68–83. New York: Palgrave.

Smith, Daniel Jordan. 2007. *A Culture of Corruption: Everyday Deception and Popular Discontent in Nigeria.* Princeton: Princeton University Press.

Smith, Jackie. 2008. *Social Movements for Global Democracy*. Baltimore: Johns Hopkins University Press.

———. 2010. "Economic Globalization and Strategic Peacebuilding." In *Strategies of Peace: Transforming Conflict in a Violent World*, edited by D. Philpott and G. F. Powers, 247–70. New York: Oxford University Press.

Smith, Jackie, S. Byrd, E. Reese, and E. Smythe, eds. 2011. *Handbook of the World Social Forums*. Boulder, CO: Paradigm.

Smith, Jackie, and Nicole Doerr. 2011. "Democratic Innovation in the U.S. and European Social Forums." In Smith et al., *Handbook of the World Social Forums*, 339–59.

Smith, Jackie, Marina Karides, Marc Becker, Dorval Brunelle, Christopher Chase-Dunn, Donatella della Porta, Rosalba Icaza, Jeffrey Juris, Lorenzo Mosca, Ellen Reese, Peter Jay Smith, and Rolando Vászuez. 2007. *Global Democracy and the World Social Forums*. Boulder, CO: Paradigm.

Smith, Jackie, and Rachel Kutz-Flamenbaum. 2010. "Prisoners of Our Concepts: Liberating the Study of Social Movements." In *The Transnational Condition: Protest Dynamics in an Entangled Europe*, edited by Simon Teune, 211–27. Berlin: Berghahn Press.

Smith, Jackie, and Dawn Wiest. 2012. *Social Movements in the World-System*. New York: Russell Sage.

Smith, M. F. 1994. *Hard Times on Kairiru Island: Poverty, Development, and Morality in a Papua New Guinea Village*. Honolulu: University of Hawaii Press.

Southall, A. 1988. "Small Urban Centers in Rural Development: What Else Is Development Other Than Helping Your Own Home Town?" *African Studies Review* 31, no. 3: 1–15.

Spear, Joanna. Forthcoming [2014]. *State-Firm Relations in the Contemporary Defence Trade*.

Spiegel, Samuel, and Philippe Le Billon. 2009. "China's Weapons Trade: From Ships of Shame to the Ethics of Global Resistance." *International Affairs* 85, no. 2: 323–46.

Spiers, Edward M. 1975. "The Use of the Dum Dum Bullet in Colonial Warfare." *The Journal of Imperial and Commonwealth History* 14, no. 1: 3–14.

*Stanford Enclyclopedia of Philosophy*. 2006. "Cosmopolitanism." http://plato.Stanford.edu/entires/cosmopolitanism/.

Stavrianakis, Anna. 2010. *Taking Aim at the Arms Trade: NGOs, Global Civil Society, and the World Military Order*. London: Zed Books.

Steele, Jonathan. 2008. "Is She Villain or Victim?" *The Guardian Weekly*, September 26, 23–25.

Stein, Janice Gross. 2008. "Humanitarian Organizations: Accountable—Why, to Whom, for What, and How?" In Barnett and Weiss, *Humanitariansm in Question*, 124–42.

Stohl, Rachel, and Suzette Grillot. 2009. *The International Arms Trade*. Cambridge, UK: Polity Press.

Stohl, Rachel, Matt Schroeder, and Dan Smith. 2007. *The Small Arms Trade: A Beginner's Guide*. Oxford: Oneworld.

Stone, David R. 2000. "Imperialism and Sovereignty: The League of Nations' Drive to Control the Global Arms Trade." *Journal of Contemporary History* 35, no. 2: 213–30.

Strickland, Mathew, and Robert Hardy. 2011. *The Great Warbow: From Hastings to the Mary Rose*. Sparkford, UK: Haynes.

Struett, Michael J. 2008. *The Politics of Constructing the International Criminal Court*. New York: Palgrave MacMillan.

Sud, Nikita. 2007. "From Land to the Tiller to Land Liberalisation: The Political Economy of Gujarat's Shifting Land Policy." *Modern Asian Studies* 41, no. 3: 603–37.

Sugiyama, Y. 1987. "Maintaining a Life of Subsistence in the Bemba Village in Northeastern Zambia." *African Study Monographs* 6: 15–32.

Suhrud, Tridip. 2002. "Where Do We Go from Here?" *Seagull Theatre Quarterly* 32–33: 99–102.

Sullivan, Sian. 2005. "An Other World Is Possible?: On Representation, Rationalism, and Romanticism in Social Forums." *Ephemera* 5: 370–92.

Susskind, Yifat. 2007. *Promising Democracy, Imposing Theocracy: Gender-Based Violence and the U.S. War in Iraq*. A MADRE Human Rights Report. NY: MADRE.

Sussman, Tina, and Caesar Ahmed. 2009. "Iraq Cabinet Member's Exit Raises Gender, Sectarian Issues." *Los Angeles Times*, February 12, http://articles.latimes .com/2009/feb/12/world/fg-iraq-women12.

Tanvir, Habib. 2002. "Art Alone Will Not Do." *Seagull Theatre Quarterly* 32–33: 136–43.

Taylor, Claire. 2011. EC Defense Equipment Directives, House of Common Library, Standard Note. SNA/IA/4640, June 3, http://www.parliament.uk /briefing-papers/SN04640.

Teivainen, Teivo. 2002. "The World Social Forum and Global Democratisation: Learning from Porto Alegre." *Third World Quarterly* 23: 621–32.

Terry, Fiona. 2002. *Condemned to Repeat?* Ithaca: Cornell University Press.

Thakur, Ramesh, and William Maley. 1999. "The Ottawa Convention on Landmines: A Landmark Humanitarian Treaty in Arms Control?" *Global Governance* 5: 273–302.

Thapar, Romila. 1989. "Imagined Religious Communities: Ancient History and the Modern Search for a Hindu Identity." *Modern Asian Studies* 23, no. 2: 209–31.

Thompson, James. 2008. *Rapporteur's Report of the Annual UNHCR Consultation with NGOs.* Geneva: International Council of Voluntary Agencies (ICVA).

Tickner, Ann. 1992. *Gender in International Relations: Feminist Perspectives on Achieving Global Security.* New York: Columbia University Press.

Tilly, Charles. 1990. *Coercion, Capital, and European States, AD 990–1990.* Cambridge, MA: Blackwell.

Tirman, John. 2009. "Iraq's Shocking Human Toll." *The Nation,* February 2, http://www.alternet.org/story/123818.

Trebilcock, Clive. 1970. "Legends of the British Armament Industry 1890–1914: A Revision." *Journal of Contemporary History* 5, no. 4: 3–19.

UK Working Group on Arms Export Control. 2009. "Written Evidence Submitted by the UK Working Group on Arms." In House of Commons Business, Innovation and Skills, Defense, Foreign Affairs, and International Development Committees, *Scrutiny of Arms Export Controls (2010): UK Strategic Export Controls Annual Report 2008, Quarterly Reports for 2009, Licensing Policy and Review of Export Control Legislation.* First Joint Report of Session 2009–10, HC 202, March 16, Minutes of Evidence, p. 38, para. 30.

UN. 1992. "An Agenda for Peace: Preventive Diplomacy, Peacemaking, and Peace-Keeping." Washington, DC: United Nations.

UN. 2008. "Security Council Condemns Acts of Piracy." Resolution 1816. New York: United Nations Security Council. http://www.un.org/News/Press /docs/2008/sc9344.doc.htm.

UN. 2009. "With Unity Government Installed in Somalia, 'New Paradigm' Needed to Guide Effort." New York: United Nations.

UNDP. 1990. *The Human Development Report.* NY: Oxford University Press.

UNDP. 1994. *Human Development Report 1994: New Dimensions of Human Security.* NY: Oxford University Press.

UNDP. 2000. *Human Development Report 2000: Human Rights and Human Development.* NY: Oxford University Press.

UNDP. 2004. *Afghanistan Human Development Report 2004: Security with a Human Face.* NY: Oxford University Press.

UNDP. 2009. *Arab Human Development Report 2009: Challenges to Human Security in the Arab Region.* NY: United Nations Development Programme. http://hdr .undp.org/en/reports/regionalreports/arabstates/ahdr2009e.pdf.

UNEP. 2005. "VOA-UN: Nuclear Waste Being Released on Somalia's Shores after Tsunami." In *The Environment in the News: United Nations Environment Programme,* http://www.voanews.com/content/a-13-2005-02-23-voa23/309291 .html.

United Nations Commission on Human Security. 2003. *Human Security Now.* http://www.humansecurity-chs.org/finalreport/index.html.

United Nations Security Council. 2008. "Security Council Decides States, Regional Organizations May Use 'All Necessary Means' to Fight Piracy off Somalia Coast for Twelve-Month Period." Resolution 1846. New York: United Nations.

USA Today. 2010. "Push onto Protect New Troops from IEDS." April 14, http:// www.usatoday.com/news/military/2010-04-18-mrap_N.htm.

Useem, B. 1998. "Breakdown Theories of Collective Action." *Annual Review of Sociology* 24: 215–38.

Utas, M. 2005. "Building a Future?: The Reintegration and Remarginalization of Youth in Liberia." In *No Peace, No War: An Anthropology of Contemporary Armed Conflicts,* edited by P. Richards, 137–54. Athens: Ohio University Press.

Uvin, Peter. 1998. *Aiding Violence: The Development Enterprise in Rwanda.* West Hartford, CT: Kumarian Press.

———. 2002. "The Development/Peacebuilding Nexus: A Typology and History of Changing Paradigms." *Journal of Peacebuilding and Development* 1: 5–24.

———. 2003. "Global Dreams and Local Anger: From Structural to Acute Violence in a Globalizing World." In *Rethinking Global Political Economy: Emerging Issues, Unfolding Odysseys,* edited by Mary Ann Tetreault, Robert A. Denemark, Kenneth P. Thomas, and Kurt Burch, 147–62. London: Routledge.

Vanaik, Achin. 2009. "India's Paradigmatic Communal Violence." In Panitch and Leys, *Violence Today,* 141–62.

Varshney, Ashutosh. 2002. *Ethnic Conflict and Civic Life: Hindus and Muslims in India.* New Haven: Yale University Press.

Vines, Alex. 2007. "Can UN Arms Embargoes in Africa Be Effective?" *International Affairs* 83, no. 6: 1107–21.

Vivian, Lord. 1890. "Statement Made Respecting the Transit Clause in Article IX." In F.O. 881/6197, Part 2: Further Correspondence respecting the Conference relating to the Slave Trade Held at Brussels, January 30, inclosure no. 2, in no. 61, 49–50. London: National Archives.

Wallerstein, Immanuel. 2003. *The Decline of American Power: The U.S. in a Chaotic World*. New York: New Press.

Walls, Michael. 2009. "The Emergence of a Somali State: Building Peace from Civil War in Somaliland." *African Affairs* 108, no. 432: 371–89.

Wander, Andrew. 2010. "The Spreading Somali Pirate Threat." Aljazera.com, March 25, http://www.aljazeera.com/focus/2010/03/2010323132216997663.html.

Wapner, Paul. 1996. *Environmental Activism and World Civic Politics*. Binghamton: State University of New York Press.

Webster, Linda, and Douglas A. Perkins. 2001. "Redressing Structural Violence against Children." In *Peace, Conflict, and Violence: Peace Psychology for the Twenty-first Century*, edited by D. J. Christie, R. V. Wagner, and D. A. Winter, 330–40. Englewood Cliffs, NJ: Prentice-Hall.

Wehrenfennig, Daniel. 2008. "Conflict Management and Communicative Action: Second Track Diplomacy from a Habermasian Perspective." *Communication Theory* 18, no. 3: 356–75.

Weisbrot, Mark, Dean Baker, Egor Kraev, and Judy Chen. 2002. "The Scorecard on Globalization 1980–2000: Twenty Years of Diminished Progress." *International Journal of Health Sciences* 32: 229–53.

West, H. 1998. "This Neighbor Is Not My Uncle!: Changing Relations of Power and Authority on the Mueda Plateau." *Journal of Southern African Studies* 24, no. 1: 141–60.

Western Cape Anti-Eviction Campaign. 2010. "Solidarity: Standing with the Poor Peoples' Alliance at the 2010 U.S. Social Forum." http://antieviction.org.za /2010/07/07/solidarity-standing-with-the-poor-peoples-alliance-at-the-2010 -us-social-forum/.

WIDE. 2007. *New Aid, Expanding Trade: What Do Women Have to Say?* Report of the WIDE Annual Conference, Madrid, June 14–16. Brussels: Women in Development Europe.

Williams, Jody. 2008. "New Approaches in a Changing World: The Human Security Agenda." In Williams, Goose, and Wareham, *Banning Landmines*, 281–98.

Williams, Jody, Stephen D. Goose, and Mary Wareham, eds. *Banning Landmines: Disarmament, Citizen Diplomacy, and Human Security*. Lanham, MD: Rowman & Littlefield.

Wood, Elisabeth. 2004. *Insurgent Collective Action and Civil War in El Salvador*. New York: Cambridge University Press.

Young, T. 2003. *Readings in African Politics*. Bloomington: Indiana University Press.

# Contributors

**James Bohman** is Danforth Professor of Philosophy and Professor of International Studies at Saint Louis University. He is the author of *Democracy across Borders* (2007), *Public Deliberation: Pluralism, Complexity, and Democracy* (1996), and *New Philosophy of Social Science: Problems of Indeterminacy* (1991). He is currently working on a book on why democracies have difficulties in solving particular kinds of problems, including obligations to future generations and to noncitizens.

**Catherine Bolten** is Assistant Professor of Anthropology and Peace Studies at the University of Notre Dame. Her book, *I Did It to Save My Life: Love and Survival in Sierra Leone,* was published by the University of California Press in 2012. Her articles appear in *American Anthropologist* (2012), *Journal of Modern African Studies* (2009), and *Journal of Political Ecology* (2009).

**Rebecca Burns** is an assistant editor at *In These Times* magazine. She holds an MA in peace studies from the Kroc Institute for International Peace Studies, University of Notre Dame, where her research focused on global land and housing rights.

**Neil Cooper** is Professor of International Relations and Security Studies at the University of Bradford. He is coeditor of the refereed journal *International Peacekeeping* as well as coauthor of *War Economies in a Regional Context* (2004), coeditor of *Whose Peace?: Critical Perspectives on the Political Economy of Peacebuilding* (2008), and also coeditor of a special issue of *Contemporary Security Policy: Arms Control for the 21st Century* (2011). The latter has also been published as *Reconceptualising Arms Control: Controlling the Means of Violence* (2011). He is currently engaged in research for a monograph on the history of arms trade regulation.

**Dia Da Costa** is in the Department of Global Development Studies, Queen's University, Canada, developing research and teaching at the intersection of political economy and cultural studies. She is the author of *Development Dramas: Reimagining Rural Political Action in Eastern India* (2010) and has articles in *Third World Quarterly* (2010), *Globalizations* (2007), *Signs* (2008), and *Contributions to Indian Sociology* (2007). She is working on a second book tentatively titled *The Work of Theatre in an Age of Precarious Labour.*

**Isaac Kamola** is currently an Assistant Professor of Political Science at Trinity College in Hartford, Connecticut. His scholarly work has appeared in *Third World Quarterly, The British Journal of Politics and International Relations, International Political Sociology, Polygraph, Transitions,* and the *Journal of Higher Education in Africa.* He received his PhD in political science from the University of Minnesota in 2010.

**Cecelia Lynch** is Professor of Political Science at the University of California, Irvine. She is the author of *Beyond Appeasement: Interpreting Interwar Peace Movements in World Politics* (1999), coauthor with Audie Klotz of *Strategies for Research in Constructivist International Relations* (2007), and coeditor of *Law and Moral Action in World Politics* (2000) and *On Rules, Politics, and Knowledge: Friedrich Kratochwil and the Study of International Relations* (2010).

**Rachel Miller** holds an MA in peace studies from the Kroc Institute for International Peace Studies, University of Notre Dame. She is a Senior Information Officer with USAID's Office of US Foreign Disaster Assistance (USAID/OFDA), where she reports on humanitarian emergencies, focusing on Sudan, South Sudan, and the Democratic Republic of the Congo. Rachel has also worked on land rights and gender justice issues in Uganda and the West Bank, environmental justice with indigenous communities in Latin America, and food security in Bolivia.

**Valentine M. Moghadam** is Professor of Sociology and Director of International Affairs at Northeastern University. Prior to this she was Professor of Sociology and Women's Studies, and Director of the Women's Studies Program at Purdue University. She is the author of *Modernizing Women: Gender and Social Change in the Middle East* (1993, 2003, 2013); *Globalizing Women: Transnational Feminist Networks,* winner of APSA's Victoria Schuck Award for best book on women and politics (2005); *Globalization and Social Movements: Islamism, Feminism, and the Global Justice Movement* (2009, 2012); and coeditor of *Social Policy in the Middle East: Economic, Political, and Gender Dynamics* (2006).

**Jackie Smith** is Professor of Sociology at the University of Pittsburgh. She is the author of *Social Movements for Global Democracy* (2008), coauthor of *Social Movements in the World-System: The Politics of Crisis and Transformation* (2012), and coeditor of several books on transnational activism, including *Coalitions Across Borders* (with Joe Bandy, 2005) and *A Handbook of World Social Forum Activism* (with Scott Byrd, Ellen Reese, and Elizabeth Smythe, 2011).

**Ernesto Verdeja** is Assistant Professor of Political Science and Peace Studies at the University of Notre Dame. He is the author of *Unchopping a Tree: Reconciliation in the Aftermath of Political Violence* (2009), and coeditor of volumes on genocide and mass atrocities. He has published articles in *Perspectives on Politics, Constellations, The Review of Politics, Contemporary Political Theory, The European Journal of Political Theory, Genocide Studies and Prevention, Metaphilosophy, Res Publica,* and *Contemporary Politics.*

# Index

democracy: deliberative, 241; feminist, 124; formal, 6, 8, 101, 113; and human rights, 10–11; minimum requirements for, 193; neoliberal, 51, 64, 98, 159–60, 164; peacebuilding and, 195; Sierra Leone experience, 174–75, 178–83, 186; socialization for, 208
deregulation, 223
Deshpande, G. P., 86–87
Detroit to Dakar, 221
Development Alternatives with Women for a New Era (DAWN), 118, 120
De Waal, Alex, 47, 52
diamonds, 105
discursive demobilization, 9, 12, 48–50, 226, 239
discursive opportunity structure, 220
discursive space, 33
Disraeli, Benjamin, 146
Dole Fruit, 152
donors: ideology, 50, 180; influence, 47, 53, 108–11, 233–34; patronage and, 169–78, 183; relationships to NGOs, 57–60; relationship to states, 57; requirements of, 66, 108, 151, 160n1, 162–63, 166; and transformative peacebuilding, 184–86
drugs, illicit trade, 111, 130
Dunant, Henri, 55

ecology. *See* environment
economic crisis of 2008, 2n1
Elizabeth I, 35
emancipation, 15, 50, 65
emergencies, 51, 55
empowerment, 15
environment, 15, 51, 98, 210, 221, 244
environmental justice, 226
Eritrea, 146
Ethiopia, 140, 142, 148, 150

ethnicity, 86
ethnic violence, 70
European Social Forum, 215, 226
European Union, 38–39, 44, 57, 108, 142, 191
Evans, Jodie, 121
exclusion. *See* social exclusion
exports, 103

failed states. *See* state failure
*Faina*, 154
Farmer, Paul, 219
fascism, 76, 81
Federal Government of Somalia (FGS), 140–43
feminist counterhegemony, 124, 240
feminist research, 67, 68, 98, 103
feminization of poverty, 62
Fetherston, A. B., 213–14, 225, 237
financial crisis of 2008, 129
food sovereignty, 220–21
Fraser, Nancy, 201

Galtung, Johan, 10, 211
Gandhi, Mohandas K., 78, 82
Gbenda, Theophilus, 178
gender, 98, 100, 128
gender apartheid, 107
gender justice, 12–13, 16, 100, 128–30, 133
General Motors, 152
Gilani, Fauzia, 108
global civil society, 24, 29, 56
globalization project, 14
Global Justice Movement (GJM), 117, 129, 220, 123
Godhra, 81
governmentality, 9, 49, 64
Great Lakes region, 46

structural violence, 1, 3n2, 6, 8–9, 16, 48, 87, 98, 209, 236; defined, 209n2, 219; demystifying, 71; role in Somalia, 136, 155; social exclusion and, 224; world-system as source of, 216; and world-systems analysis, 103
Suez Canal, 137–38, 146
sustainability, 52–53, 68, 124, 197

Taj Mahal, 85
Take Back the Land, 223–24
Taliban, 97, 101, 107–9, 111, 116, 123–25
Thatcher, Margaret, 225
Tobin Tax, 129–30
Total Oil Company, 152
toxic dumping, 137
track-two diplomacy. *See* multi-track peacebuilding
trade liberalization, 6–7, 13
trade unions, 46, 73, 82
tradition: and gender, 106
transformative peacebuilding, 213–17, 223, 229–30, 233, 243
Transition Federal Government (TFG), 140–41, 143, 155
Transition National Government (TNG), 139, 140
translation, 203–4, 226
transnational advocacy networks, 118, 210
transnational corporations, 102, 110
transnational feminist networks, 17, 117–18, 120–22, 129
transnational society, 190, 194–200, 204–5
Tripartite Agreement on Arms Sales to Middle East, 32
Truth and Reconciliation Commission of South Africa, 191
truth commissions, 219

Uganda Agreement of 1900, 30
unfreedoms, 161, 184–86, 242
Union of Youth Groups, 174
United for Peace and Justice, 121, 123
United Kingdom House of Commons Foreign Affairs Committee, 34
United Nations, 2, 29, 34, 111, 149; *Afghanistan Human Development Report*, 108, 127; Afghanistan peace agreement, 99n1; Arms Register, 38; Commission on Human Security, 127n18; General Assembly, 140; Human Development Index, 109; *Human Development Report*, 126, Program of Action on Small Arms, 38; Sanctions, 101; Security Council, 156; Security Council resolution 1325 and 1820, 106, 106n5; Security Council Resolution 814, 139; and Sierra Leone patronage networks, 180; UNICEF, 119; UNOSOM II, 139
United Progressive Alliance (UPA), 74
United States: Agency for International Development, 57, 110; Clinton administration, 38; cluster bomb use, 32; Defense Trade Security Initiative, 38; Department of Defense, 38, 114; energy dependence, 112–13; export control system, 39; Government Accountability Office, 114; limits of power, 113; military-industrial complex, 79; National Security Council, 135; Obama administration, 39, 125
United States Food Sovereignty Alliance, 221
United States Social Forum (USSF), 214, 226–27; Atlanta (2007), 222; Detroit (2010), 215, 221, 223, 225; National Planning Committee, 215, 222, 226
US Human Rights Network, 223